Praise for Von Allan

Stargazer Volume (

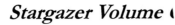

"*Stargazer Volume One* is a black-and-white graphic novel following three girls stranded on a faraway alien world. Young Marni has recently lost her grandmother, with whom she was very close. Her grandmother had also bequeathed a mysterious "Artifact" upon her - and it is this object that transports Marni and her friends, Sophie and Elora, far away from any home they have ever known. The three girls must pool their courage and resources to learn more about this unreal new world, and the strange things within it - a robot, a faraway tower, and an unknown monster hidden in shadows. *Stargazer* is a story of wonder, exploration, determination, and inward as well as outward challenge, and is highly recommended for readers of all ages."

- The Midwest Book Review

"This book is definitely something that should be on the radar of parents out there that are looking for something innocuous. The book isn't just for kids, though. When read, it took me back to the days of my youth when everything including life itself was much more simplistic. Definitely give Von Allan's *Stargazer* a look for yourself, or anyone needing a great gift for the holidays! Again, kudos to Von Allan and his smooth style of writing a simple story in a world where it seems everything is interweaving like a spiderweb and sometimes too hard to follow. Let's face it, a story doesn't need to span a lifetime or contain forty different characters to be good."

- Comic Attack

"Anyway, this book deals with a young girl who is very distraught about the recent death of her grandmother. The early moments of the book are all about this and the family dynamic that comes from it, but don't worry, that title comes into effect before too long. Marni (the main character) eventually has a sleepover with friends, they end up camping in the backyard and eat too much pizza… then things get weird. Marni has inherited an odd artifact from her grandma, and they're all poking around at it when something flashes and they find themselves in a strange land. Oh, and the artifact is gone. The rest of the book is essentially them trying to get acclimated to this new place, as they find an old statue, a tiny robot guy, a boat and a few other things I probably shouldn't get into…The art is amazing (although I'm thinking future volumes will give Von more of a chance to flex his artistic muscles), the writing was excellent overall and I can't wait to see what happens next, so that sure sounds like a success to me."

- Optical Sloth

Stargazer

Book Two

by Von Allan

a von allan studio book

Ottawa

Library and Archives Canada Cataloguing in Publication

Allan, Von, 1974-
     Stargazer / by Von Allan.

ISBN 978-0-9781237-4-1 (pbk. : bk. 2)

     I. Title.

PN6733.A46S83 2010   741.5'971   C2010-902254-8

Published by Von Allan Studio, P.O. Box 20520, 390 Rideau Street, Ottawa, Ontario, Canada K1N 1A3. Email: von@vonallan.com Web: http://www.vonallan.com Phone: 613-236-9957

v 1.0

For Sammy, again

Previously in *Stargazer Volume One*

In Volume One we are introduced to Marni, a young girl struggling to cope with the recent death of her beloved grandmother. Marni has been bequeathed her grandmother's favourite possession, a mysterious and somewhat unearthly artifact. With this treasure as a memento of her grandmother, and with the support of her two best friends, Sophie and Elora, Marni is just beginning to deal with her grief when suddenly her life takes a fantastical turn. While the three girls are examining the artifact on a backyard camping trip, the object suddenly transports the friends and their tent to a faraway place. When they recover from their initial shock, Marni, Sophie, and Elora discover that the artifact has vanished, leaving them all alone.

Once the the friends gather their courage and explore their surroundings, they find an alien and strangely empty world. Eventually, they spot a mysterious tower in the distance and decide to travel to it in the hopes of finding help. However, as they gather their belongings to start the trip, they are startled by a deafening roar from an unseen monster in the nearby woods. Terrified, they run for their lives, abandoning all of their belongings, except for the knapsacks on their backs. They escape the monster but are afraid to return to the area; they decide to leave the tent behind and press on towards the tower.

On this first leg of their adventure, the girls make a number of strange discoveries, including a mysterious robot and a seemingly endless supply of food in an otherwise empty building. The building's inhabitants are nowhere to be found and, since the robot seems friendly, the girls decide to sleep there rather than in the dark woods. That night, Marni has an unsettling night-time encounter with a silent and shadowy child. Marni is convinced the child is trying to communicate with her; however, the next morning, uncertain whether the experience was a dream or not, she decides to keep it to herself.

After leaving the shelter, this time accompanied by the friendly little robot, the girls stumble across an abandoned Viking-like longboat. While exploring its cargo hold, Marni discovers a sword and decides to keep it in case the monster comes back. Feeling safe on the boat, the girls agree that it also seems like a faster way to get to the far-off tower, so they set sail with the help of the robot. That night, Marni has another night-time encounter with a dream-like figure; however, this time it's an older woman and Marni is convinced that this is her grandmother reborn.

As Volume One ended, the longboat was approaching the tower and the three girls were fervently hoping they would fine help there...and a way home.

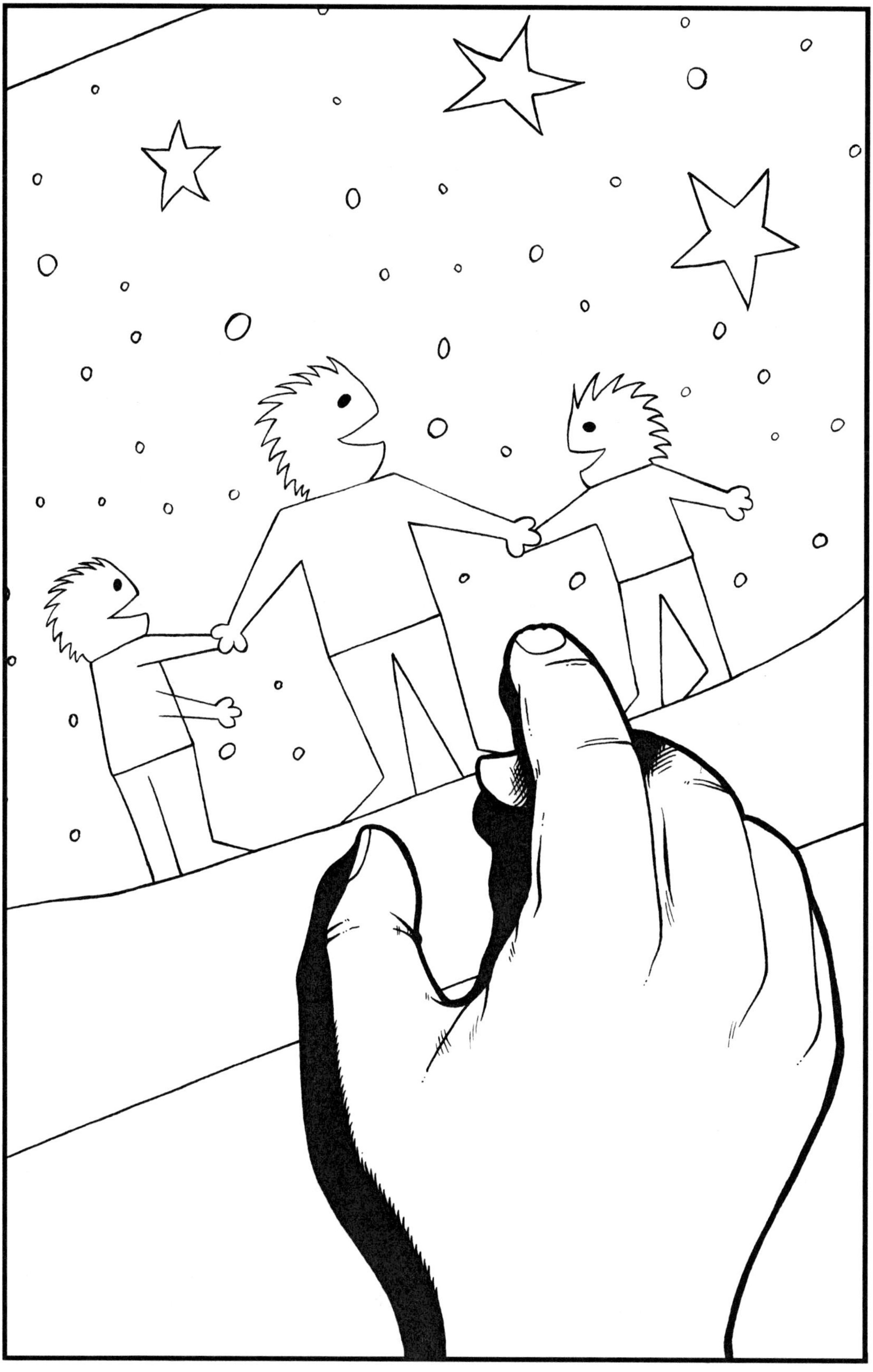

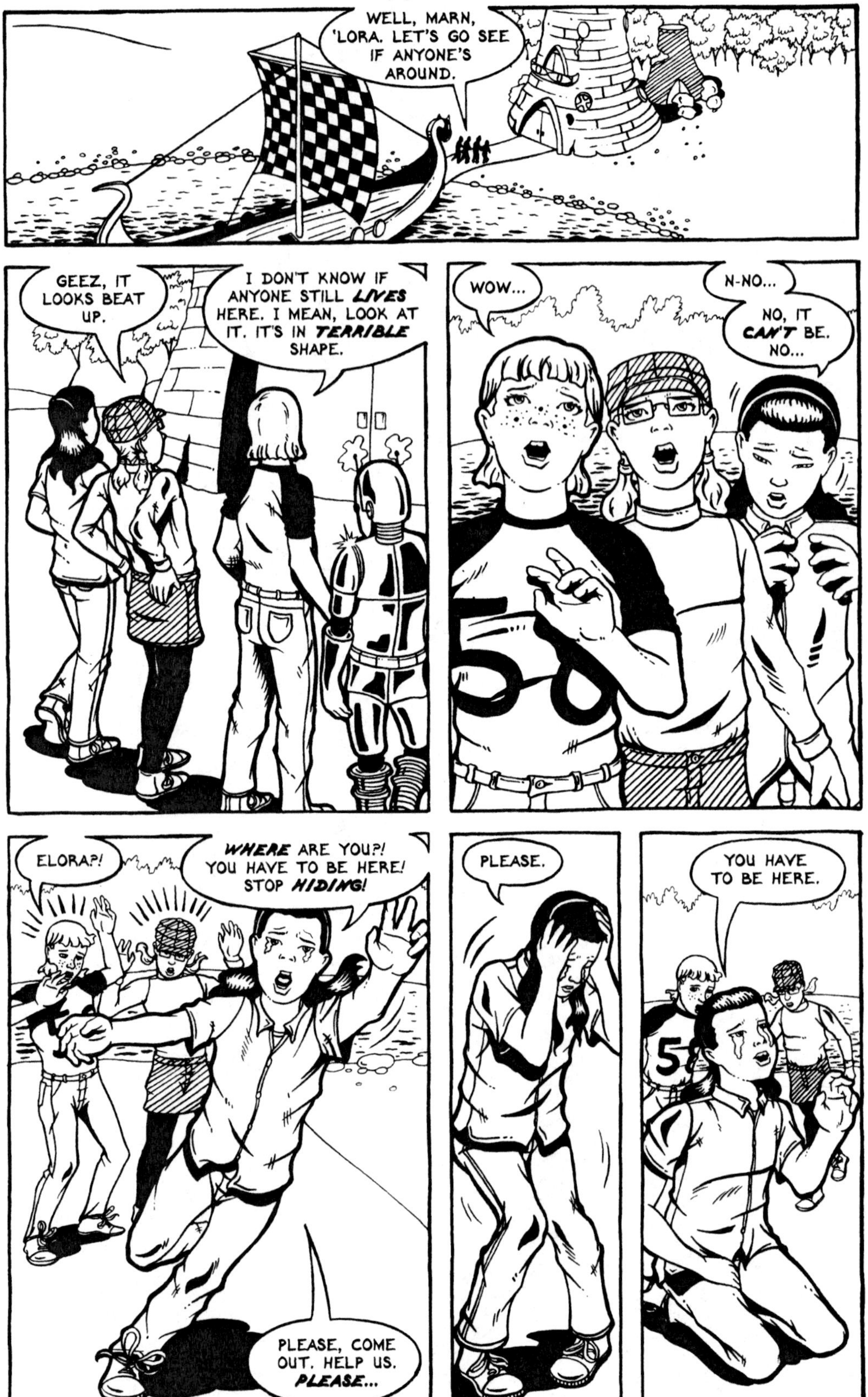
WELL, MARN, 'LORA. LET'S GO SEE IF ANYONE'S AROUND.
GEEZ, IT LOOKS BEAT UP.
I DON'T KNOW IF ANYONE STILL *LIVES* HERE. I MEAN, LOOK AT IT. IT'S IN *TERRIBLE* SHAPE.
WOW...
N-NO...
NO, IT *CAN'T* BE. NO...
ELORA?!
WHERE ARE YOU?! YOU HAVE TO BE HERE! STOP *HIDING*!
PLEASE, COME OUT. HELP US. *PLEASE*...
PLEASE.
YOU HAVE TO BE HERE.

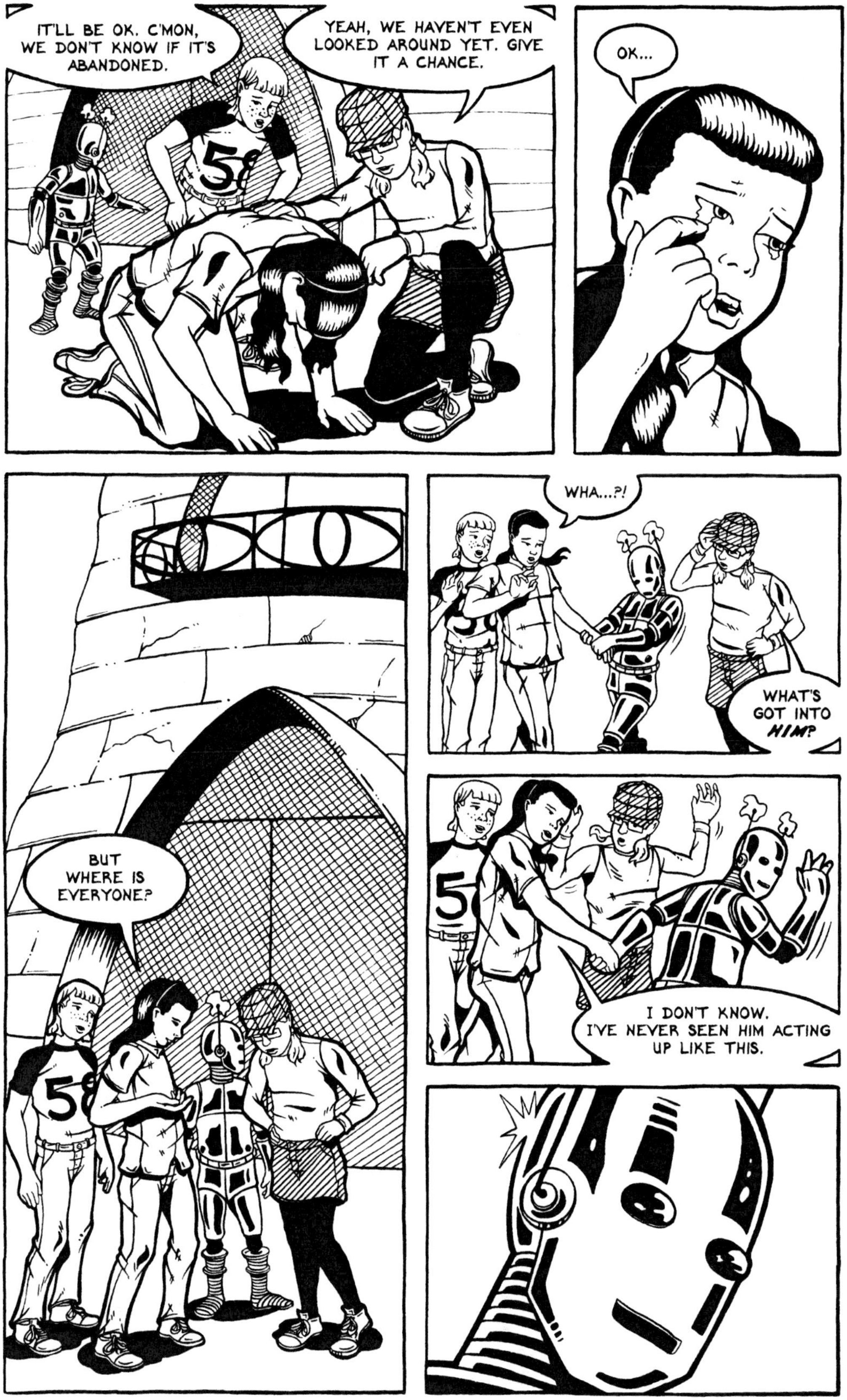
IT'LL BE OK. C'MON, WE DON'T KNOW IF IT'S ABANDONED.
YEAH, WE HAVEN'T EVEN LOOKED AROUND YET. GIVE IT A CHANCE.
OK...
BUT WHERE IS EVERYONE?
WHA...?!
WHAT'S GOT INTO *HIM*?
I DON'T KNOW. I'VE NEVER SEEN HIM ACTING UP LIKE THIS.

"WHOA!"
LOOK AT 'EM ALL!
I KNOW, THIS IS CRAZY! WHERE'D THEY ALL COME FROM? WERE THEY HIDING?
I KNEW THERE'D BE SOMEONE HERE! I JUST KNEW IT!

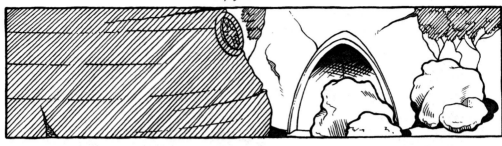

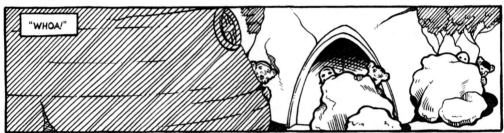

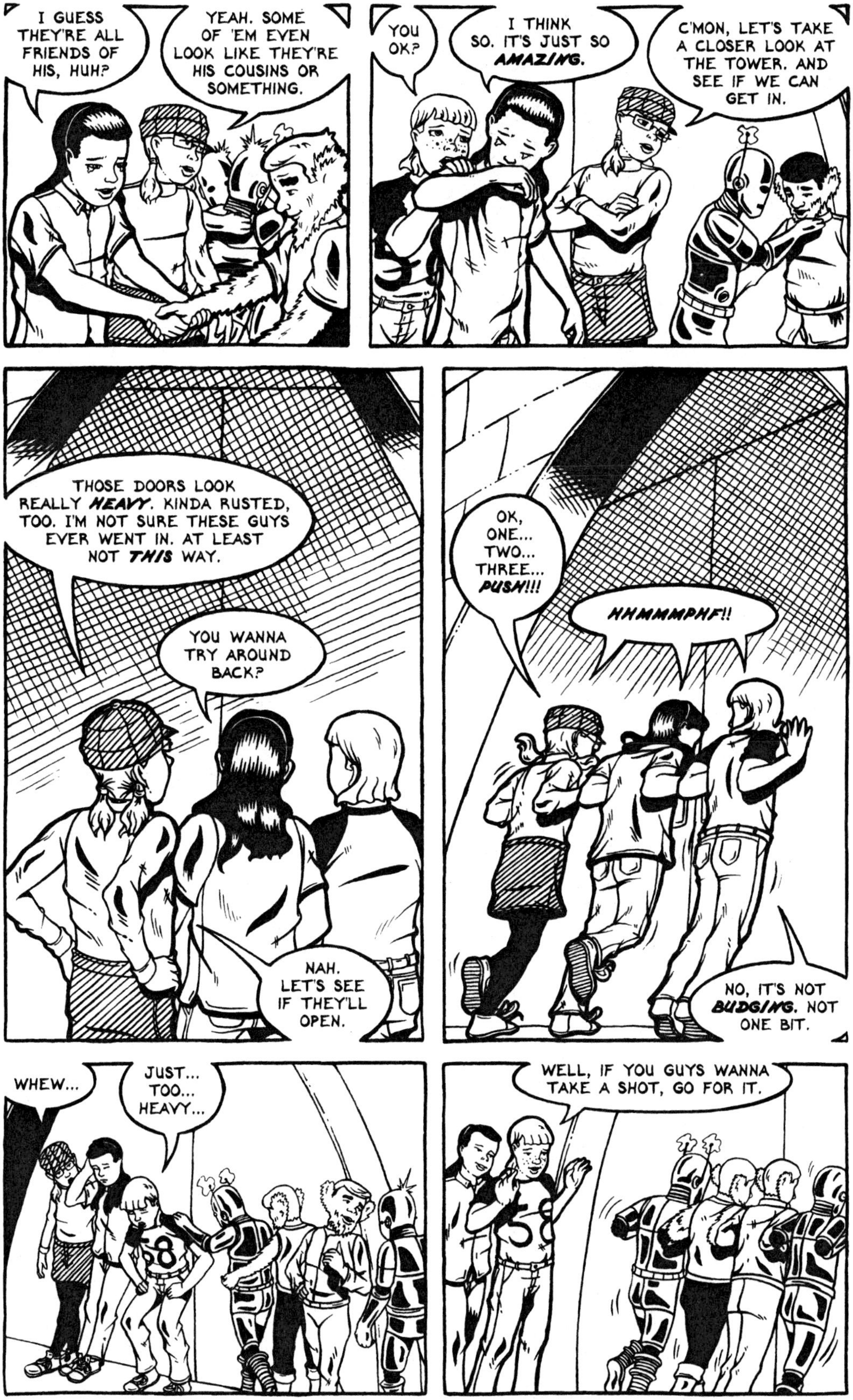
I GUESS THEY'RE ALL FRIENDS OF HIS, HUH?
YEAH. SOME OF 'EM EVEN LOOK LIKE THEY'RE HIS COUSINS OR SOMETHING.
YOU OK?
I THINK SO. IT'S JUST SO AMAZING.
C'MON, LET'S TAKE A CLOSER LOOK AT THE TOWER. AND SEE IF WE CAN GET IN.
THOSE DOORS LOOK REALLY HEAVY. KINDA RUSTED, TOO. I'M NOT SURE THESE GUYS EVER WENT IN. AT LEAST NOT THIS WAY.
YOU WANNA TRY AROUND BACK?
NAH. LET'S SEE IF THEY'LL OPEN.
OK, ONE... TWO... THREE... PUSH!!!
HHMMMMPHF!!
NO, IT'S NOT BUDGING. NOT ONE BIT.
WHEW...
JUST... TOO... HEAVY...
WELL, IF YOU GUYS WANNA TAKE A SHOT, GO FOR IT.

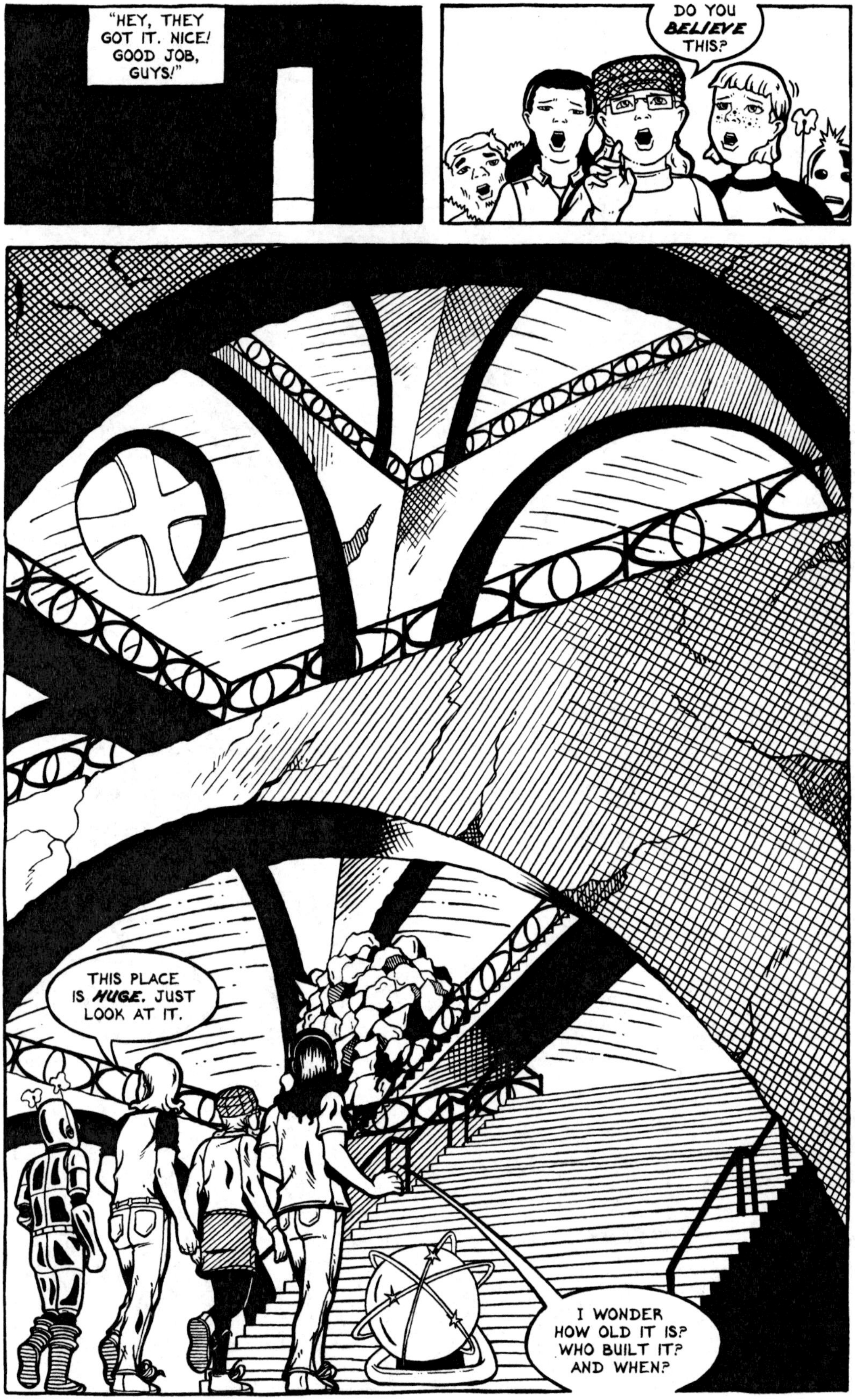
"HEY, THEY GOT IT. NICE! GOOD JOB, GUYS!"
DO YOU *BELIEVE* THIS?
THIS PLACE IS *HUGE*. JUST LOOK AT IT.
I WONDER HOW OLD IT IS? WHO BUILT IT? AND WHEN?

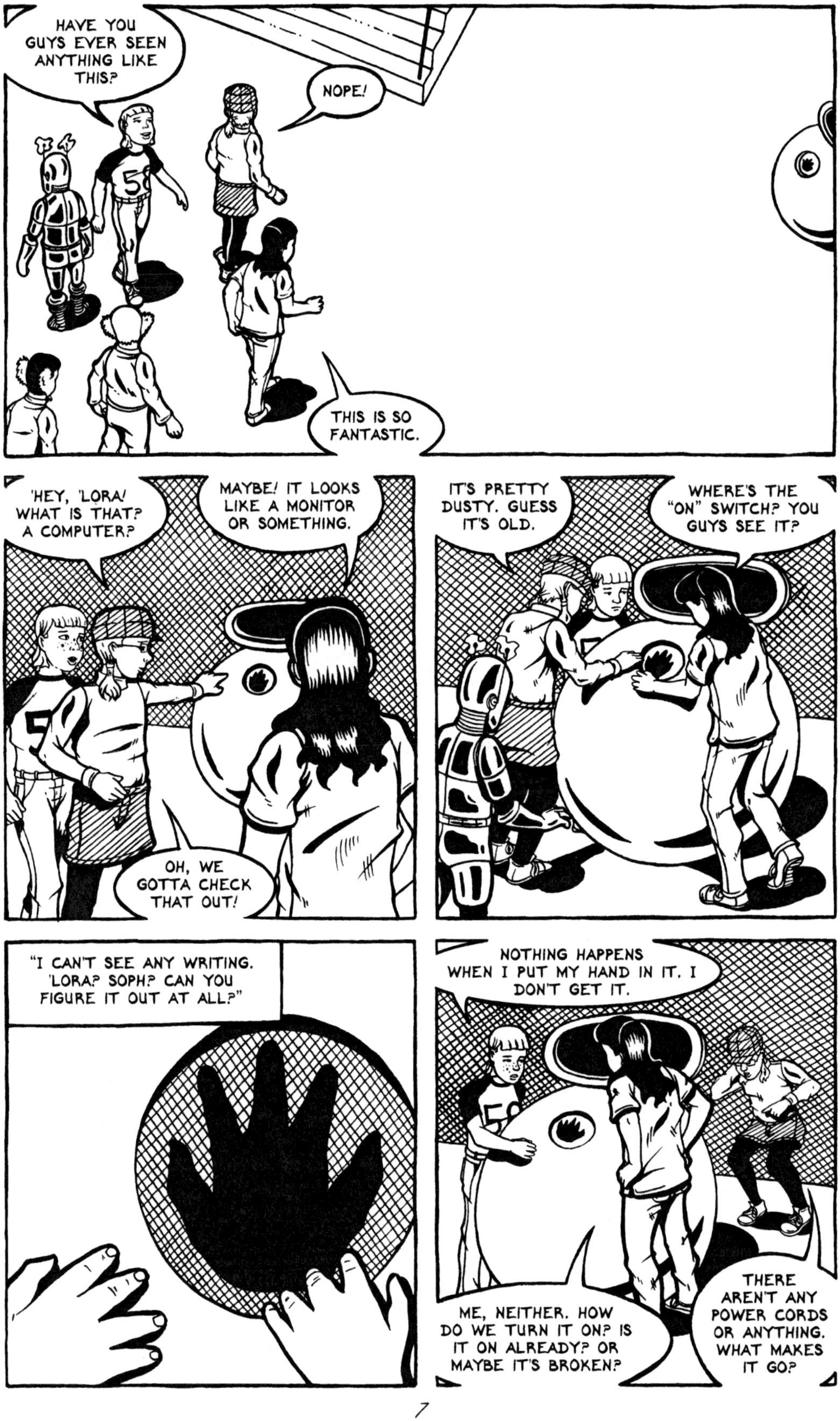
HAVE YOU GUYS EVER SEEN ANYTHING LIKE THIS?
NOPE!
THIS IS SO FANTASTIC.
'HEY, 'LORA! WHAT IS THAT? A COMPUTER?
MAYBE! IT LOOKS LIKE A MONITOR OR SOMETHING.
OH, WE GOTTA CHECK THAT OUT!
IT'S PRETTY DUSTY. GUESS IT'S OLD.
WHERE'S THE "ON" SWITCH? YOU GUYS SEE IT?
"I CAN'T SEE ANY WRITING. 'LORA? SOPH? CAN YOU FIGURE IT OUT AT ALL?"
NOTHING HAPPENS WHEN I PUT MY HAND IN IT. I DON'T GET IT.
ME, NEITHER. HOW DO WE TURN IT ON? IS IT ON ALREADY? OR MAYBE IT'S BROKEN?
THERE AREN'T ANY POWER CORDS OR ANYTHING. WHAT MAKES IT GO?

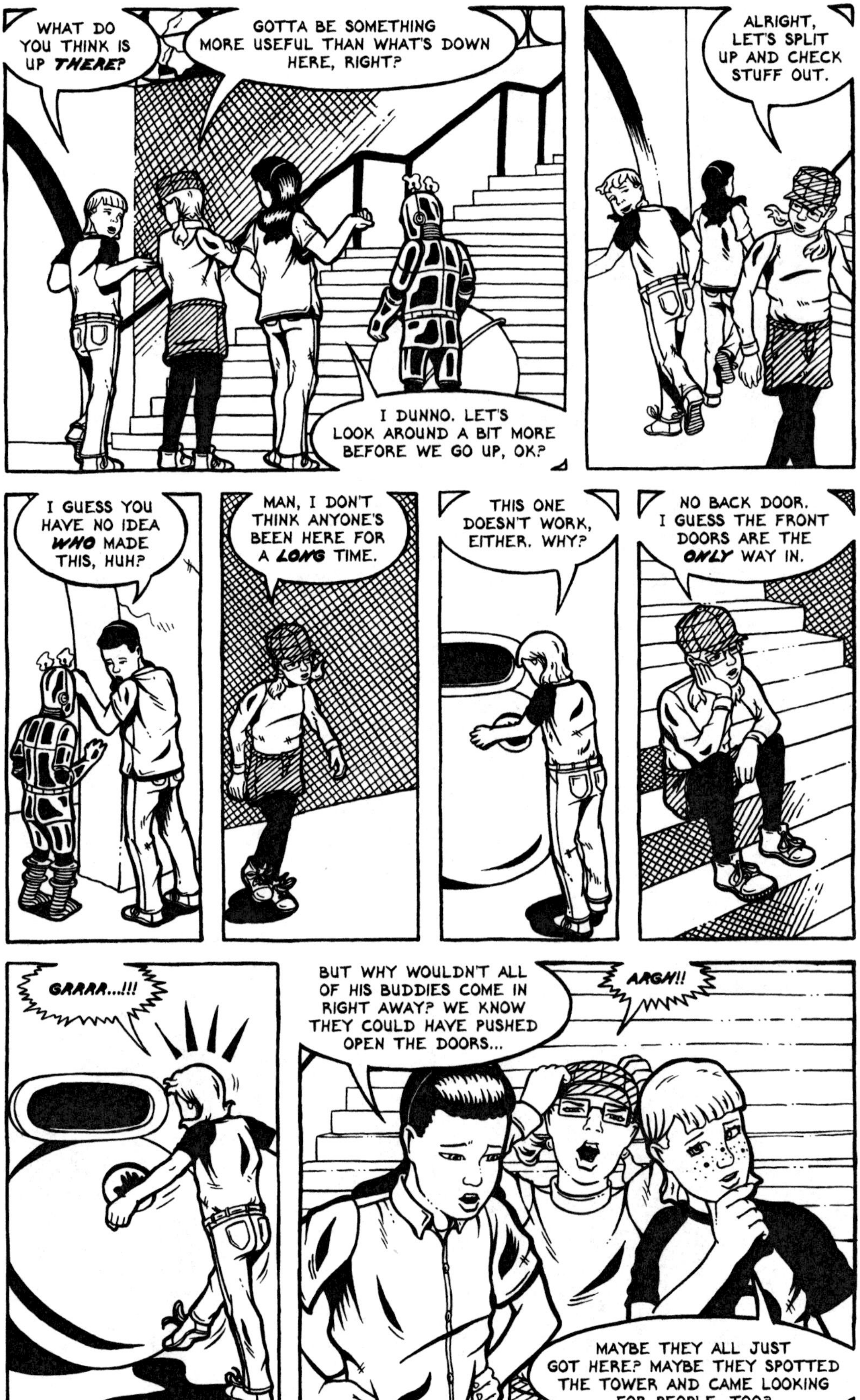
WHAT DO YOU THINK IS UP THERE?
GOTTA BE SOMETHING MORE USEFUL THAN WHAT'S DOWN HERE, RIGHT?
I DUNNO. LET'S LOOK AROUND A BIT MORE BEFORE WE GO UP, OK?
ALRIGHT, LET'S SPLIT UP AND CHECK STUFF OUT.
I GUESS YOU HAVE NO IDEA WHO MADE THIS, HUH?
MAN, I DON'T THINK ANYONE'S BEEN HERE FOR A LONG TIME.
THIS ONE DOESN'T WORK, EITHER. WHY?
NO BACK DOOR. I GUESS THE FRONT DOORS ARE THE ONLY WAY IN.
GRRRR...!!!
BUT WHY WOULDN'T ALL OF HIS BUDDIES COME IN RIGHT AWAY? WE KNOW THEY COULD HAVE PUSHED OPEN THE DOORS...
ARGH!!
MAYBE THEY ALL JUST GOT HERE? MAYBE THEY SPOTTED THE TOWER AND CAME LOOKING FOR PEOPLE, TOO?

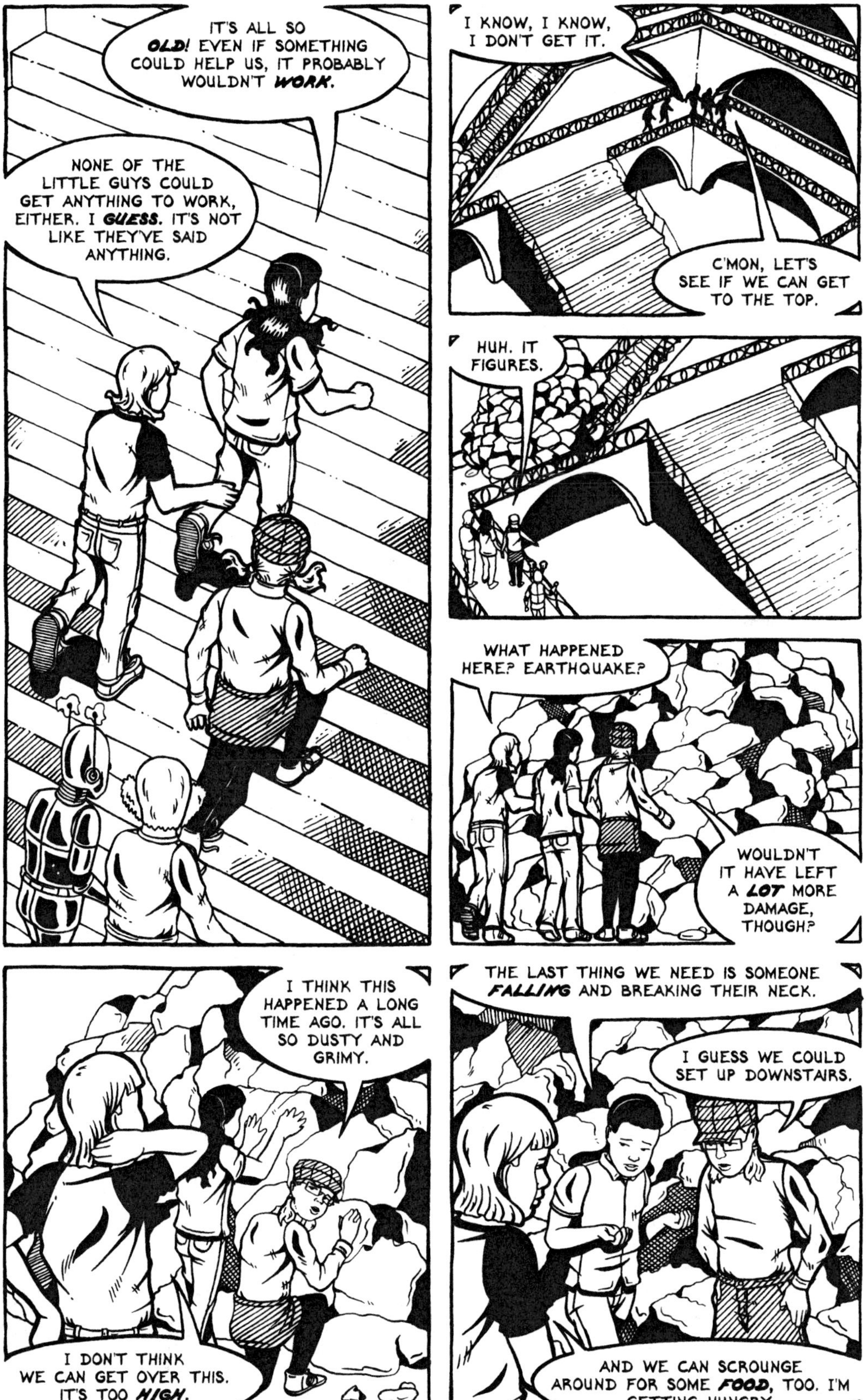
IT'S ALL SO OLD! EVEN IF SOMETHING COULD HELP US, IT PROBABLY WOULDN'T WORK.
NONE OF THE LITTLE GUYS COULD GET ANYTHING TO WORK, EITHER. I GUESS. IT'S NOT LIKE THEY'VE SAID ANYTHING.
I KNOW, I KNOW, I DON'T GET IT.
C'MON, LET'S SEE IF WE CAN GET TO THE TOP.
HUH. IT FIGURES.
WHAT HAPPENED HERE? EARTHQUAKE?
WOULDN'T IT HAVE LEFT A LOT MORE DAMAGE, THOUGH?
I THINK THIS HAPPENED A LONG TIME AGO. IT'S ALL SO DUSTY AND GRIMY.
I DON'T THINK WE CAN GET OVER THIS. IT'S TOO HIGH.
THE LAST THING WE NEED IS SOMEONE FALLING AND BREAKING THEIR NECK.
I GUESS WE COULD SET UP DOWNSTAIRS.
AND WE CAN SCROUNGE AROUND FOR SOME FOOD, TOO. I'M GETTING HUNGRY.

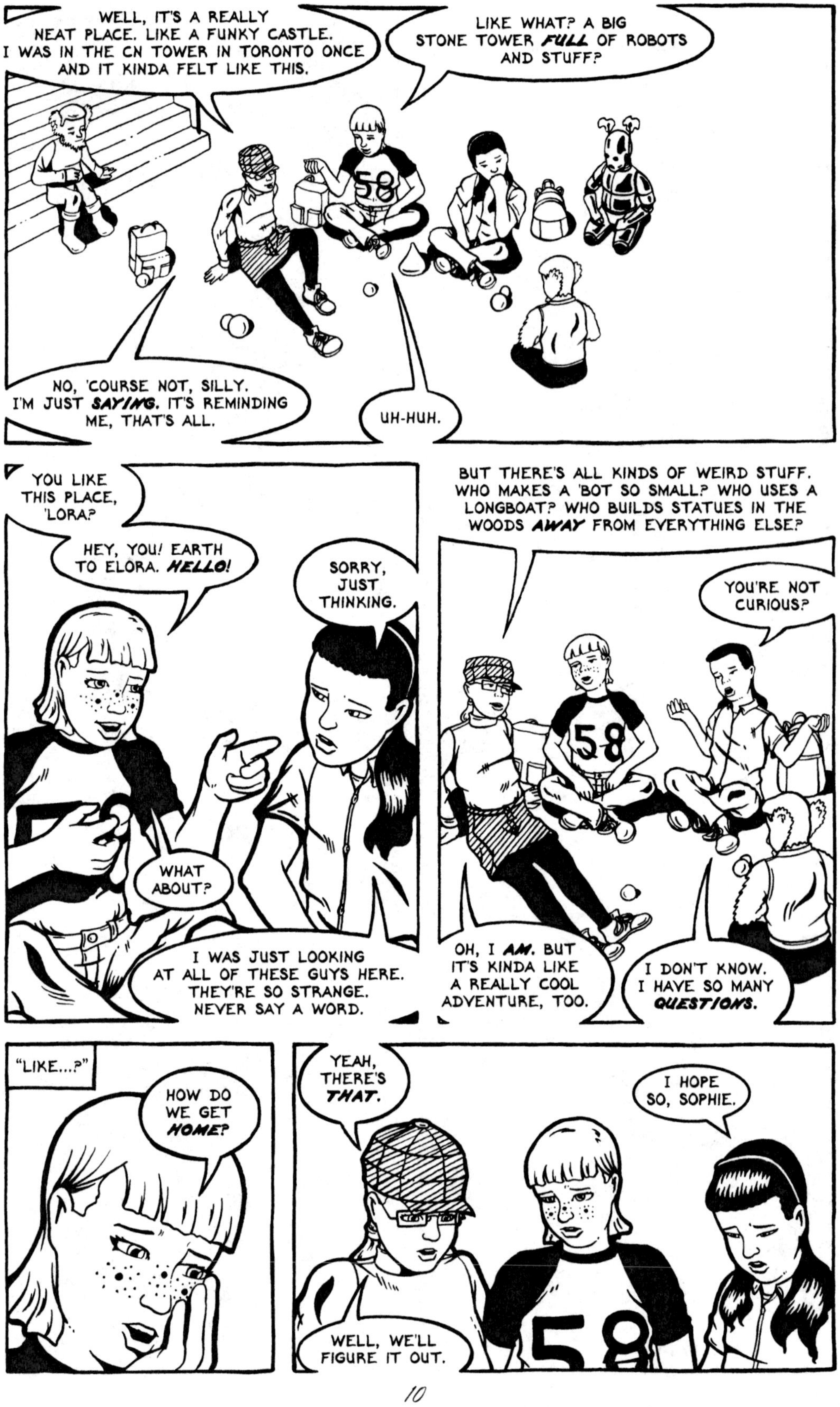
WELL, IT'S A REALLY NEAT PLACE. LIKE A FUNKY CASTLE. I WAS IN THE CN TOWER IN TORONTO ONCE AND IT KINDA FELT LIKE THIS.
LIKE WHAT? A BIG STONE TOWER FULL OF ROBOTS AND STUFF?
NO, 'COURSE NOT, SILLY. I'M JUST SAYING. IT'S REMINDING ME, THAT'S ALL.
UH-HUH.
YOU LIKE THIS PLACE, 'LORA?
HEY, YOU! EARTH TO ELORA. HELLO!
SORRY, JUST THINKING.
WHAT ABOUT?
I WAS JUST LOOKING AT ALL OF THESE GUYS HERE. THEY'RE SO STRANGE. NEVER SAY A WORD.
BUT THERE'S ALL KINDS OF WEIRD STUFF. WHO MAKES A 'BOT SO SMALL? WHO USES A LONGBOAT? WHO BUILDS STATUES IN THE WOODS AWAY FROM EVERYTHING ELSE?
YOU'RE NOT CURIOUS?
OH, I AM. BUT IT'S KINDA LIKE A REALLY COOL ADVENTURE, TOO.
I DON'T KNOW. I HAVE SO MANY QUESTIONS.
"LIKE...?"
HOW DO WE GET HOME?
YEAH, THERE'S THAT.
I HOPE SO, SOPHIE.
WELL, WE'LL FIGURE IT OUT.

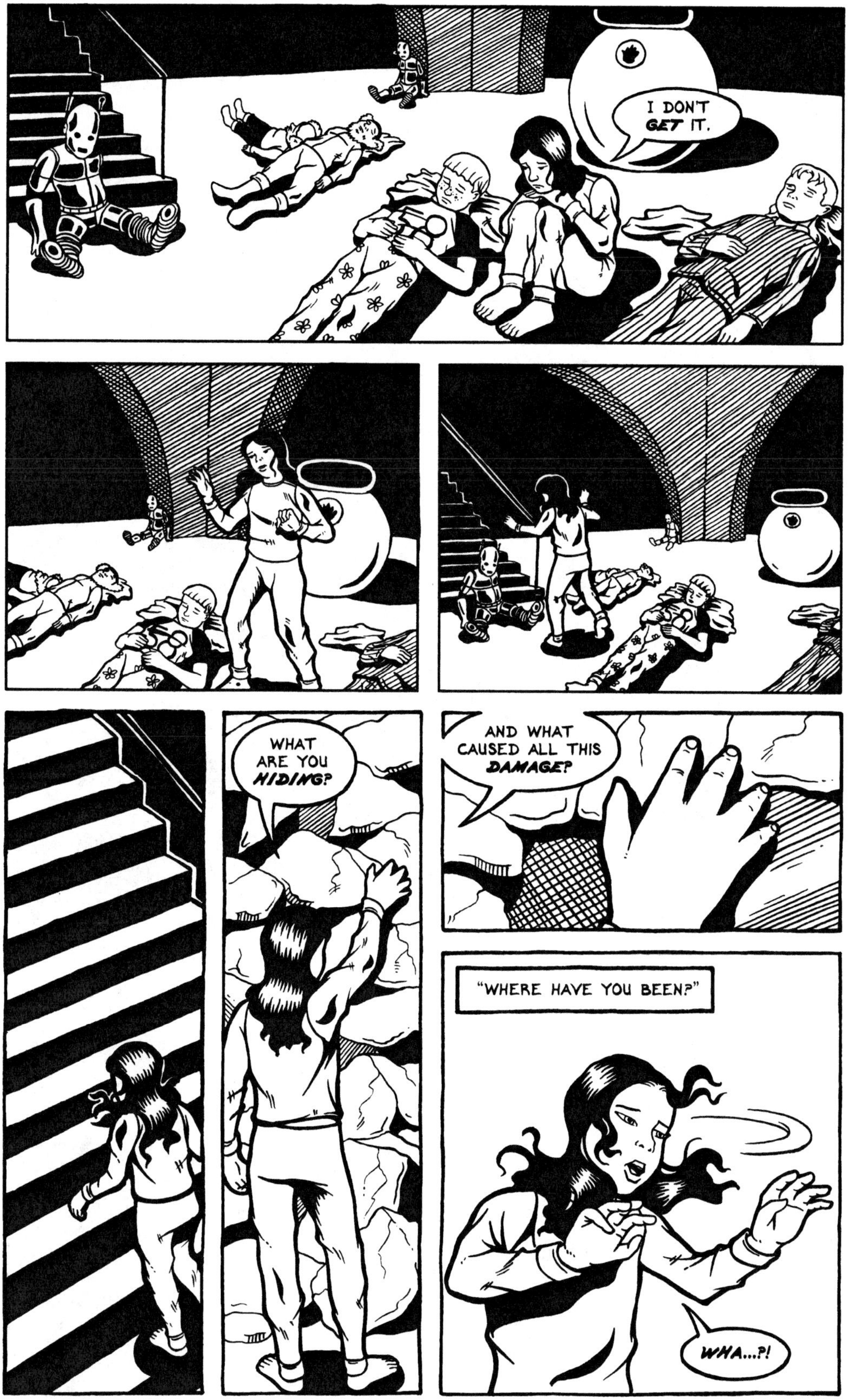
I DON'T GET IT.
WHAT ARE YOU HIDING?
AND WHAT CAUSED ALL THIS DAMAGE?
"WHERE HAVE YOU BEEN?"
WHA...?!

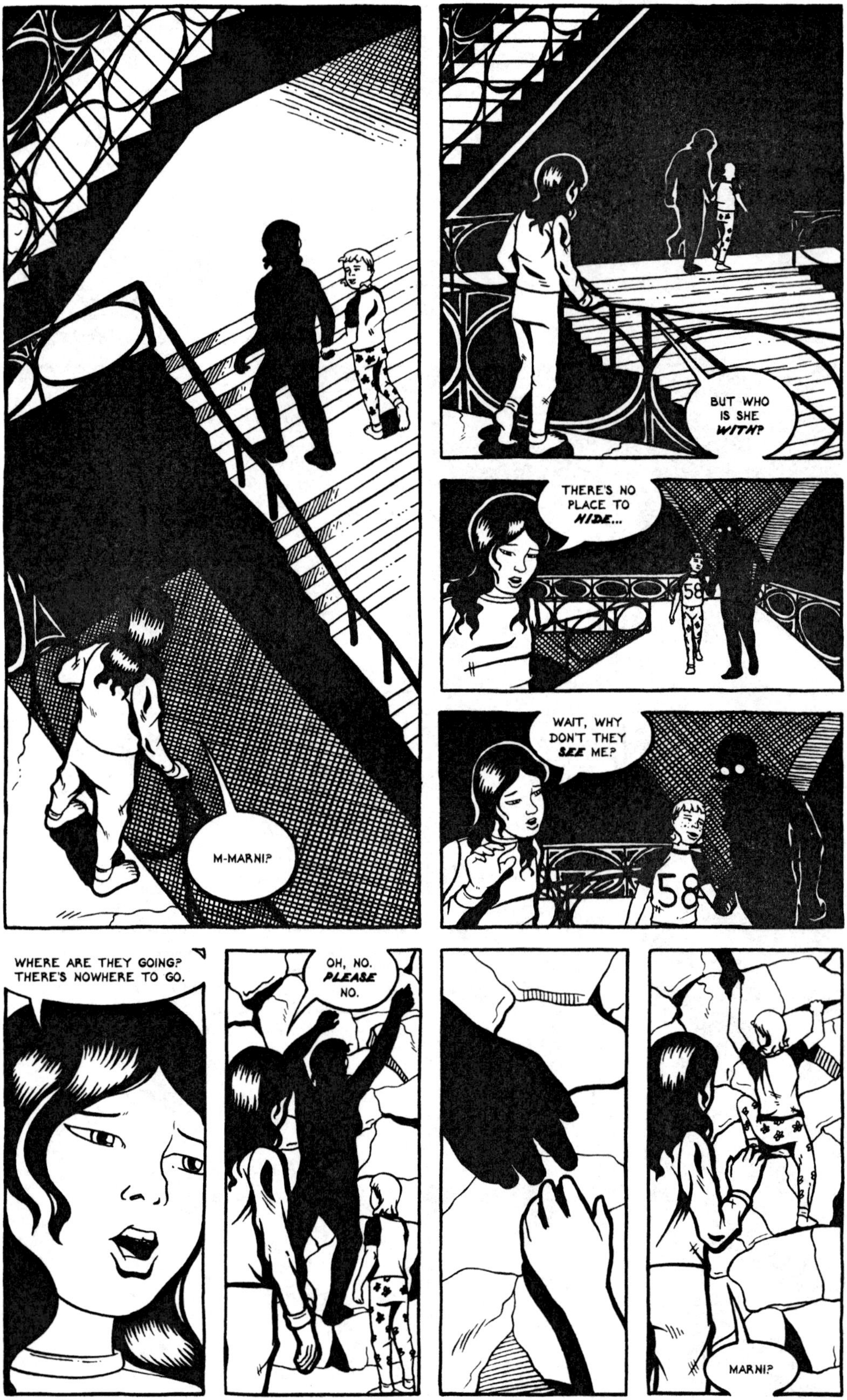
M-MARNI?
BUT WHO IS SHE WITH?
THERE'S NO PLACE TO HIDE...
58
WAIT, WHY DON'T THEY SEE ME?
58
WHERE ARE THEY GOING? THERE'S NOWHERE TO GO.
OH, NO. PLEASE NO.
MARNI?

MARNI!
MARNI! WAIT!
OH, WHAT DO I DO?
I-I HAVE TO CATCH HER.
C'MON, C'MON! I'VE GOTTA GO FASTER!
"NO!"
AAAAAAAAAAH!

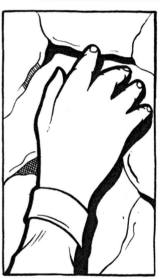

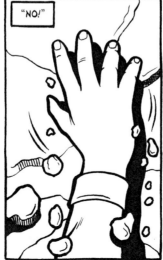

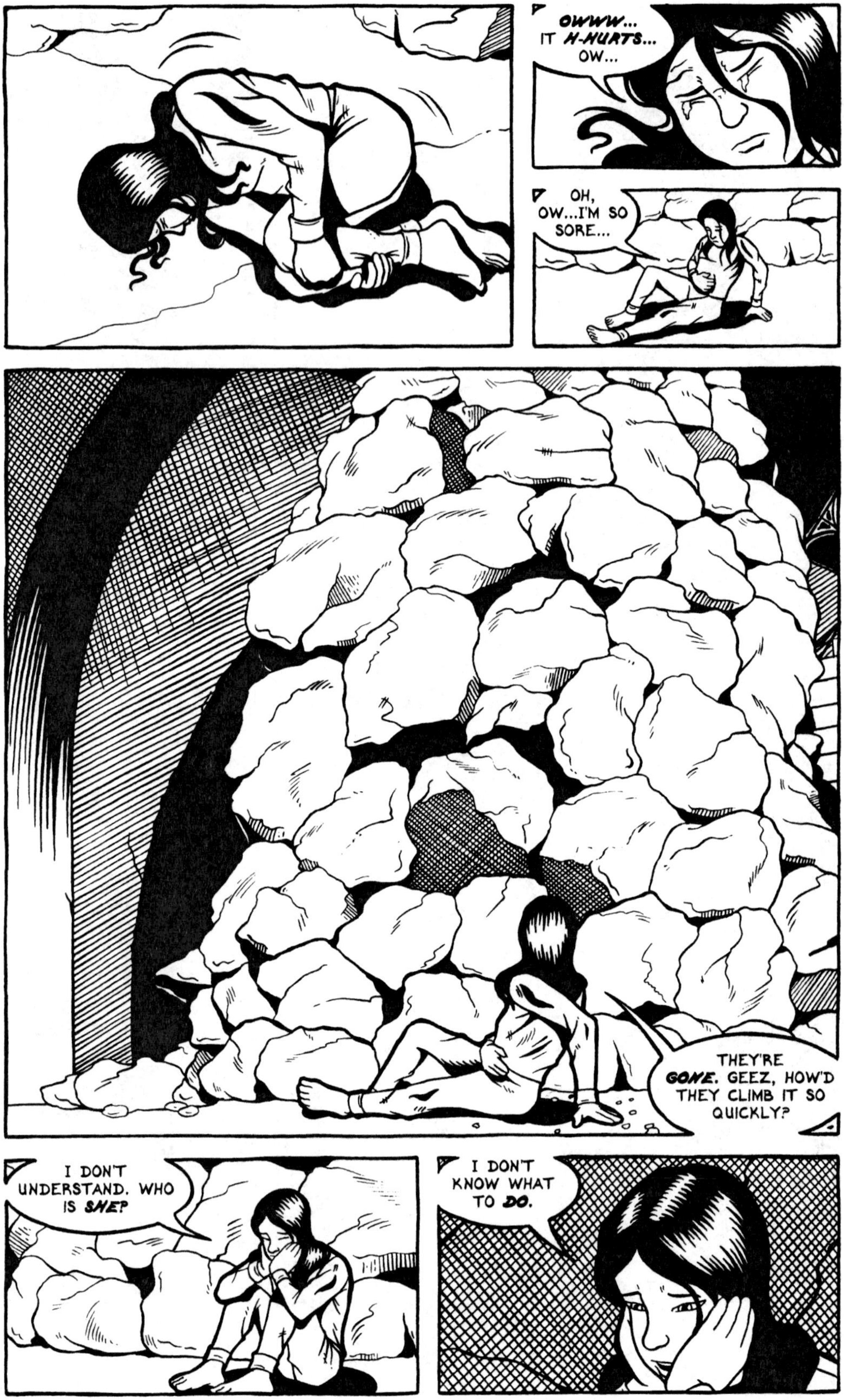
OWWW... IT H-HURTS... OW...
OH, OW...I'M SO SORE...
THEY'RE GONE. GEEZ, HOW'D THEY CLIMB IT SO QUICKLY?
I DON'T UNDERSTAND. WHO IS SHE?
I DON'T KNOW WHAT TO DO.

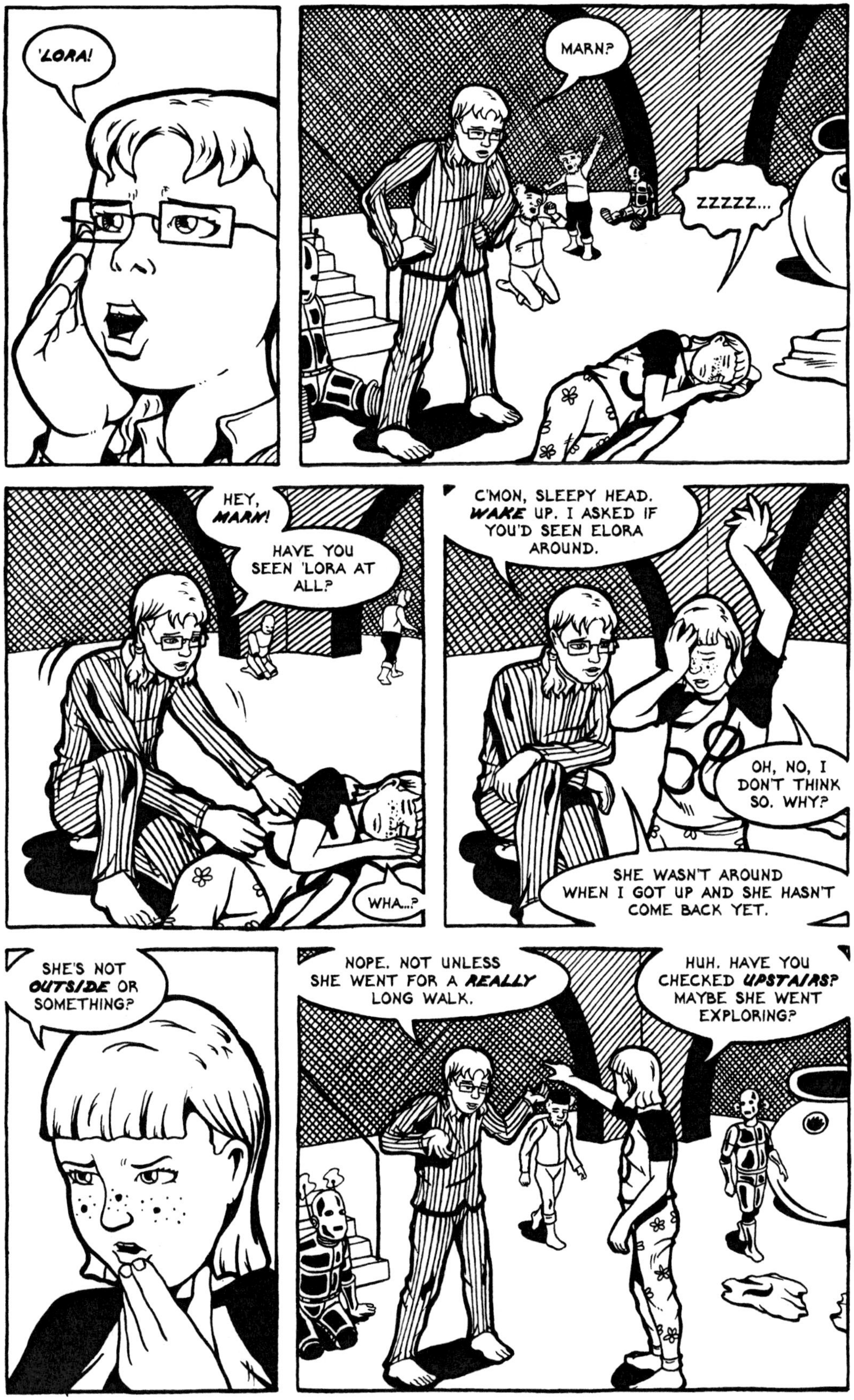
'LORA!
MARN?
ZZZZZ...
HEY, *MARN*!
HAVE YOU SEEN 'LORA AT ALL?
WHA...?
C'MON, SLEEPY HEAD. *WAKE* UP. I ASKED IF YOU'D SEEN ELORA AROUND.
OH, NO, I DON'T THINK SO. WHY?
SHE WASN'T AROUND WHEN I GOT UP AND SHE HASN'T COME BACK YET.
SHE'S NOT *OUTSIDE* OR SOMETHING?
NOPE. NOT UNLESS SHE WENT FOR A *REALLY* LONG WALK.
HUH. HAVE YOU CHECKED *UPSTAIRS*? MAYBE SHE WENT EXPLORING?

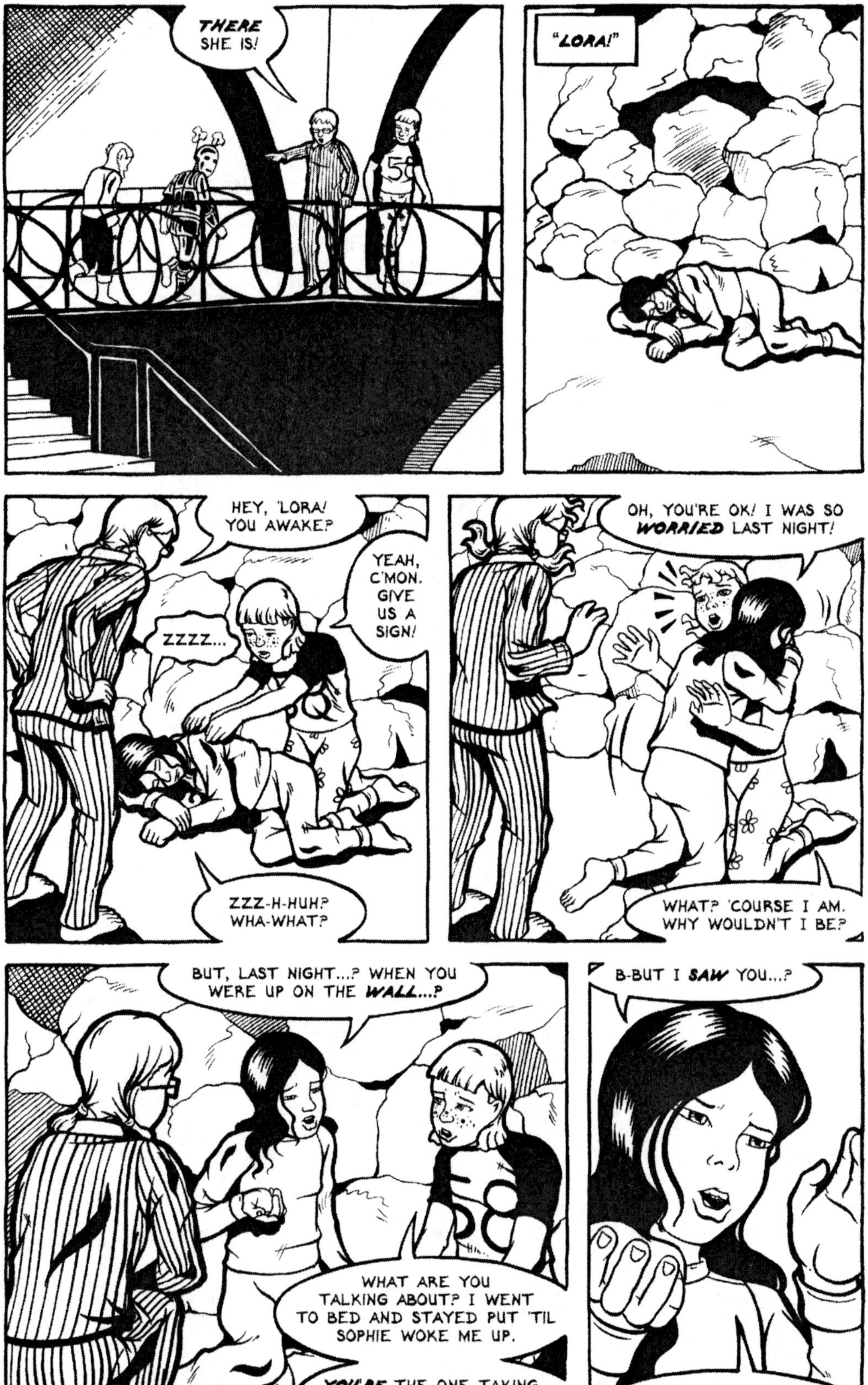
THERE SHE IS!
"LORA!"
HEY, 'LORA! YOU AWAKE?
YEAH, C'MON. GIVE US A SIGN!
ZZZZ...
ZZZ-H-HUH? WHA-WHAT?
OH, YOU'RE OK! I WAS SO WORRIED LAST NIGHT!
WHAT? 'COURSE I AM. WHY WOULDN'T I BE?
BUT, LAST NIGHT...? WHEN YOU WERE UP ON THE WALL...?
WHAT ARE YOU TALKING ABOUT? I WENT TO BED AND STAYED PUT 'TIL SOPHIE WOKE ME UP.
YOU'RE THE ONE TAKING THE LATE NIGHT WALKS.
B-BUT I SAW YOU...?
I'M SURE I SAW YOU.

WHOA! GUESS THIS MEANS HE MISSED YOU, TOO, HUH?

I-I...

IT'S OK, LITTLE GUY. I'M *F-FINE.* REALLY. I'M FINE.

SO, *WHY* WERE YOU UP HERE AGAIN?

I THOUGHT I SAW...

AH, FORGET IT. I MUST HAVE IMAGINED IT OR SOMETHING.

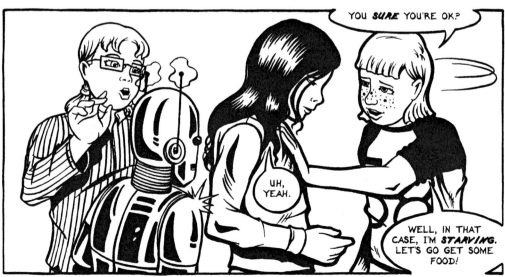

YOU *SURE* YOU'RE OK?

UH, YEAH.

WELL, IN THAT CASE, I'M *STARVING.* LET'S GO GET SOME FOOD!

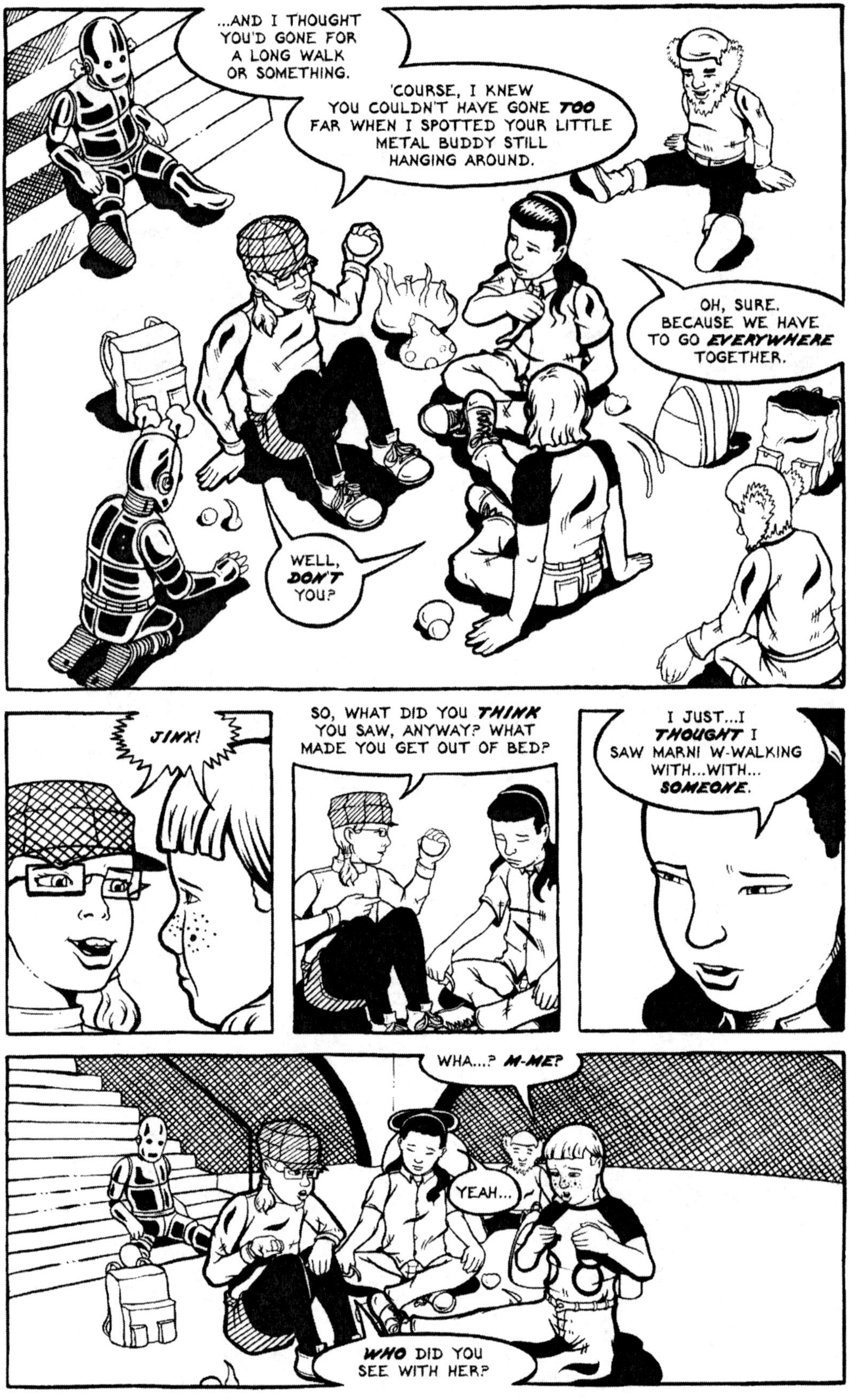
...AND I THOUGHT YOU'D GONE FOR A LONG WALK OR SOMETHING.
'COURSE, I KNEW YOU COULDN'T HAVE GONE *TOO* FAR WHEN I SPOTTED YOUR LITTLE METAL BUDDY STILL HANGING AROUND.
OH, SURE. BECAUSE WE HAVE TO GO *EVERYWHERE* TOGETHER.
WELL, *DON'T* YOU?
JINX!
SO, WHAT DID YOU *THINK* YOU SAW, ANYWAY? WHAT MADE YOU GET OUT OF BED?
I JUST...I *THOUGHT* I SAW MARNI W-WALKING WITH...WITH... *SOMEONE*.
WHA...? *M-ME?*
YEAH...
WHO DID YOU SEE WITH HER?

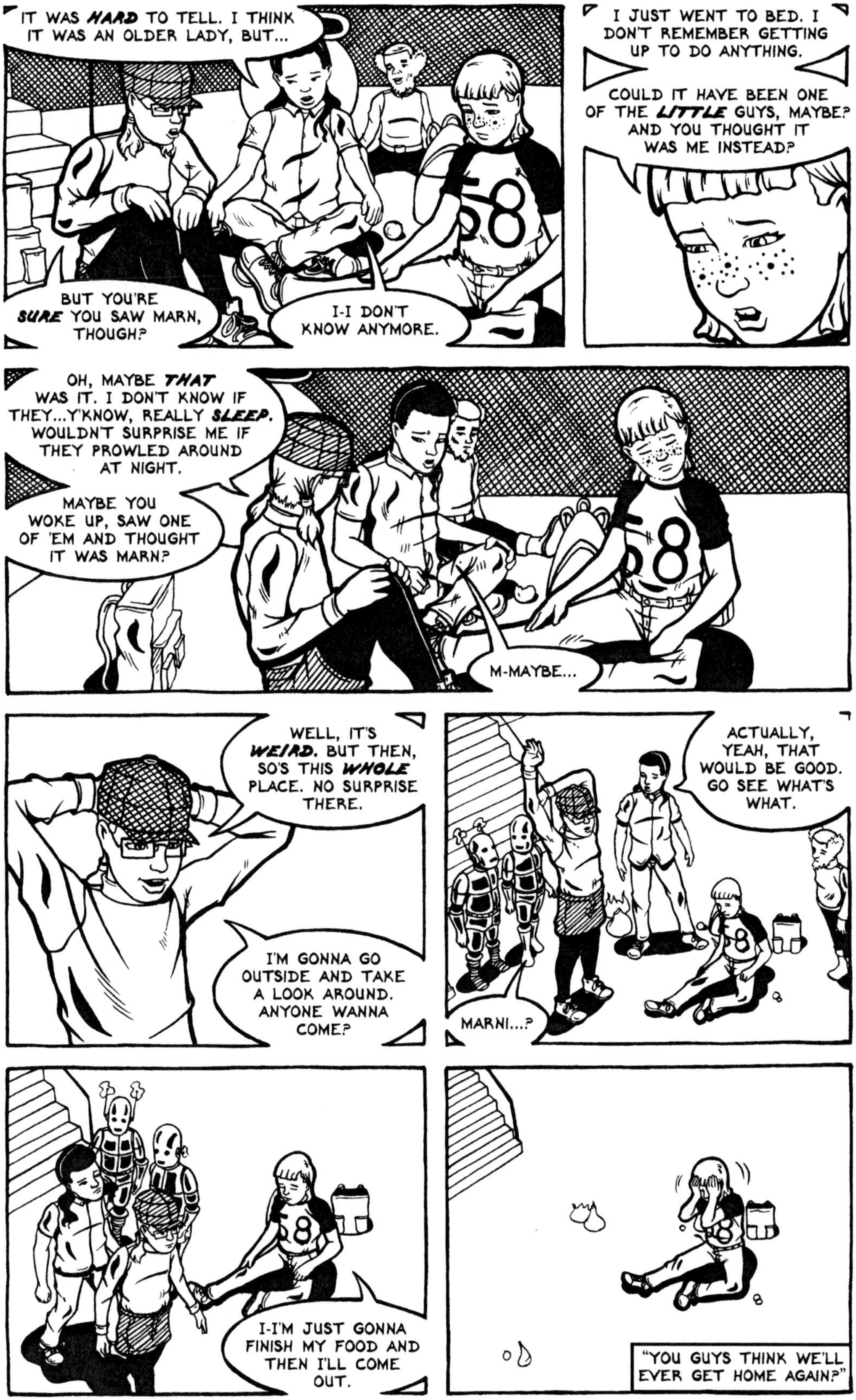
IT WAS HARD TO TELL. I THINK IT WAS AN OLDER LADY, BUT...
BUT YOU'RE SURE YOU SAW MARN, THOUGH?
I-I DON'T KNOW ANYMORE.
I JUST WENT TO BED. I DON'T REMEMBER GETTING UP TO DO ANYTHING.
COULD IT HAVE BEEN ONE OF THE LITTLE GUYS, MAYBE? AND YOU THOUGHT IT WAS ME INSTEAD?
OH, MAYBE THAT WAS IT. I DON'T KNOW IF THEY...Y'KNOW, REALLY SLEEP. WOULDN'T SURPRISE ME IF THEY PROWLED AROUND AT NIGHT.
MAYBE YOU WOKE UP, SAW ONE OF 'EM AND THOUGHT IT WAS MARN?
M-MAYBE...
WELL, IT'S WEIRD. BUT THEN, SO'S THIS WHOLE PLACE. NO SURPRISE THERE.
I'M GONNA GO OUTSIDE AND TAKE A LOOK AROUND. ANYONE WANNA COME?
ACTUALLY, YEAH, THAT WOULD BE GOOD. GO SEE WHAT'S WHAT.
MARNI...?
I-I'M JUST GONNA FINISH MY FOOD AND THEN I'LL COME OUT.
"YOU GUYS THINK WE'LL EVER GET HOME AGAIN?"

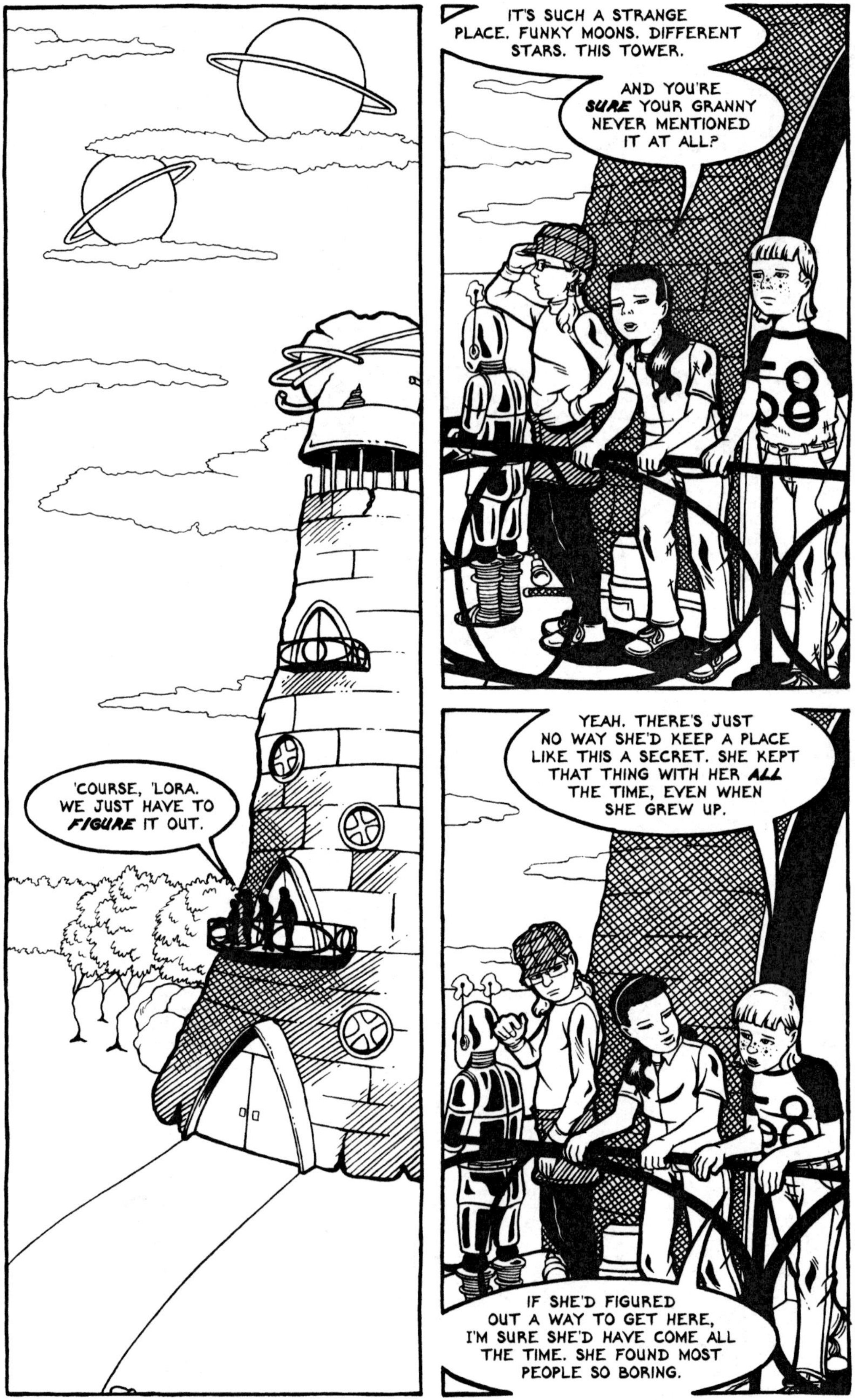
'COURSE, 'LORA. WE JUST HAVE TO FIGURE IT OUT.
IT'S SUCH A STRANGE PLACE. FUNKY MOONS. DIFFERENT STARS. THIS TOWER.
AND YOU'RE SURE YOUR GRANNY NEVER MENTIONED IT AT ALL?
YEAH. THERE'S JUST NO WAY SHE'D KEEP A PLACE LIKE THIS A SECRET. SHE KEPT THAT THING WITH HER ALL THE TIME, EVEN WHEN SHE GREW UP.
IF SHE'D FIGURED OUT A WAY TO GET HERE, I'M SURE SHE'D HAVE COME ALL THE TIME. SHE FOUND MOST PEOPLE SO BORING.

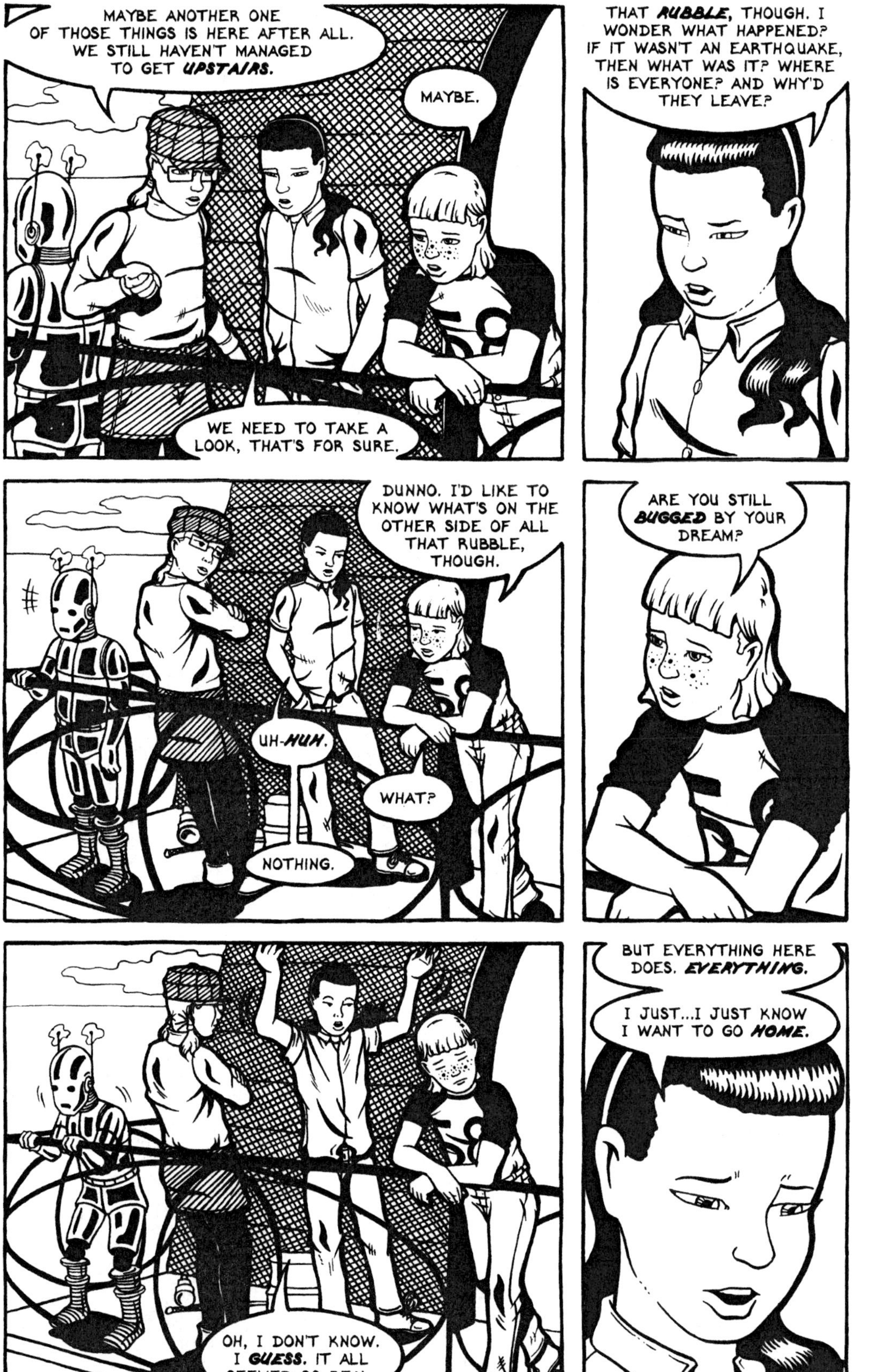
MAYBE ANOTHER ONE OF THOSE THINGS IS HERE AFTER ALL. WE STILL HAVEN'T MANAGED TO GET UPSTAIRS.
MAYBE.
WE NEED TO TAKE A LOOK, THAT'S FOR SURE.
THAT RUBBLE, THOUGH. I WONDER WHAT HAPPENED? IF IT WASN'T AN EARTHQUAKE, THEN WHAT WAS IT? WHERE IS EVERYONE? AND WHY'D THEY LEAVE?
DUNNO. I'D LIKE TO KNOW WHAT'S ON THE OTHER SIDE OF ALL THAT RUBBLE, THOUGH.
UH-HUH.
WHAT?
NOTHING.
ARE YOU STILL BUGGED BY YOUR DREAM?
OH, I DON'T KNOW. I GUESS. IT ALL SEEMED SO REAL.
BUT EVERYTHING HERE DOES. EVERYTHING.
I JUST...I JUST KNOW I WANT TO GO HOME.

WE'LL FIGURE IT OUT. WE'RE *SMART*.

MAYBE TOMORROW WE CAN REALLY START EXPLORING. SEE IF THERE'S ANYTHING *NEW* TO DISCOVER AROUND HERE.

THERE'S GOT TO BE *SOMETHING* UP THERE THAT CAN HELP US.

YOU THINK?

I'M AN OPTIMIST, WHAT CAN I SAY?

HEY, WHAT'S UP WITH THE LITTLE GUY?

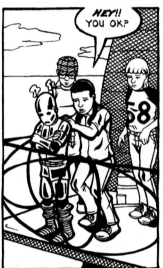

HEY!! YOU OK?

R O A R

OH, *NO*... NO, NO, NO NO...

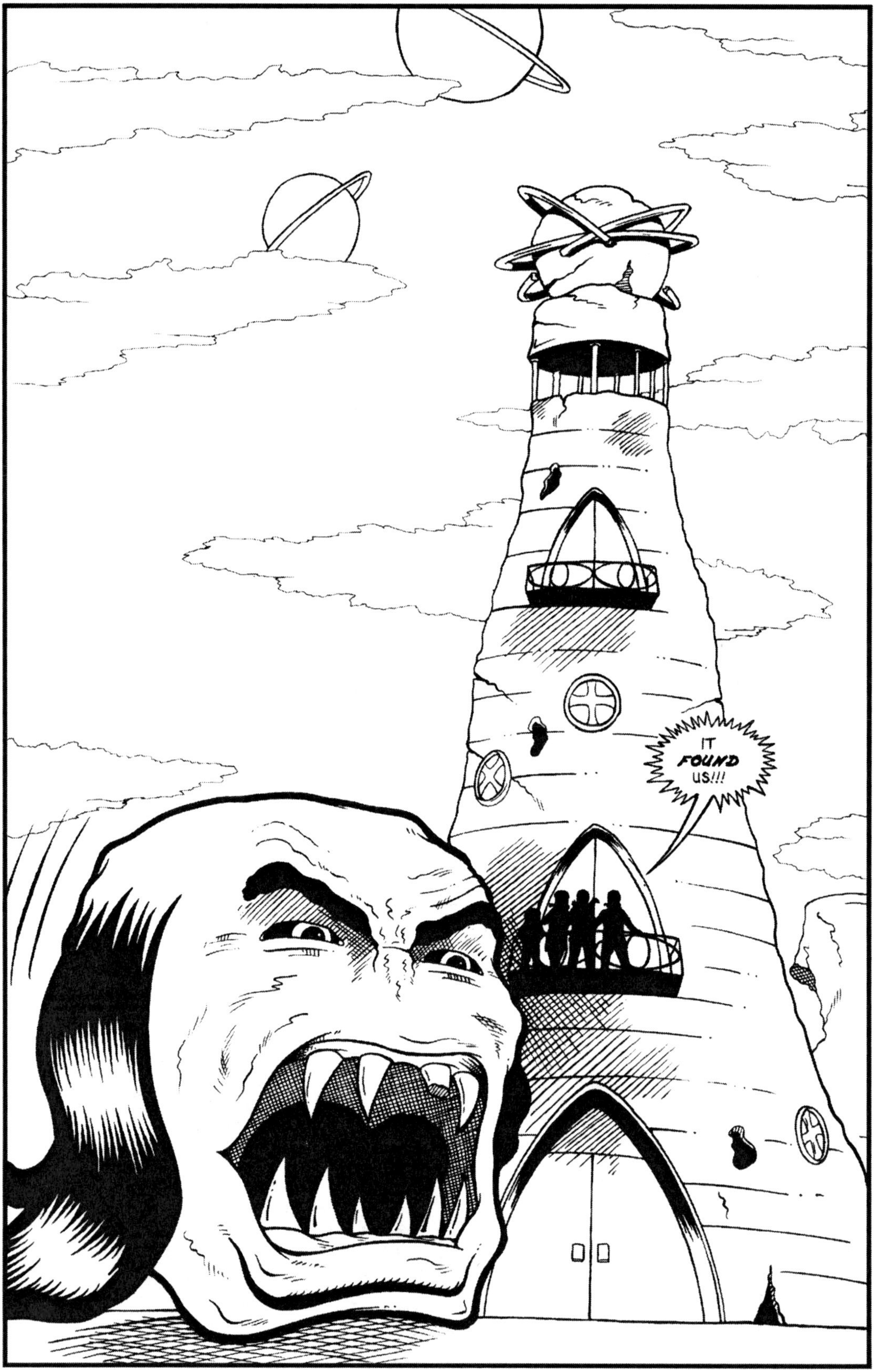
IT FOUND US!!!

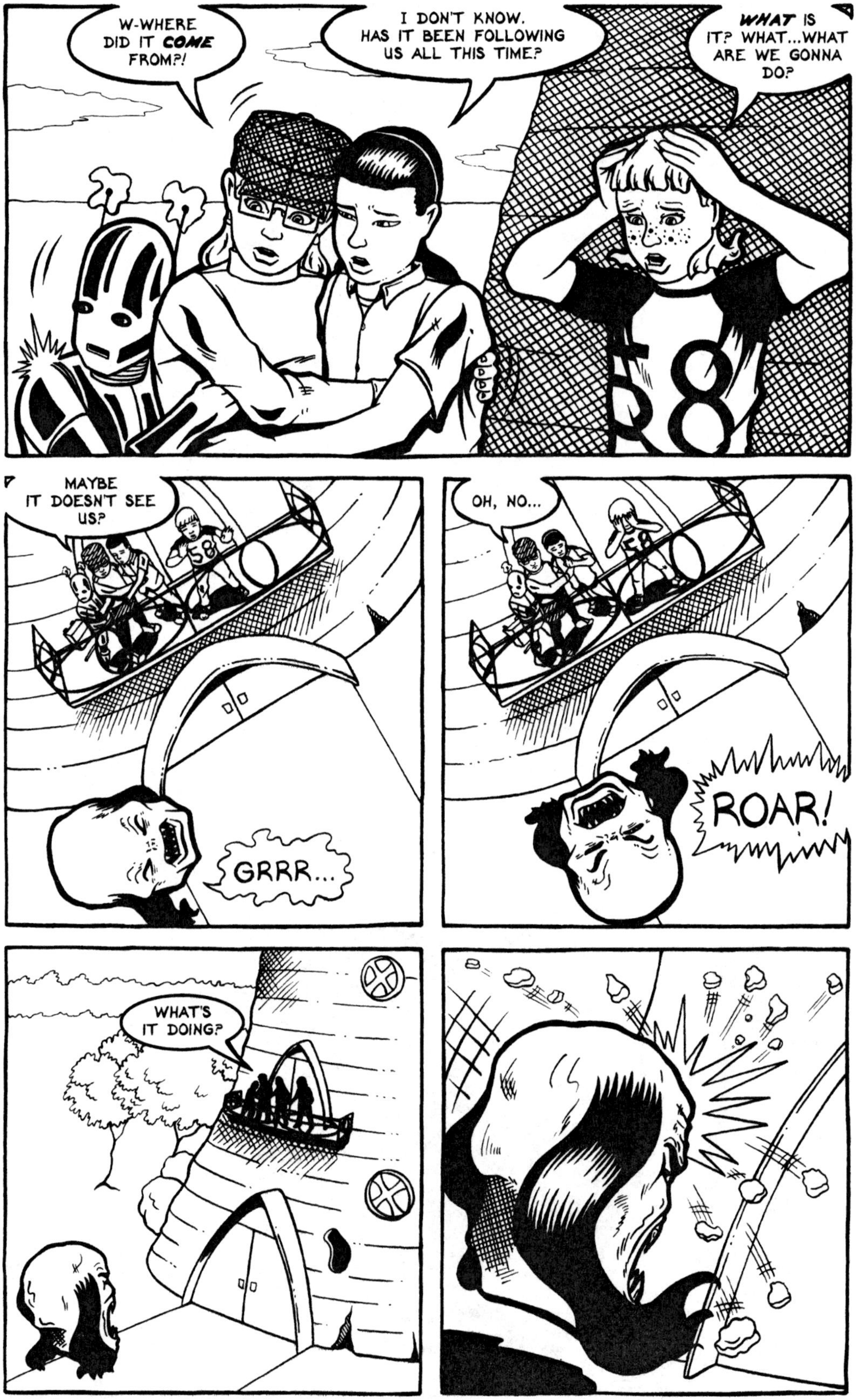
W-WHERE DID IT **COME** FROM?!
I DON'T KNOW. HAS IT BEEN FOLLOWING US ALL THIS TIME?
WHAT IS IT? WHAT...WHAT ARE WE GONNA DO?
MAYBE IT DOESN'T SEE US?
GRRR...
OH, NO...
WHAT
ROAR!
WHAT'S IT DOING?

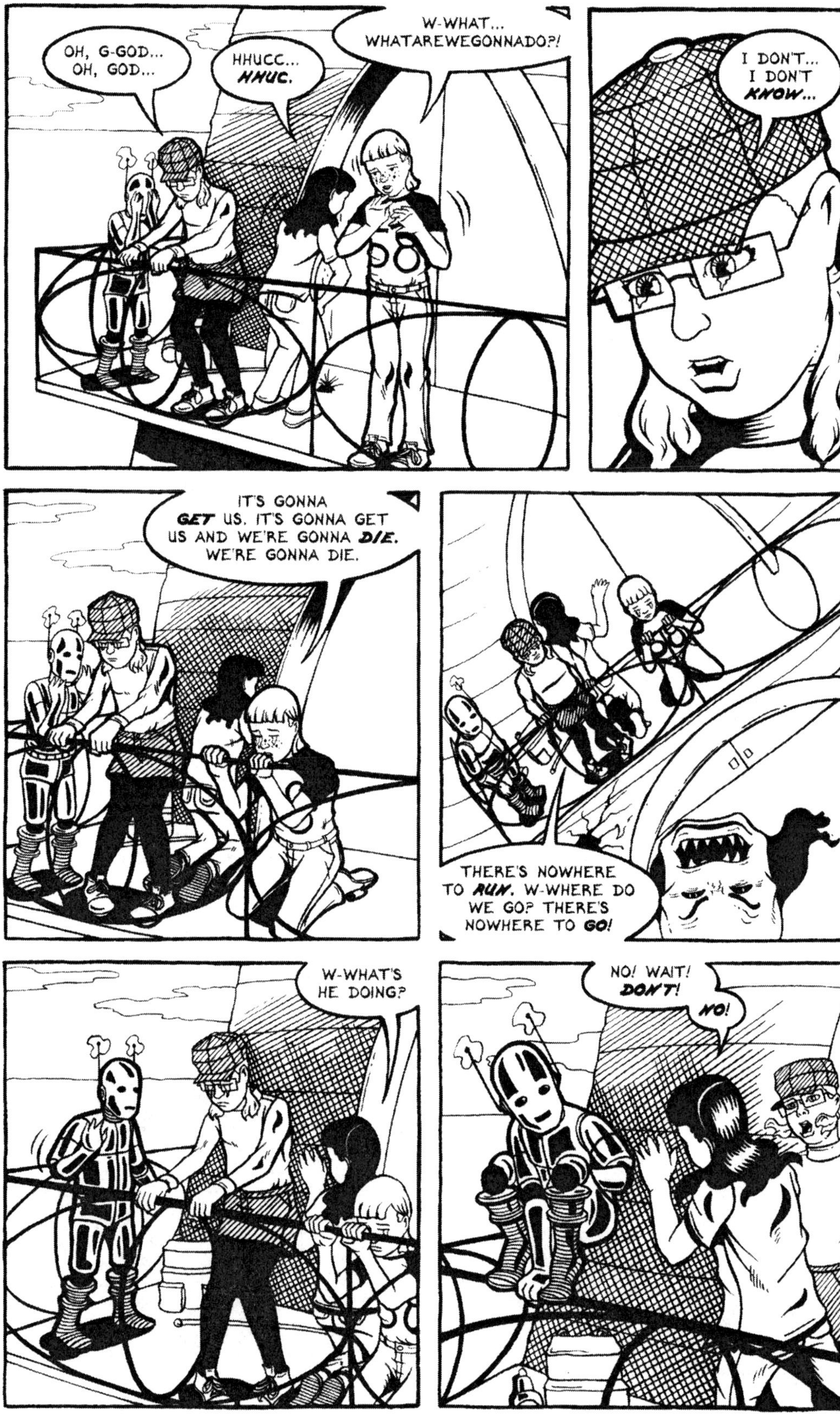
OH, G-GOD...
OH, GOD...
HHUCC...
NNUC.
W-WHAT...
WHATAREWEGONNADO?!
I DON'T...
I DON'T
KNOW...
IT'S GONNA GET US. IT'S GONNA GET US AND WE'RE GONNA DIE. WE'RE GONNA DIE.
THERE'S NOWHERE TO RUN. W-WHERE DO WE GO? THERE'S NOWHERE TO GO!
W-WHAT'S HE DOING?
NO! WAIT! DON'T!
NO!

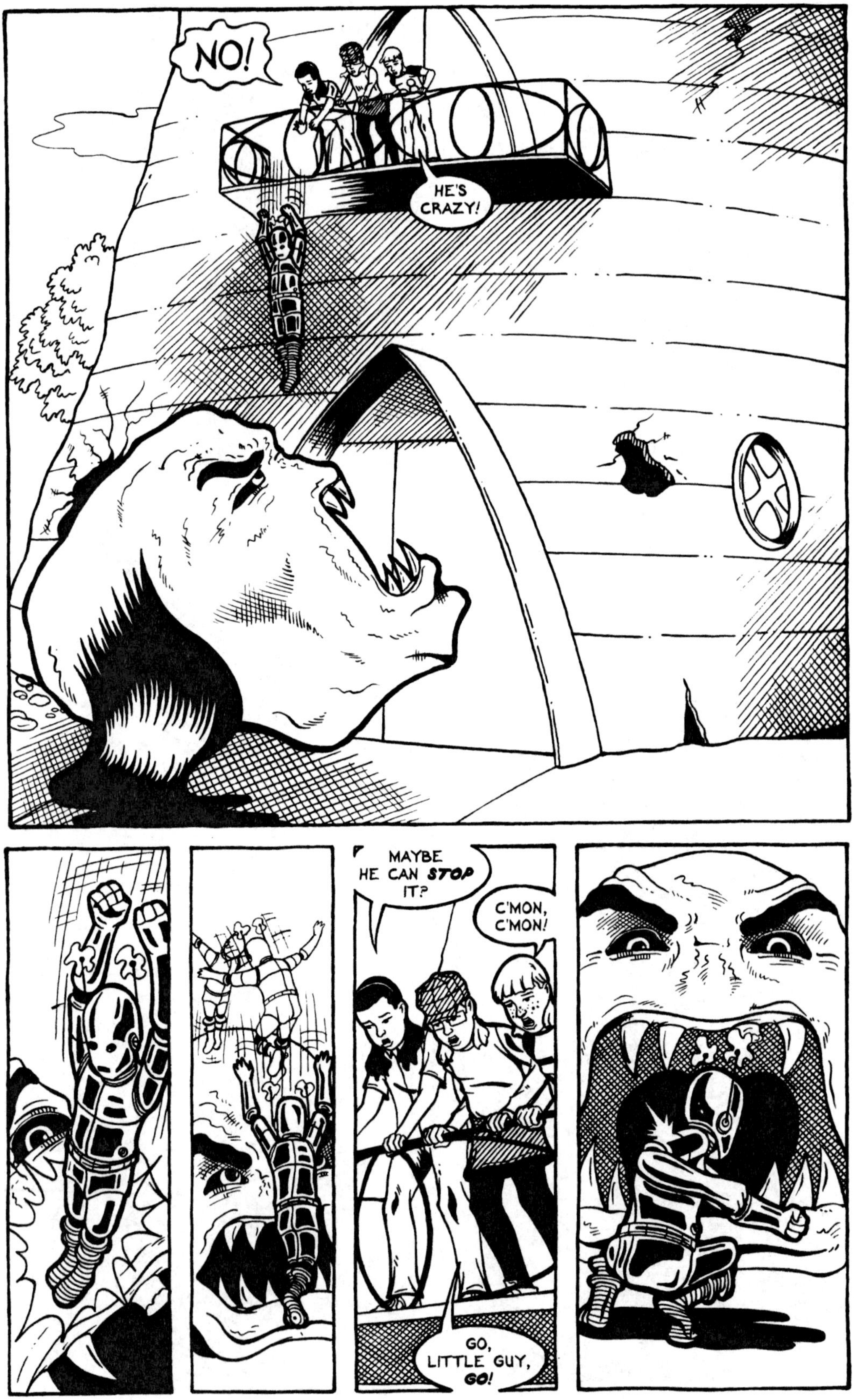
NO!
HE'S CRAZY!
MAYBE HE CAN **STOP** IT?
C'MON, C'MON!
GO, LITTLE GUY, **GO!**

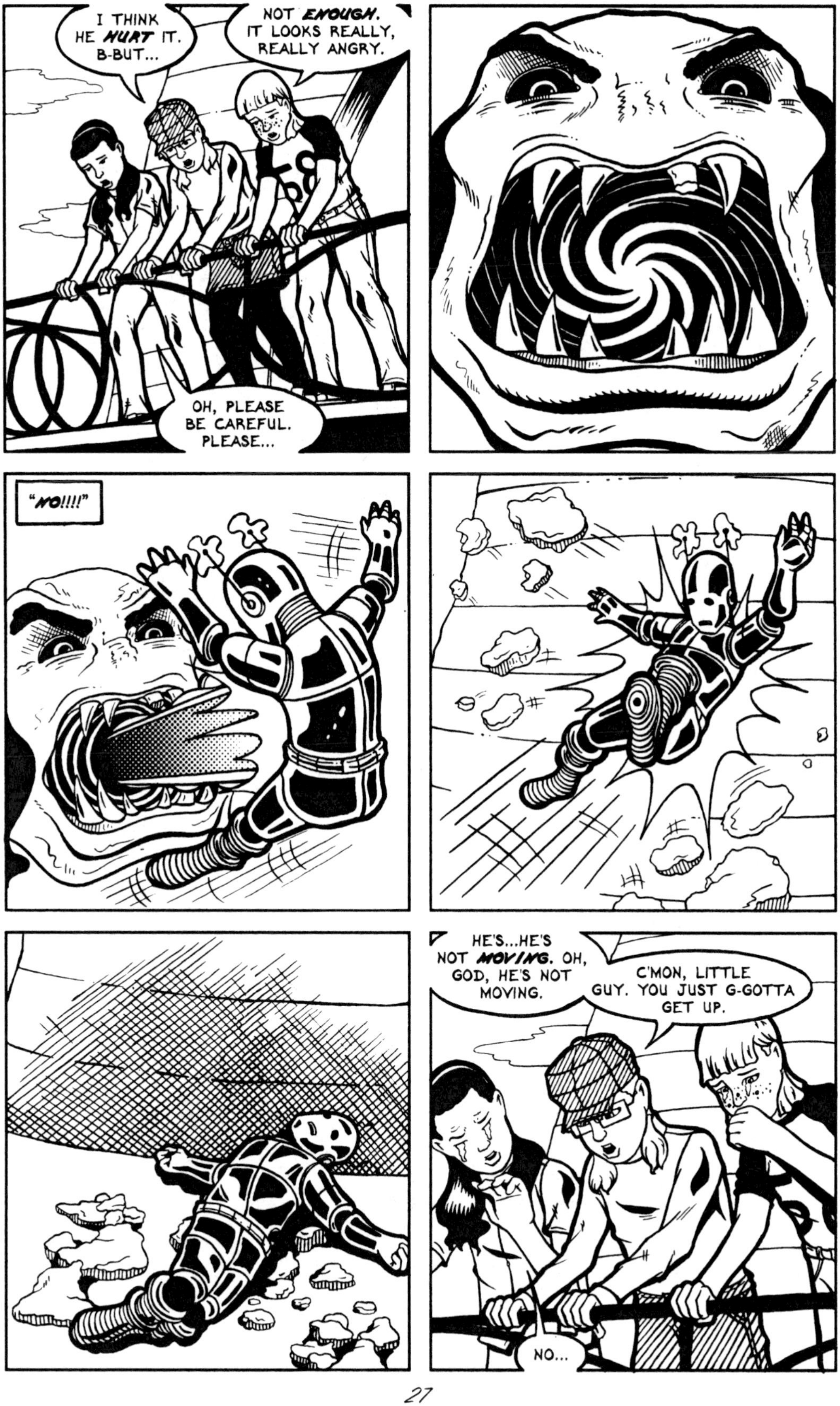
I THINK HE HURT IT. B-BUT...
NOT ENOUGH. IT LOOKS REALLY, REALLY ANGRY.
OH, PLEASE BE CAREFUL. PLEASE...
"NO!!!!"
HE'S...HE'S NOT MOVING. OH, GOD, HE'S NOT MOVING.
C'MON, LITTLE GUY. YOU JUST G-GOTTA GET UP.
NO...

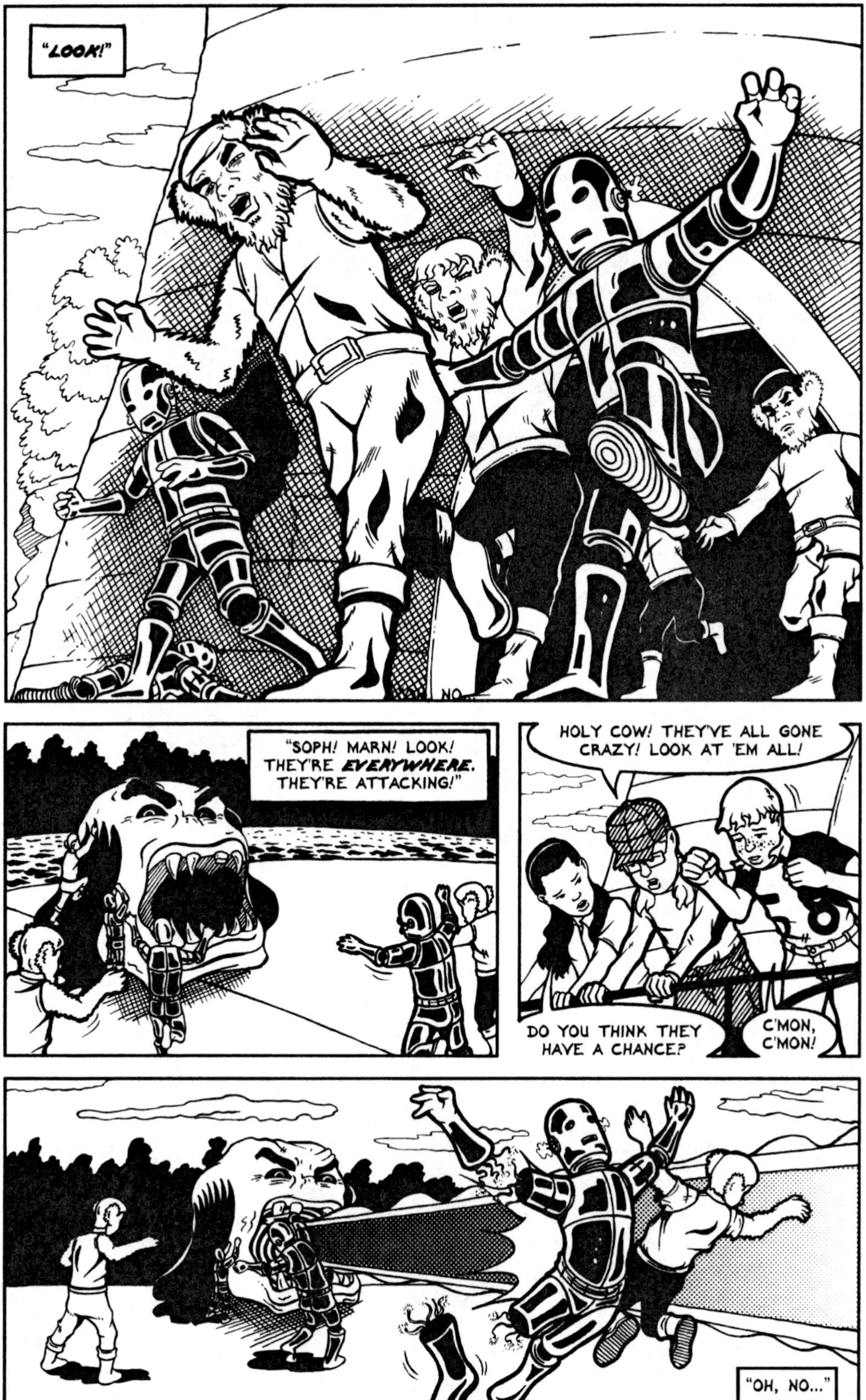
"LOOK!"
NO
"SOPH! MARN! LOOK! THEY'RE EVERYWHERE. THEY'RE ATTACKING!"
HOLY COW! THEY'VE ALL GONE CRAZY! LOOK AT 'EM ALL!
DO YOU THINK THEY HAVE A CHANCE?
C'MON, C'MON!
"OH, NO..."

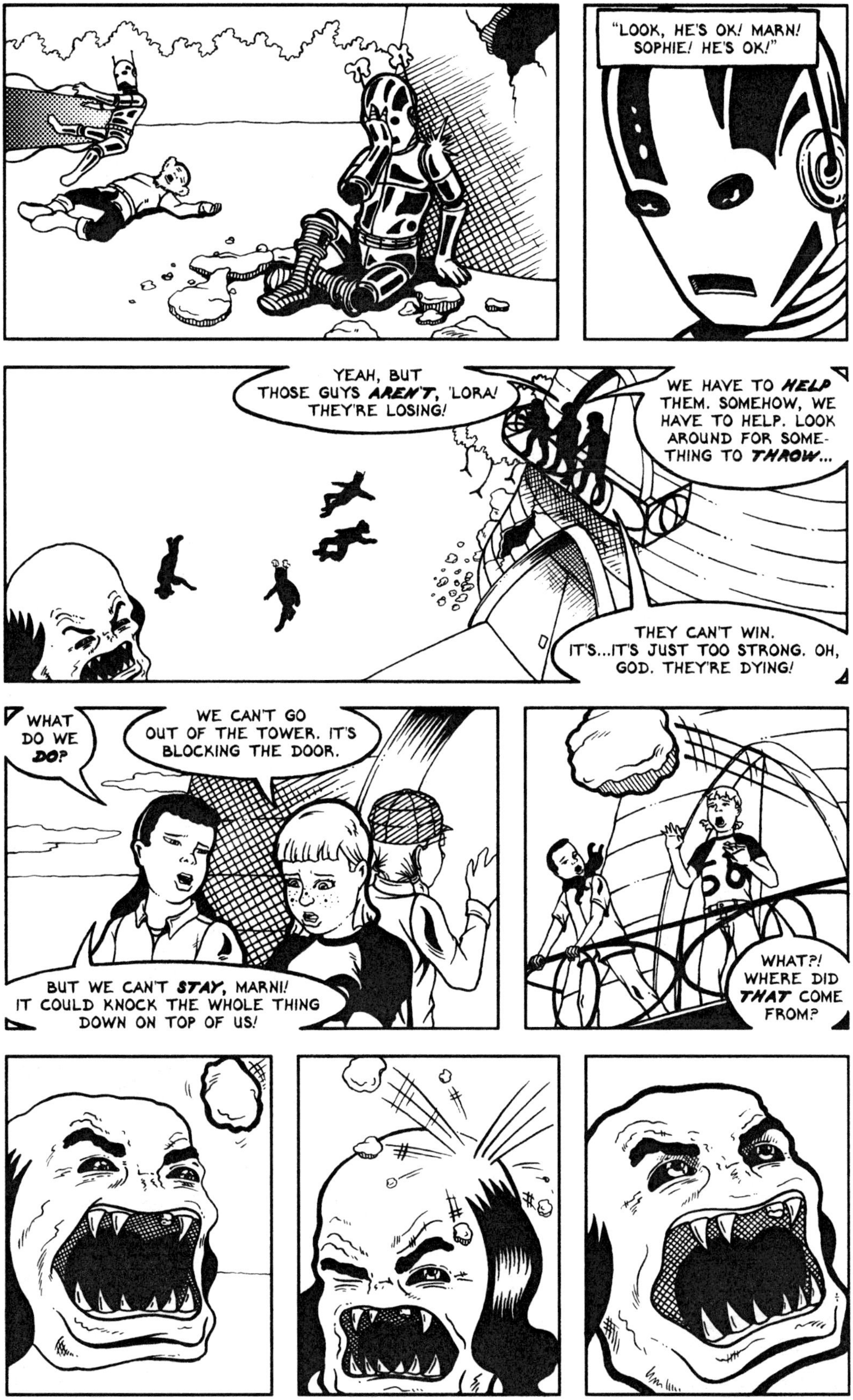
"LOOK, HE'S OK! MARN! SOPHIE! HE'S OK!"
YEAH, BUT THOSE GUYS AREN'T, 'LORA! THEY'RE LOSING!
WE HAVE TO HELP THEM. SOMEHOW, WE HAVE TO HELP. LOOK AROUND FOR SOMETHING TO THROW...
THEY CAN'T WIN. IT'S...IT'S JUST TOO STRONG. OH, GOD. THEY'RE DYING!
WHAT DO WE DO?
WE CAN'T GO OUT OF THE TOWER. IT'S BLOCKING THE DOOR.
BUT WE CAN'T STAY, MARNI! IT COULD KNOCK THE WHOLE THING DOWN ON TOP OF US!
WHAT?! WHERE DID THAT COME FROM?

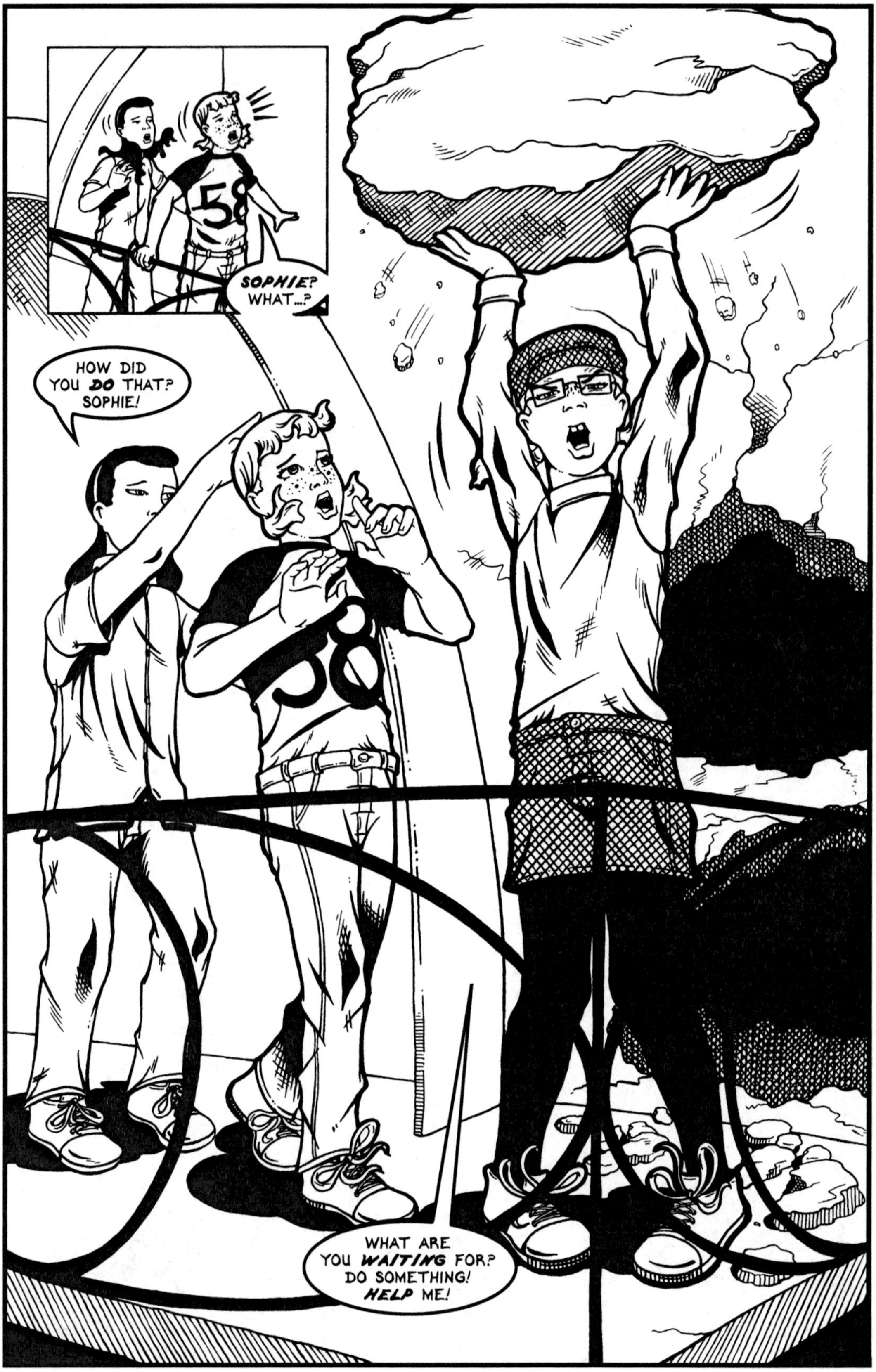
SOPHIE? WHAT...?
HOW DID YOU DO THAT? SOPHIE!
WHAT ARE YOU WAITING FOR? DO SOMETHING! HELP ME!

C'MON!

GUYS, GUYS!

YOU'VE GOT TO GET OUT OF THE WAY! NOW! *MOVE!*

MAYBE THE SWORD?

"MARN, IT'S ATTACKING THE WALLS! YOU GOTTA *HELP* US!"

WHAT USE IS A SWORD?

THINK.

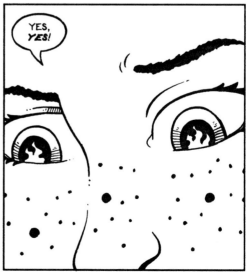

YES, *YES!*

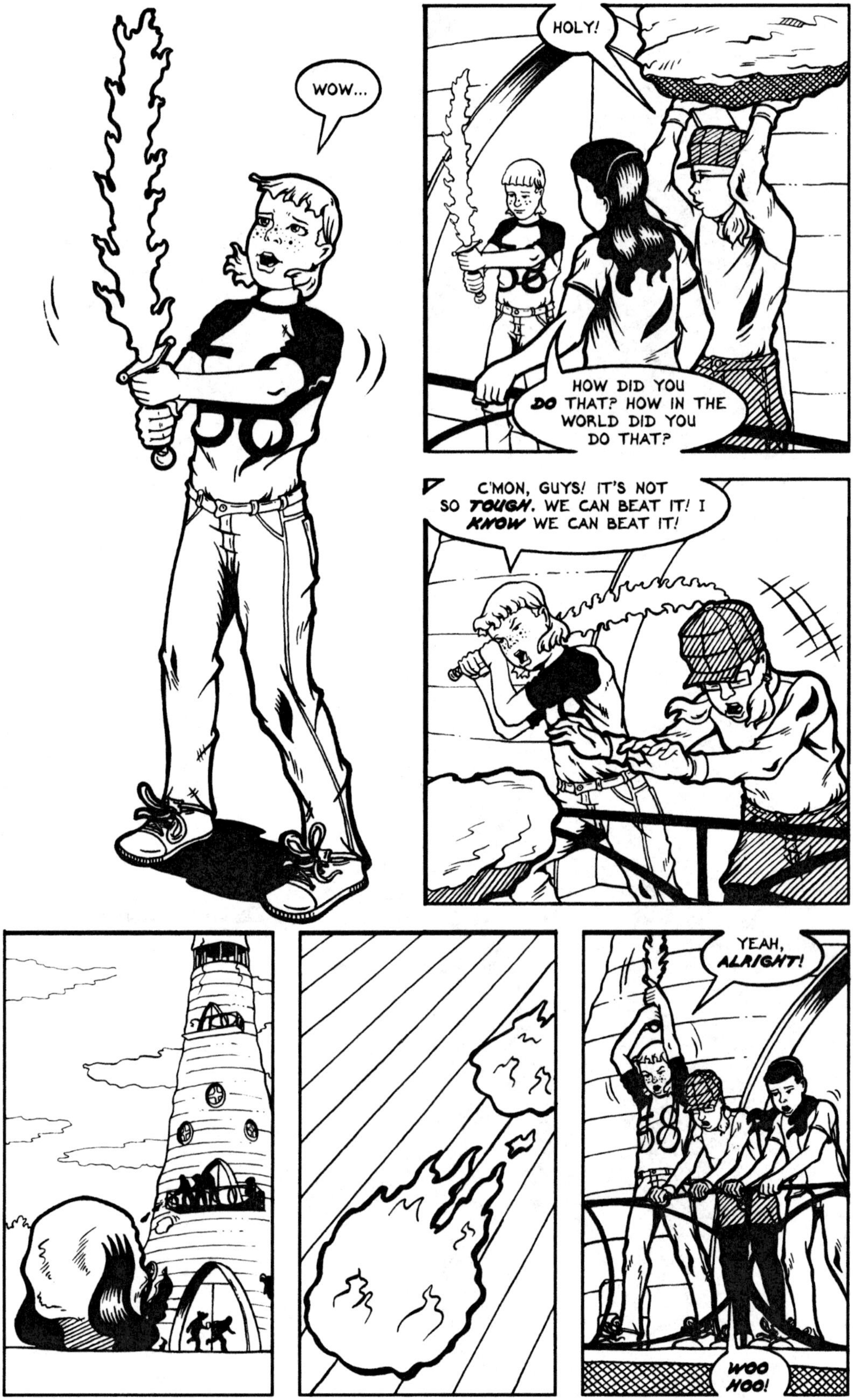
WOW...
HOLY!
HOW DID YOU DO THAT? HOW IN THE WORLD DID YOU DO THAT?
C'MON, GUYS! IT'S NOT SO TOUGH. WE CAN BEAT IT! I KNOW WE CAN BEAT IT!
YEAH, ALRIGHT!
WOO HOO!

NO, NOT *THIS* TIME.

NO!!!!

YOU'RE NOT GOING TO HURT ANY MORE OF MY FRIENDS!

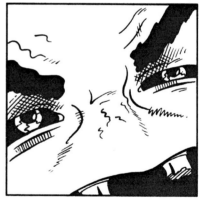

C'MON!

I HATE YOU!

"'LORA! MARN! I THINK... I THINK WE *DID* IT!"

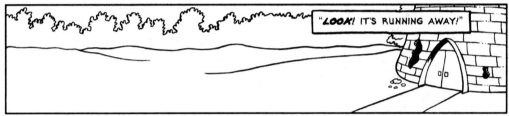

"*LOOK!* IT'S RUNNING AWAY!"

YEAH, 'LORA! IT'S *GONE.* WE DID IT!

MARNI, SOPH, YOU TWO WERE INCREDIBLE.

MARN, YOU OK?

YEAH... WE DID IT, GUYS. *WE DID IT!*

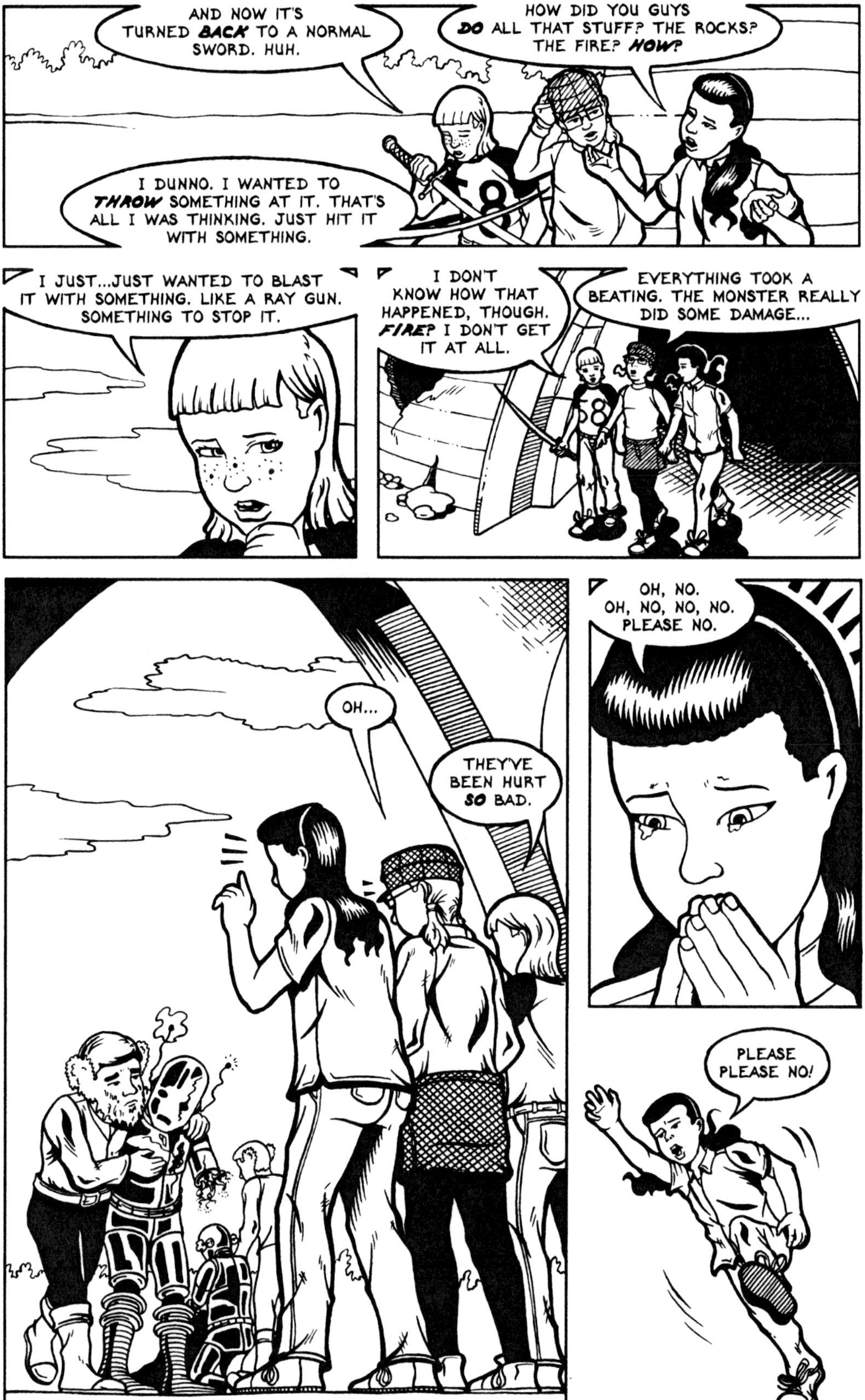
AND NOW IT'S TURNED **BACK** TO A NORMAL SWORD. HUH.
HOW DID YOU GUYS **DO** ALL THAT STUFF? THE ROCKS? THE FIRE? **HOW?**
I DUNNO. I WANTED TO **THROW** SOMETHING AT IT. THAT'S ALL I WAS THINKING. JUST HIT IT WITH SOMETHING.
I JUST...JUST WANTED TO BLAST IT WITH SOMETHING. LIKE A RAY GUN. SOMETHING TO STOP IT.
I DON'T KNOW HOW THAT HAPPENED, THOUGH. **FIRE?** I DON'T GET IT AT ALL.
EVERYTHING TOOK A BEATING. THE MONSTER REALLY DID SOME DAMAGE...
OH...
THEY'VE BEEN HURT **SO** BAD.
OH, NO. OH, NO, NO, NO. PLEASE NO.
PLEASE PLEASE NO!

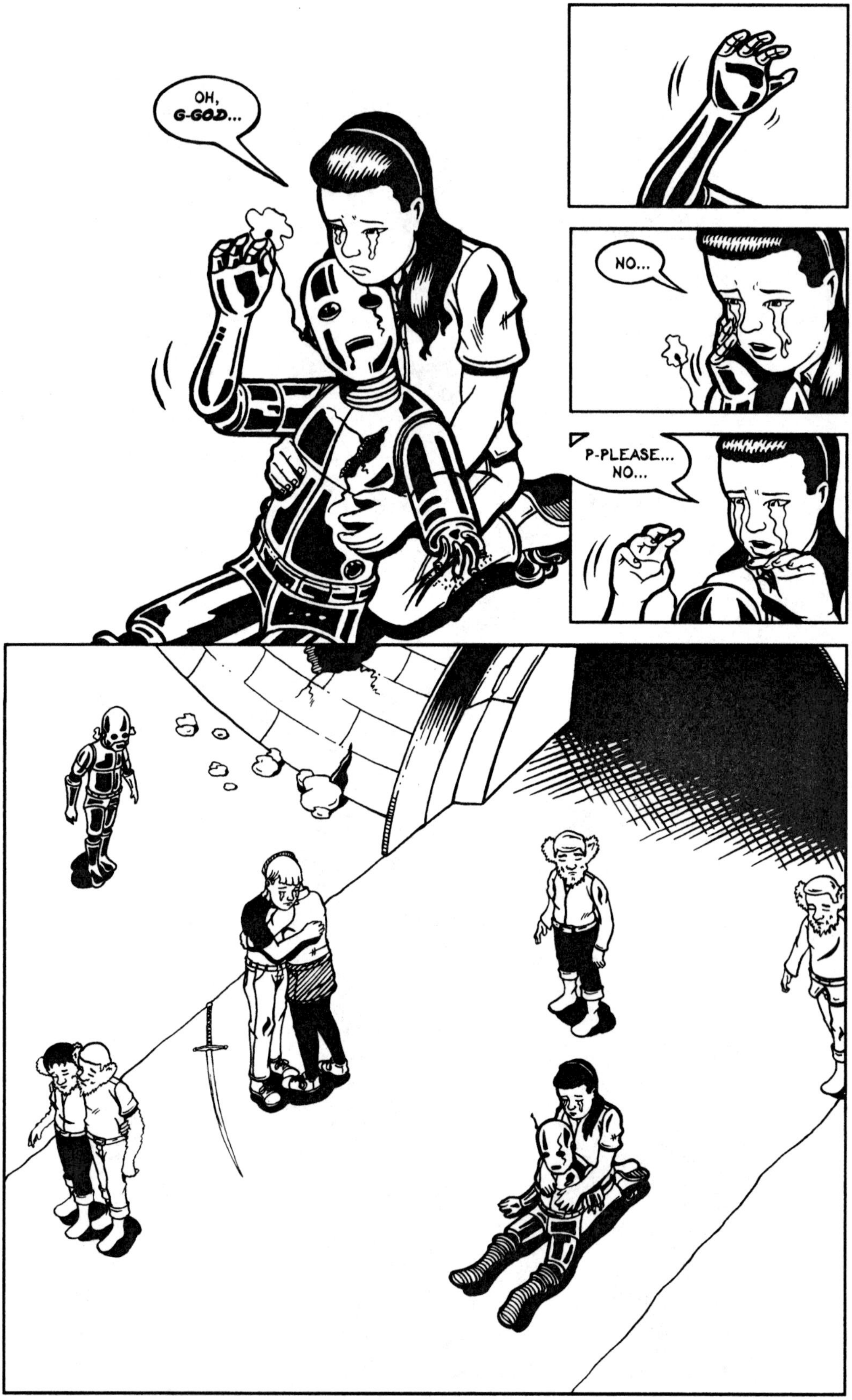
OH, G-GOD...
NO...
P-PLEASE... NO...

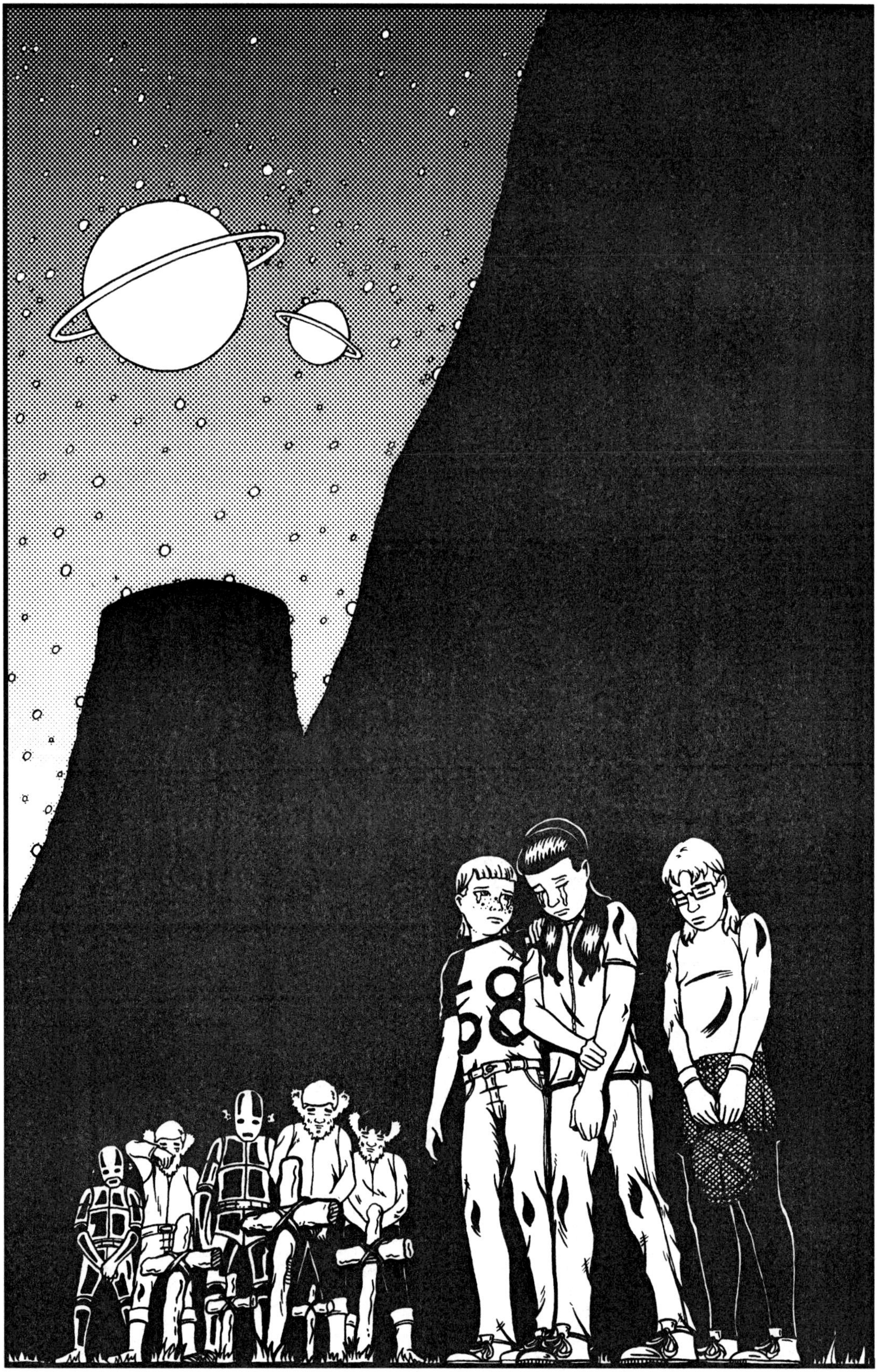
58

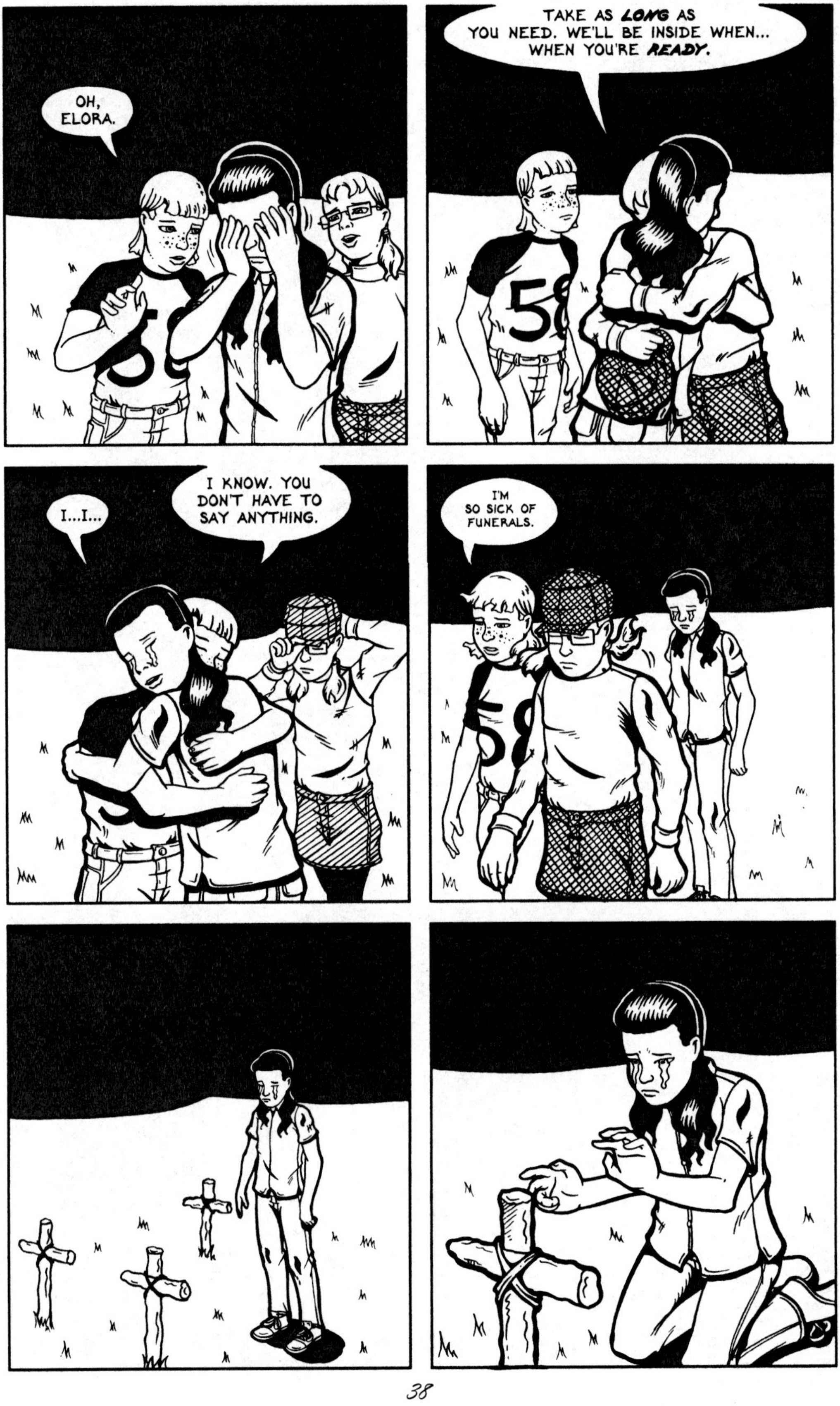
OH, ELORA.
TAKE AS LONG AS YOU NEED. WE'LL BE INSIDE WHEN... WHEN YOU'RE READY.
I...I...
I KNOW. YOU DON'T HAVE TO SAY ANYTHING.
I'M SO SICK OF FUNERALS.

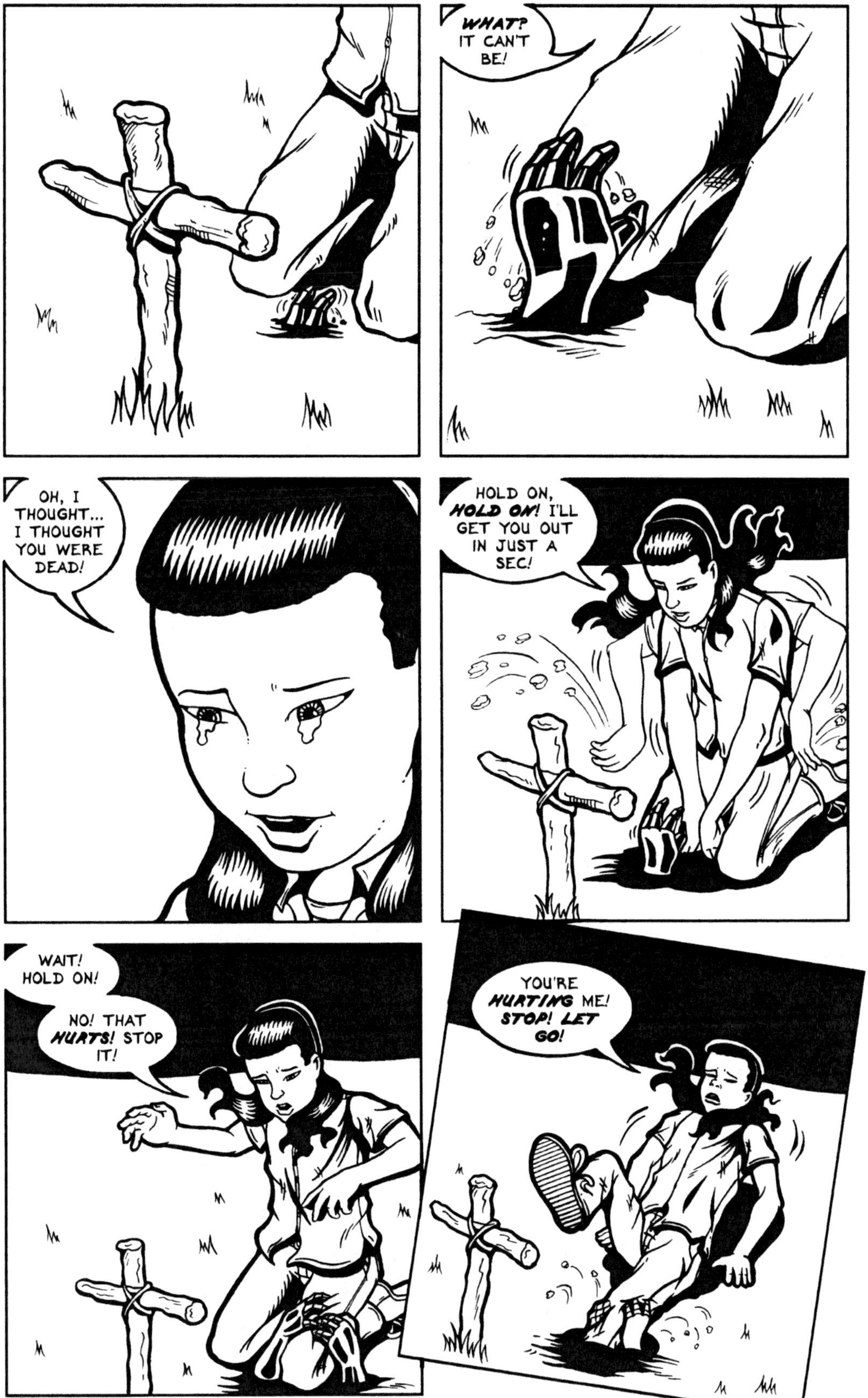
WHAT? IT CAN'T BE!
OH, I THOUGHT... I THOUGHT YOU WERE DEAD!
HOLD ON, HOLD ON! I'LL GET YOU OUT IN JUST A SEC!
WAIT! HOLD ON!
NO! THAT HURTS! STOP IT!
YOU'RE HURTING ME! STOP! LET GO!

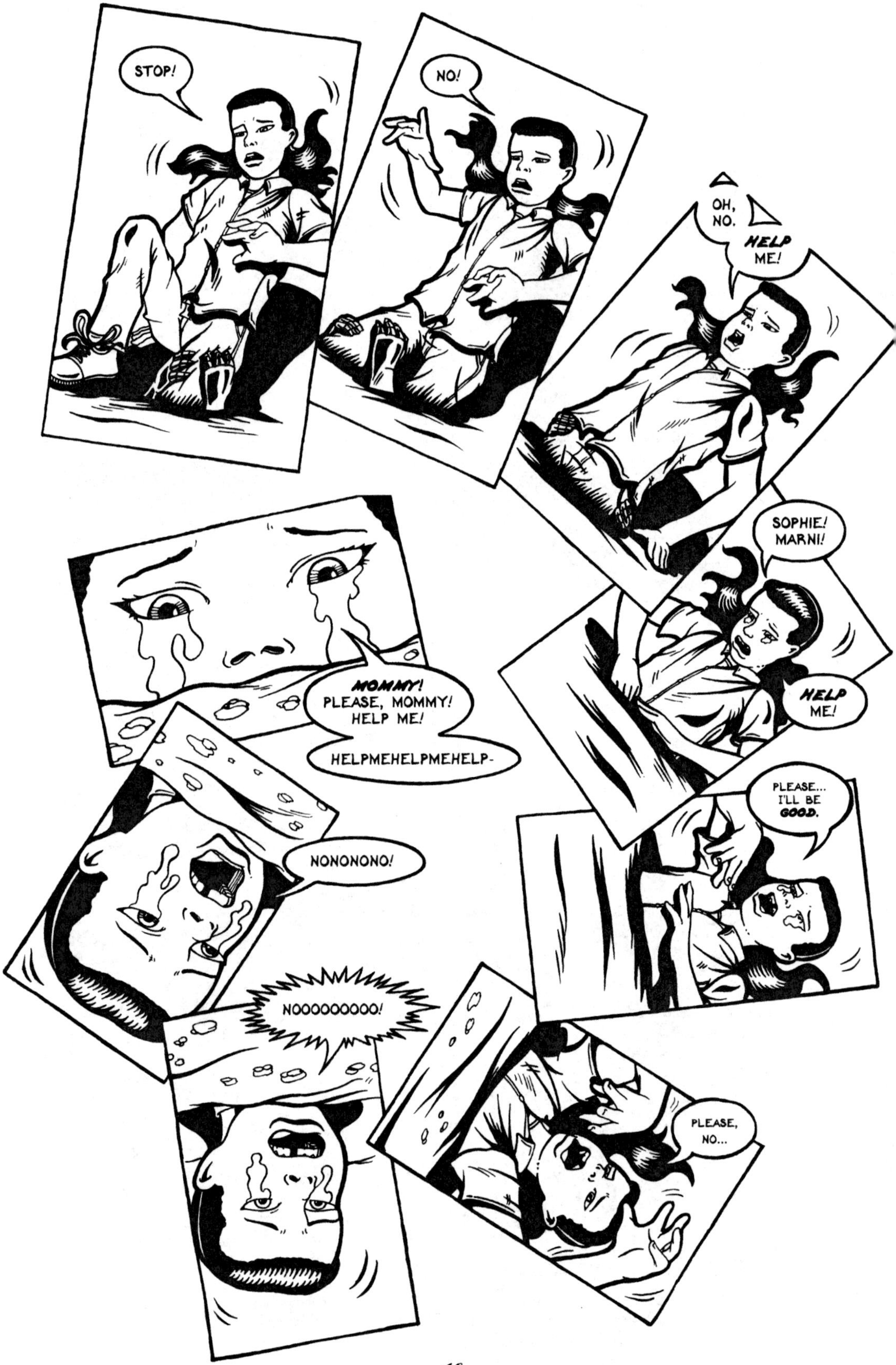
STOP!
NO!
OH, NO.
HELP ME!
SOPHIE! MARNI!
HELP ME!
MOMMY! PLEASE, MOMMY! HELP ME!
HELPMEHELPMEHELP-
PLEASE... I'LL BE GOOD.
NONONONO!
NOOOOOOOOO!
PLEASE, NO...

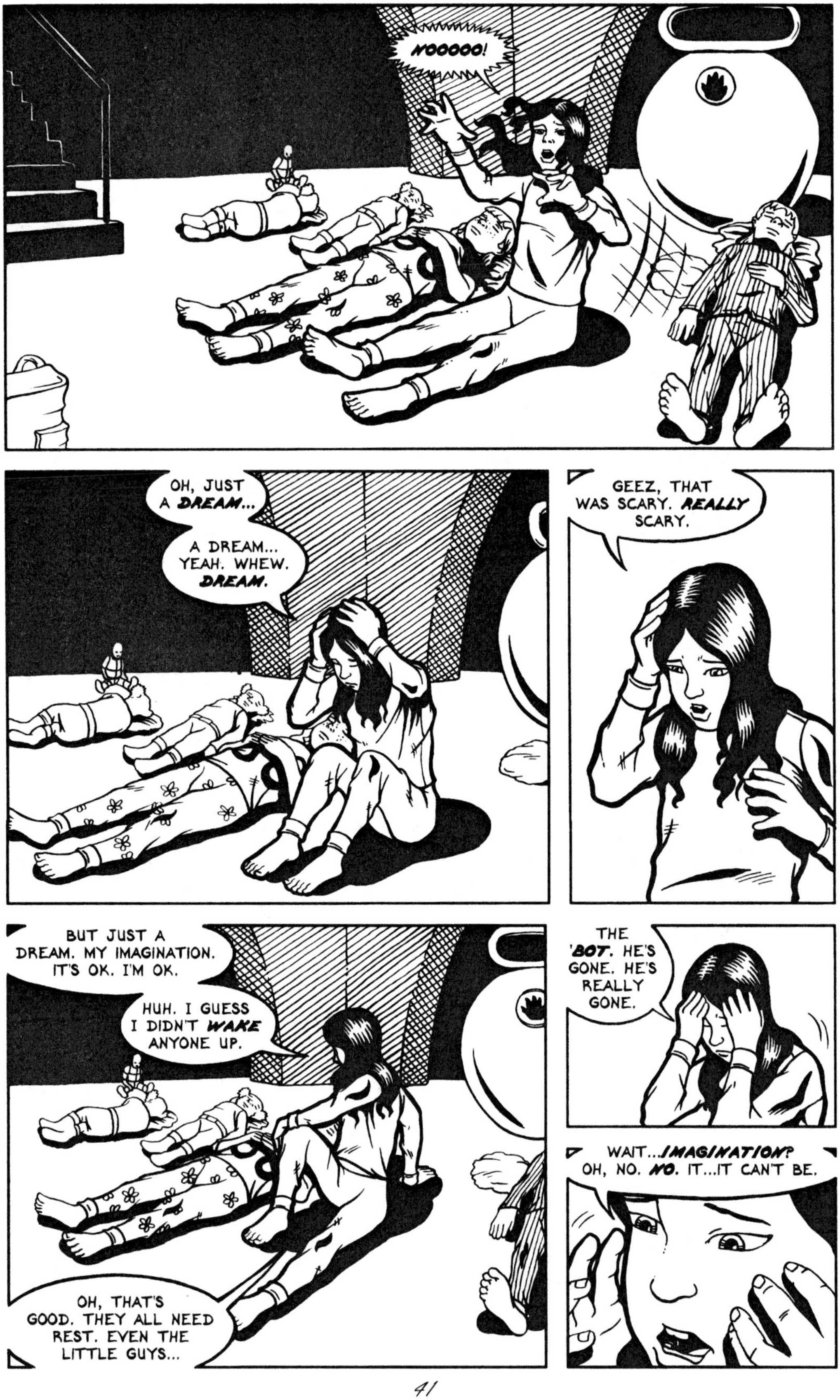
NOOOOO!
OH, JUST A DREAM...
A DREAM... YEAH. WHEW. DREAM.
GEEZ, THAT WAS SCARY. REALLY SCARY.
BUT JUST A DREAM. MY IMAGINATION. IT'S OK. I'M OK.
HUH. I GUESS I DIDN'T WAKE ANYONE UP.
OH, THAT'S GOOD. THEY ALL NEED REST. EVEN THE LITTLE GUYS...
THE 'BOT. HE'S GONE. HE'S REALLY GONE.
WAIT...IMAGINATION? OH, NO. NO. IT...IT CAN'T BE.

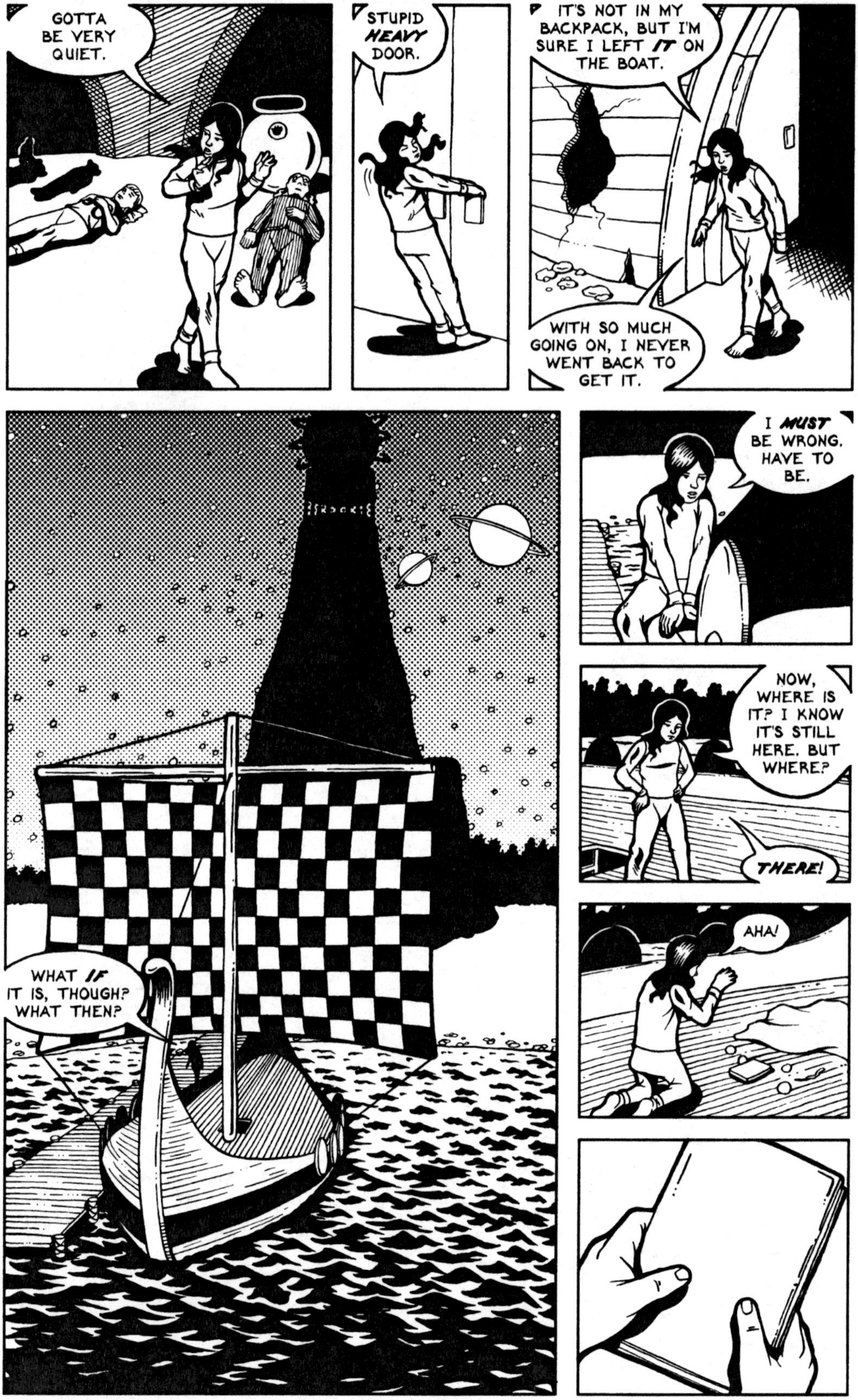
GOTTA BE VERY QUIET.
STUPID HEAVY DOOR.
IT'S NOT IN MY BACKPACK, BUT I'M SURE I LEFT IT ON THE BOAT.
WITH SO MUCH GOING ON, I NEVER WENT BACK TO GET IT.
WHAT IF IT IS, THOUGH? WHAT THEN?
I MUST BE WRONG. HAVE TO BE.
NOW, WHERE IS IT? I KNOW IT'S STILL HERE. BUT WHERE?
THERE!
AHA!

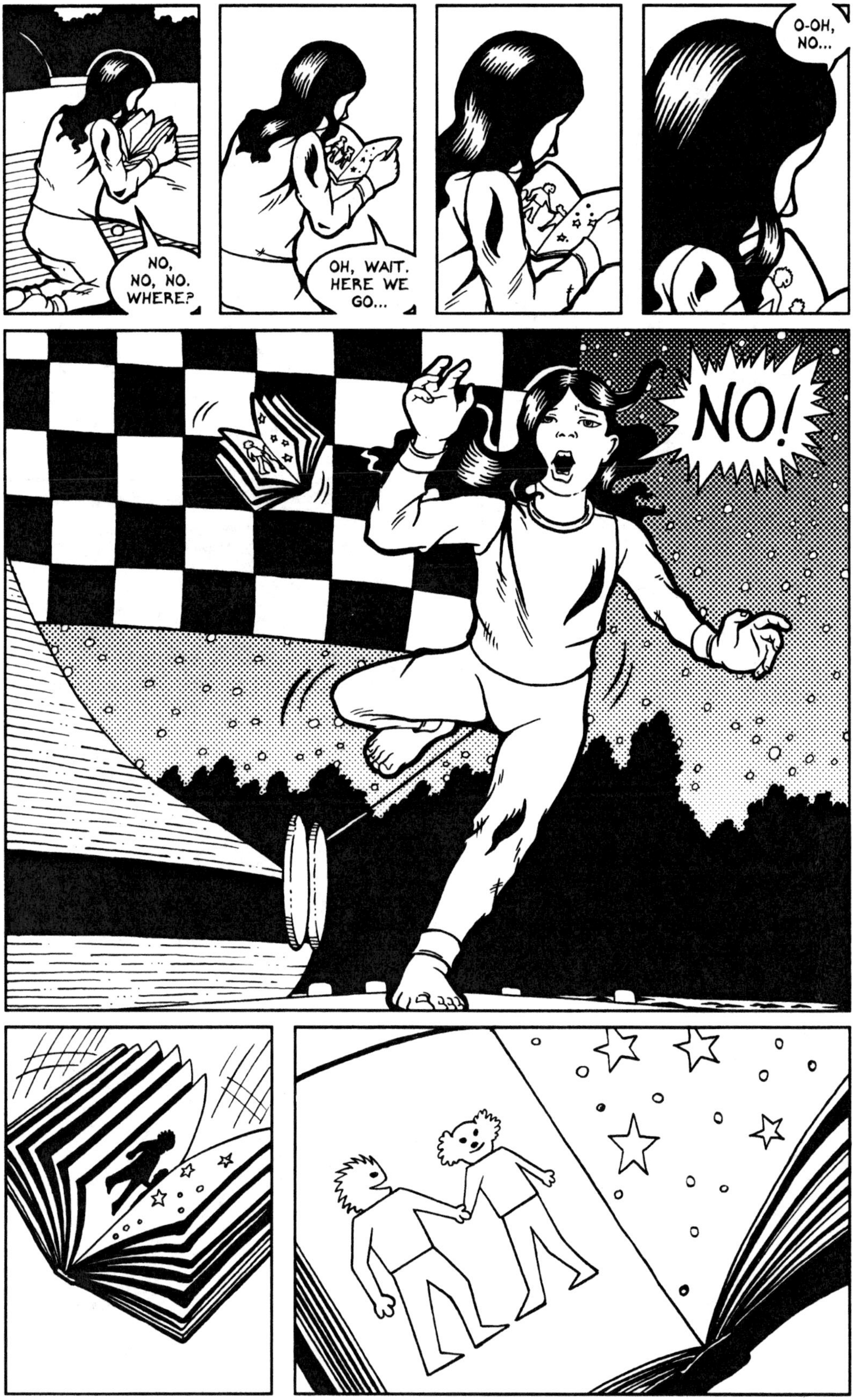
NO,
NO, NO.
WHERE?
OH, WAIT.
HERE WE
GO...
O-OH,
NO...
NO!

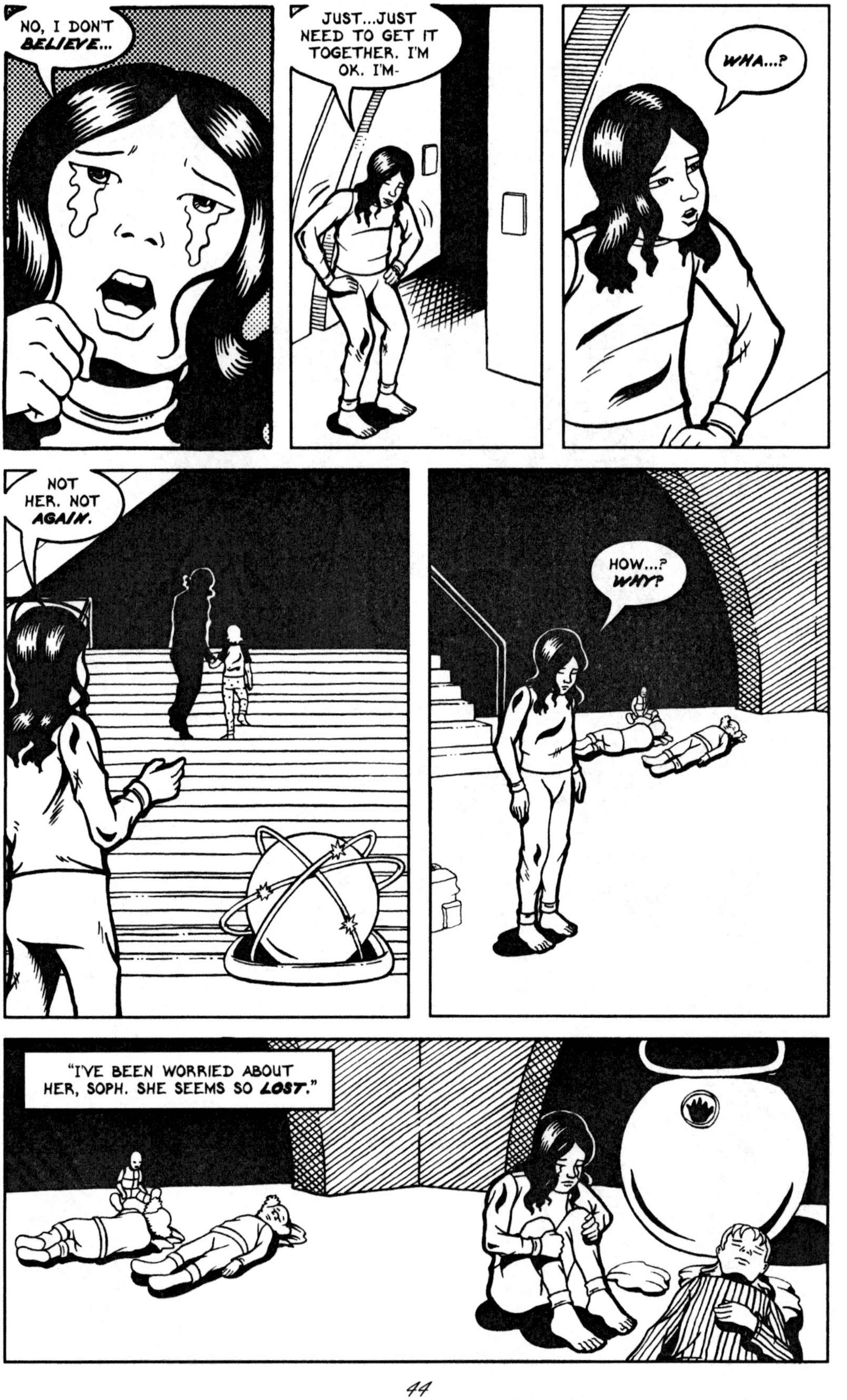
NO, I DON'T BELIEVE...
JUST...JUST NEED TO GET IT TOGETHER. I'M OK. I'M-
WHA...?
NOT HER. NOT AGAIN.
HOW...? WHY?
"I'VE BEEN WORRIED ABOUT HER, SOPH. SHE SEEMS SO LOST."

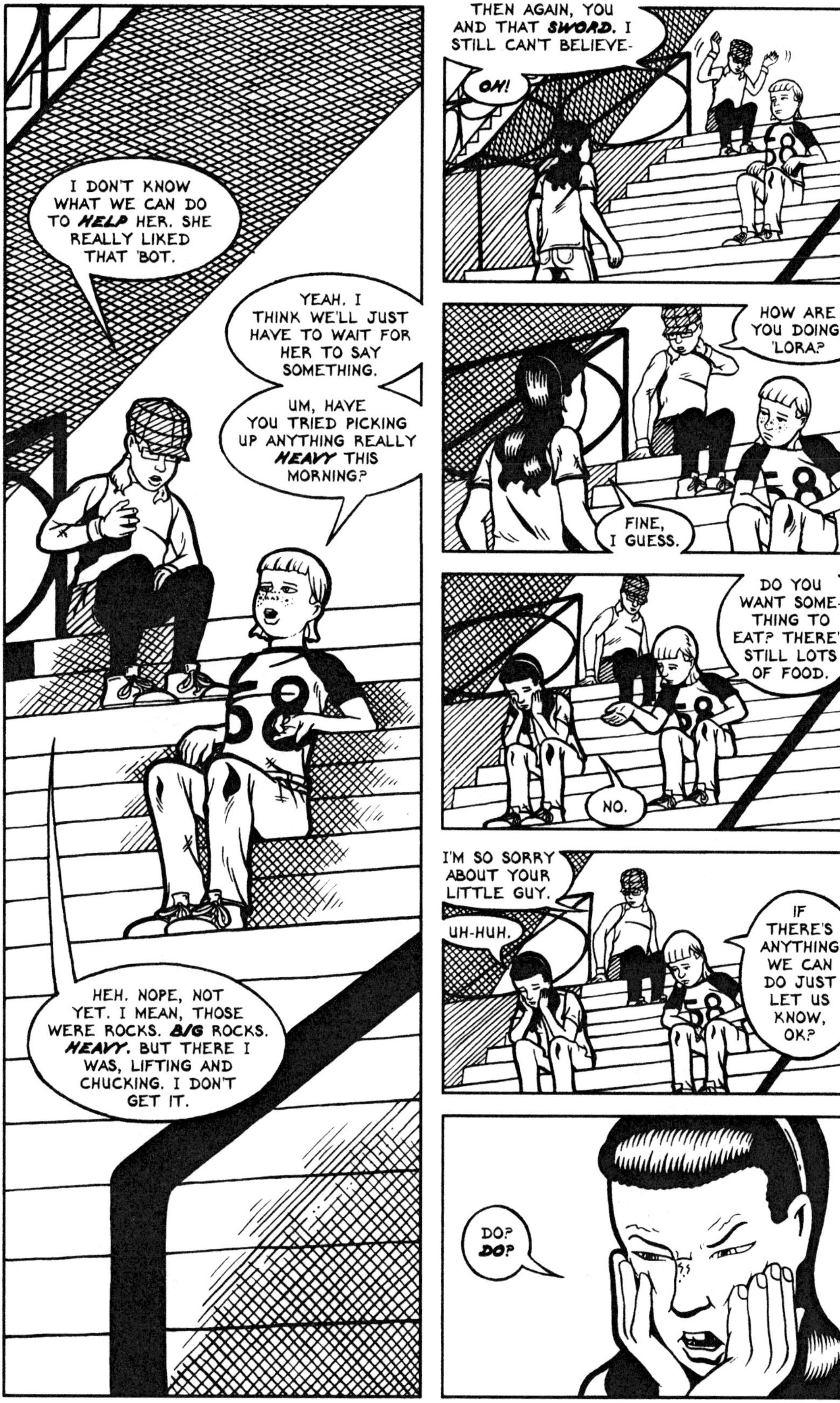
I DON'T KNOW WHAT WE CAN DO TO HELP HER. SHE REALLY LIKED THAT 'BOT.
YEAH. I THINK WE'LL JUST HAVE TO WAIT FOR HER TO SAY SOMETHING.
UM, HAVE YOU TRIED PICKING UP ANYTHING REALLY HEAVY THIS MORNING?
HEH. NOPE, NOT YET. I MEAN, THOSE WERE ROCKS. BIG ROCKS. HEAVY. BUT THERE I WAS, LIFTING AND CHUCKING. I DON'T GET IT.
THEN AGAIN, YOU AND THAT SWORD. I STILL CAN'T BELIEVE-
OH!
HOW ARE YOU DOING, 'LORA?
FINE, I GUESS.
DO YOU WANT SOMETHING TO EAT? THERE'S STILL LOTS OF FOOD.
NO.
I'M SO SORRY ABOUT YOUR LITTLE GUY.
UH-HUH.
IF THERE'S ANYTHING WE CAN DO JUST LET US KNOW, OK?
DO? DO?

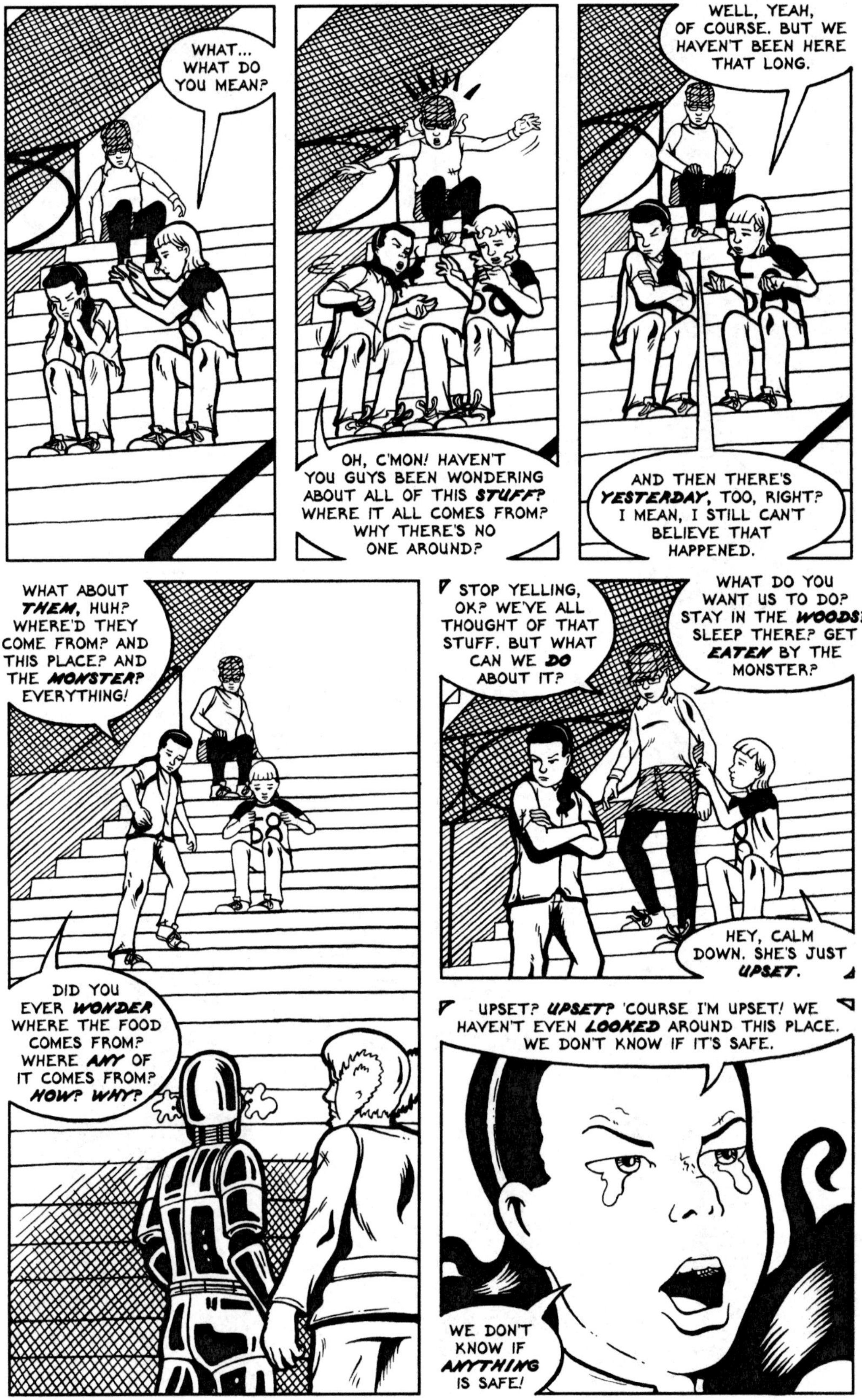
WHAT... WHAT DO YOU MEAN?
OH, C'MON! HAVEN'T YOU GUYS BEEN WONDERING ABOUT ALL OF THIS STUFF? WHERE IT ALL COMES FROM? WHY THERE'S NO ONE AROUND?
WELL, YEAH, OF COURSE. BUT WE HAVEN'T BEEN HERE THAT LONG.
AND THEN THERE'S YESTERDAY, TOO, RIGHT? I MEAN, I STILL CAN'T BELIEVE THAT HAPPENED.
WHAT ABOUT THEM, HUH? WHERE'D THEY COME FROM? AND THIS PLACE? AND THE MONSTER? EVERYTHING!
DID YOU EVER WONDER WHERE THE FOOD COMES FROM? WHERE ANY OF IT COMES FROM? HOW? WHY?
STOP YELLING, OK? WE'VE ALL THOUGHT OF THAT STUFF. BUT WHAT CAN WE DO ABOUT IT?
WHAT DO YOU WANT US TO DO? STAY IN THE WOODS? SLEEP THERE? GET EATEN BY THE MONSTER?
HEY, CALM DOWN. SHE'S JUST UPSET.
UPSET? UPSET? 'COURSE I'M UPSET! WE HAVEN'T EVEN LOOKED AROUND THIS PLACE. WE DON'T KNOW IF IT'S SAFE.
WE DON'T KNOW IF ANYTHING IS SAFE!

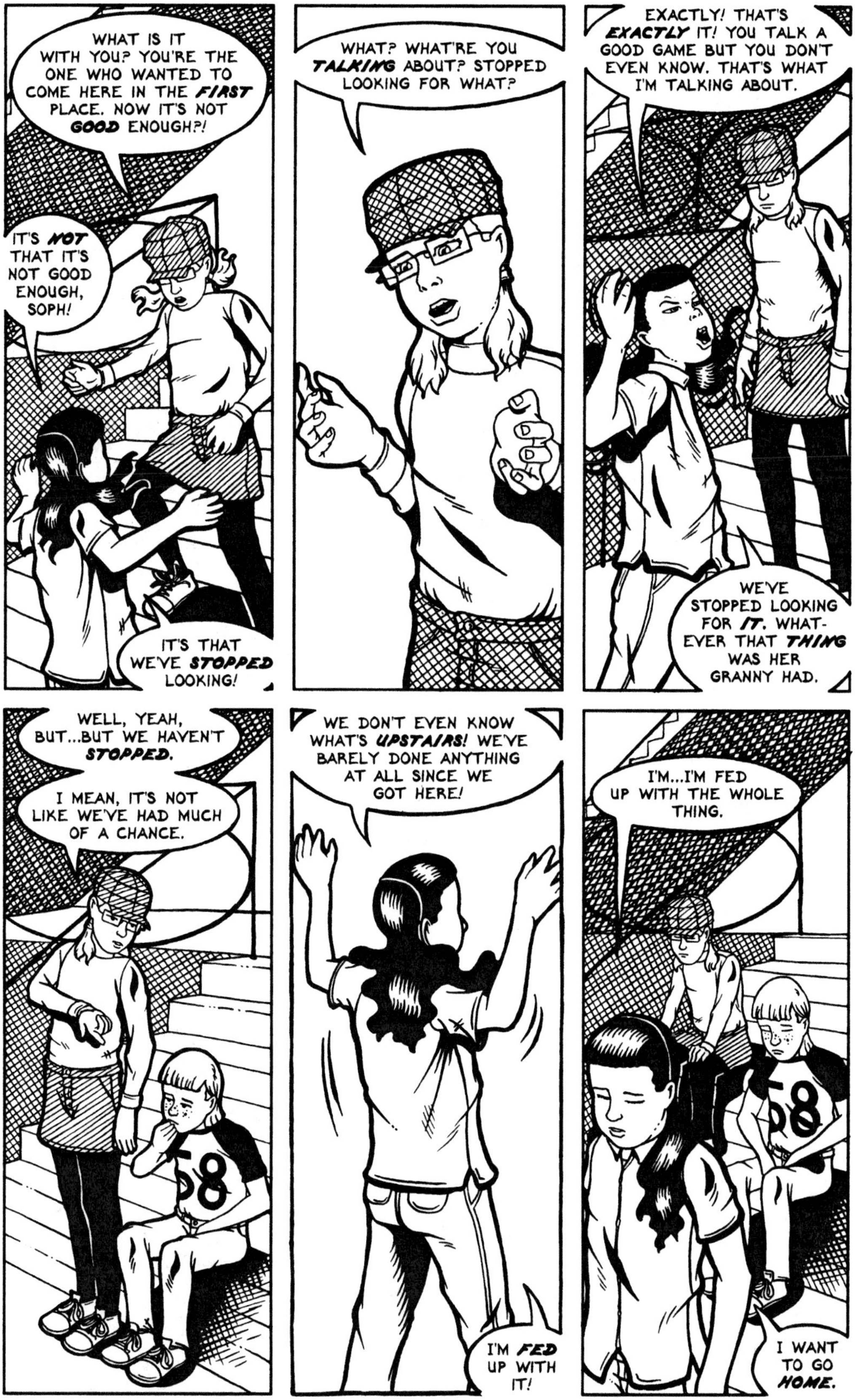
WHAT IS IT WITH YOU? YOU'RE THE ONE WHO WANTED TO COME HERE IN THE FIRST PLACE. NOW IT'S NOT GOOD ENOUGH?!
IT'S NOT THAT IT'S NOT GOOD ENOUGH, SOPH!
IT'S THAT WE'VE STOPPED LOOKING!
WHAT? WHAT'RE YOU TALKING ABOUT? STOPPED LOOKING FOR WHAT?
EXACTLY! THAT'S EXACTLY IT! YOU TALK A GOOD GAME BUT YOU DON'T EVEN KNOW. THAT'S WHAT I'M TALKING ABOUT.
WE'VE STOPPED LOOKING FOR IT. WHAT-EVER THAT THING WAS HER GRANNY HAD.
WELL, YEAH, BUT...BUT WE HAVEN'T STOPPED.
I MEAN, IT'S NOT LIKE WE'VE HAD MUCH OF A CHANCE.
WE DON'T EVEN KNOW WHAT'S UPSTAIRS! WE'VE BARELY DONE ANYTHING AT ALL SINCE WE GOT HERE!
I'M FED UP WITH IT!
I'M...I'M FED UP WITH THE WHOLE THING.
I WANT TO GO HOME.
58
58

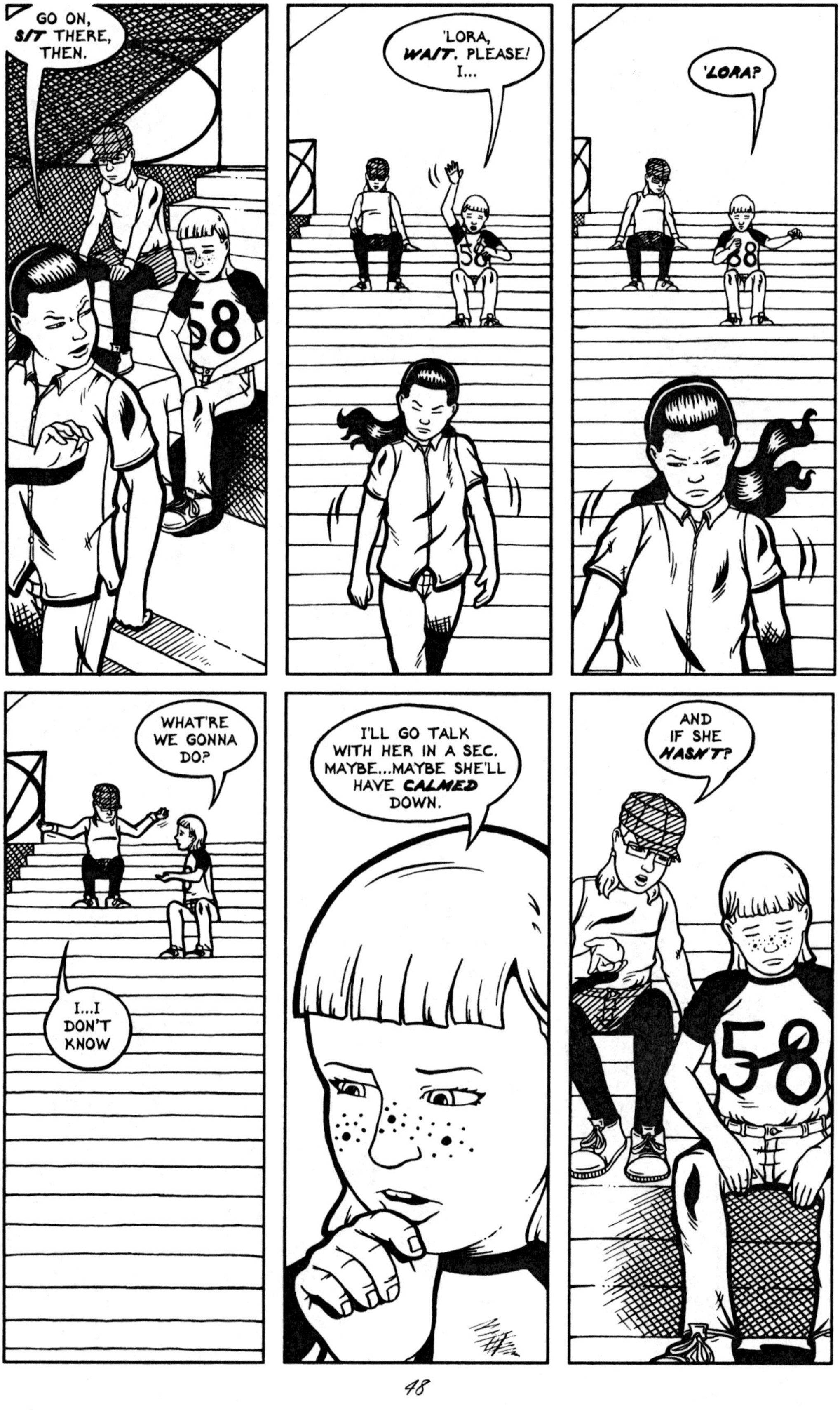
GO ON, SIT THERE, THEN.
'LORA, WAIT. PLEASE! I...
'LORA?
WHAT'RE WE GONNA DO?
I...I DON'T KNOW
I'LL GO TALK WITH HER IN A SEC. MAYBE...MAYBE SHE'LL HAVE CALMED DOWN.
AND IF SHE HASN'T?

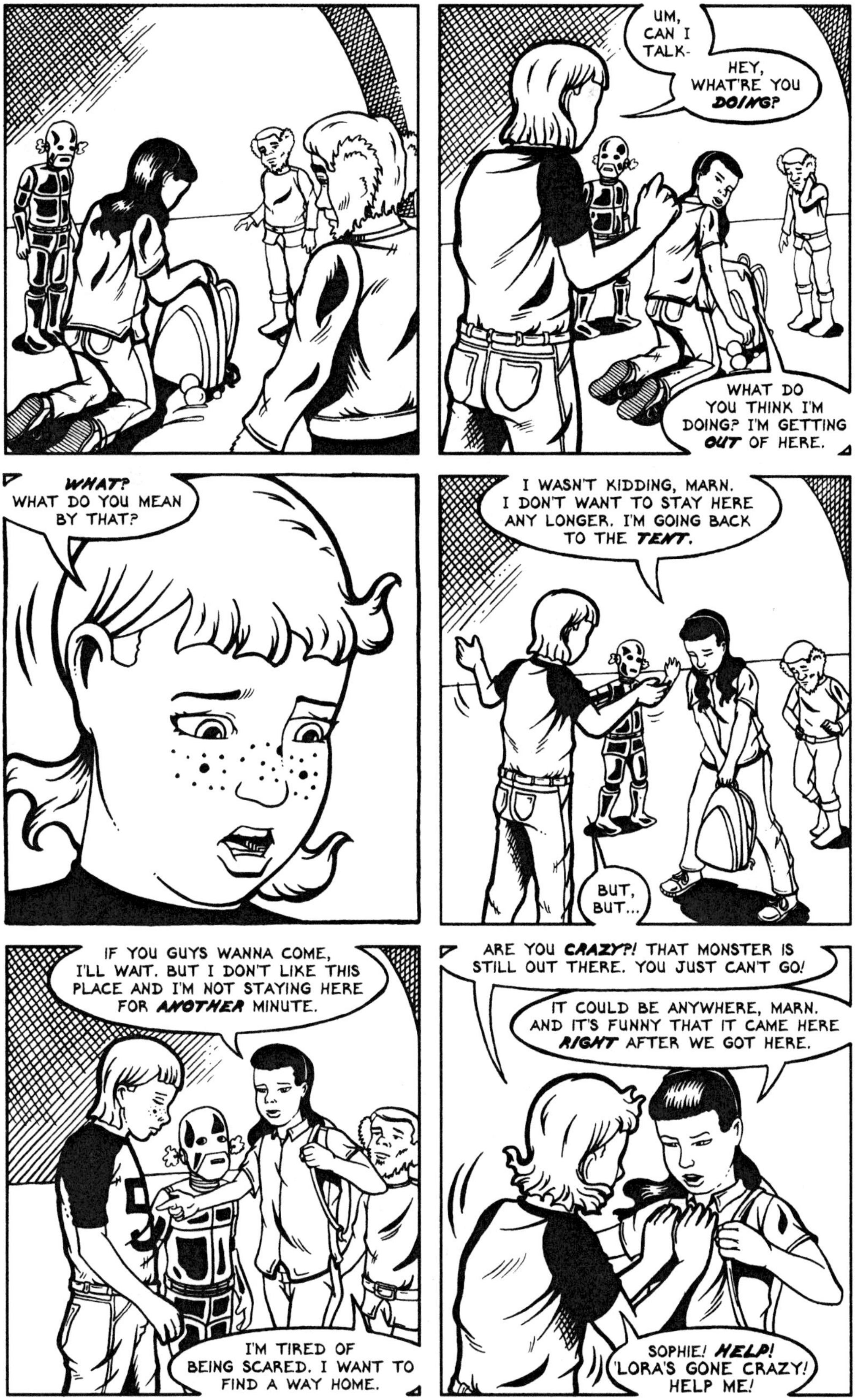
UM, CAN I TALK-
HEY, WHAT'RE YOU DOING?
WHAT DO YOU THINK I'M DOING? I'M GETTING OUT OF HERE.
WHAT? WHAT DO YOU MEAN BY THAT?
I WASN'T KIDDING, MARN. I DON'T WANT TO STAY HERE ANY LONGER. I'M GOING BACK TO THE TENT.
BUT, BUT...
IF YOU GUYS WANNA COME, I'LL WAIT. BUT I DON'T LIKE THIS PLACE AND I'M NOT STAYING HERE FOR ANOTHER MINUTE.
I'M TIRED OF BEING SCARED. I WANT TO FIND A WAY HOME.
ARE YOU CRAZY?! THAT MONSTER IS STILL OUT THERE. YOU JUST CAN'T GO!
IT COULD BE ANYWHERE, MARN. AND IT'S FUNNY THAT IT CAME HERE RIGHT AFTER WE GOT HERE.
SOPHIE! HELP! 'LORA'S GONE CRAZY! HELP ME!

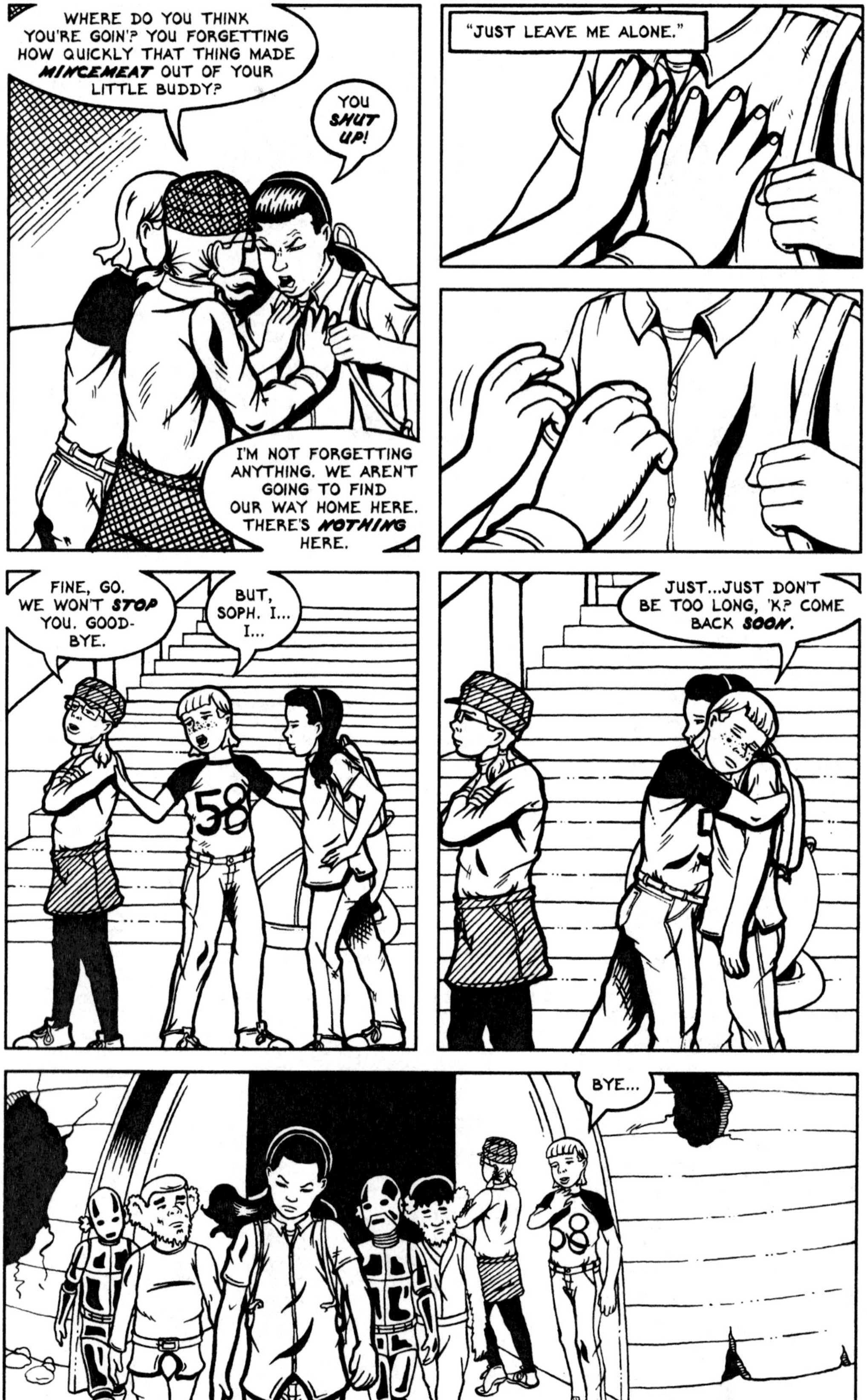
WHERE DO YOU THINK YOU'RE GOIN'? YOU FORGETTING HOW QUICKLY THAT THING MADE MINCEMEAT OUT OF YOUR LITTLE BUDDY?
YOU SHUT UP!
I'M NOT FORGETTING ANYTHING. WE AREN'T GOING TO FIND OUR WAY HOME HERE. THERE'S NOTHING HERE.
"JUST LEAVE ME ALONE."
FINE, GO. WE WON'T STOP YOU. GOOD-BYE.
BUT, SOPH. I... I...
JUST...JUST DON'T BE TOO LONG, 'K? COME BACK SOON.
BYE...

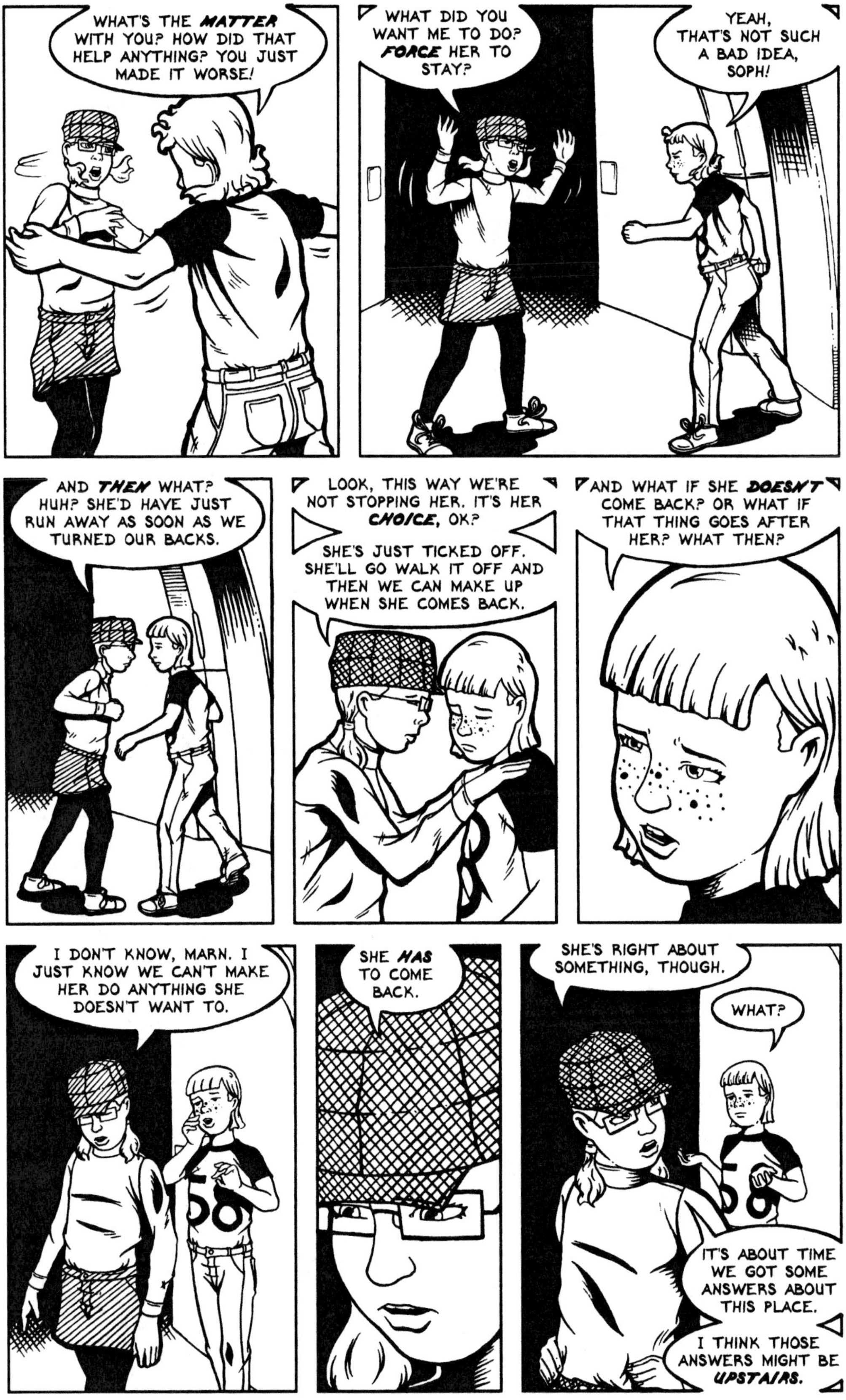
WHAT'S THE MATTER WITH YOU? HOW DID THAT HELP ANYTHING? YOU JUST MADE IT WORSE!
WHAT DID YOU WANT ME TO DO? FORCE HER TO STAY?
YEAH, THAT'S NOT SUCH A BAD IDEA, SOPH!
AND THEN WHAT? HUH? SHE'D HAVE JUST RUN AWAY AS SOON AS WE TURNED OUR BACKS.
LOOK, THIS WAY WE'RE NOT STOPPING HER. IT'S HER CHOICE, OK?
SHE'S JUST TICKED OFF. SHE'LL GO WALK IT OFF AND THEN WE CAN MAKE UP WHEN SHE COMES BACK.
AND WHAT IF SHE DOESN'T COME BACK? OR WHAT IF THAT THING GOES AFTER HER? WHAT THEN?
I DON'T KNOW, MARN. I JUST KNOW WE CAN'T MAKE HER DO ANYTHING SHE DOESN'T WANT TO.
SHE HAS TO COME BACK.
SHE'S RIGHT ABOUT SOMETHING, THOUGH.
WHAT?
IT'S ABOUT TIME WE GOT SOME ANSWERS ABOUT THIS PLACE.
I THINK THOSE ANSWERS MIGHT BE UPSTAIRS.

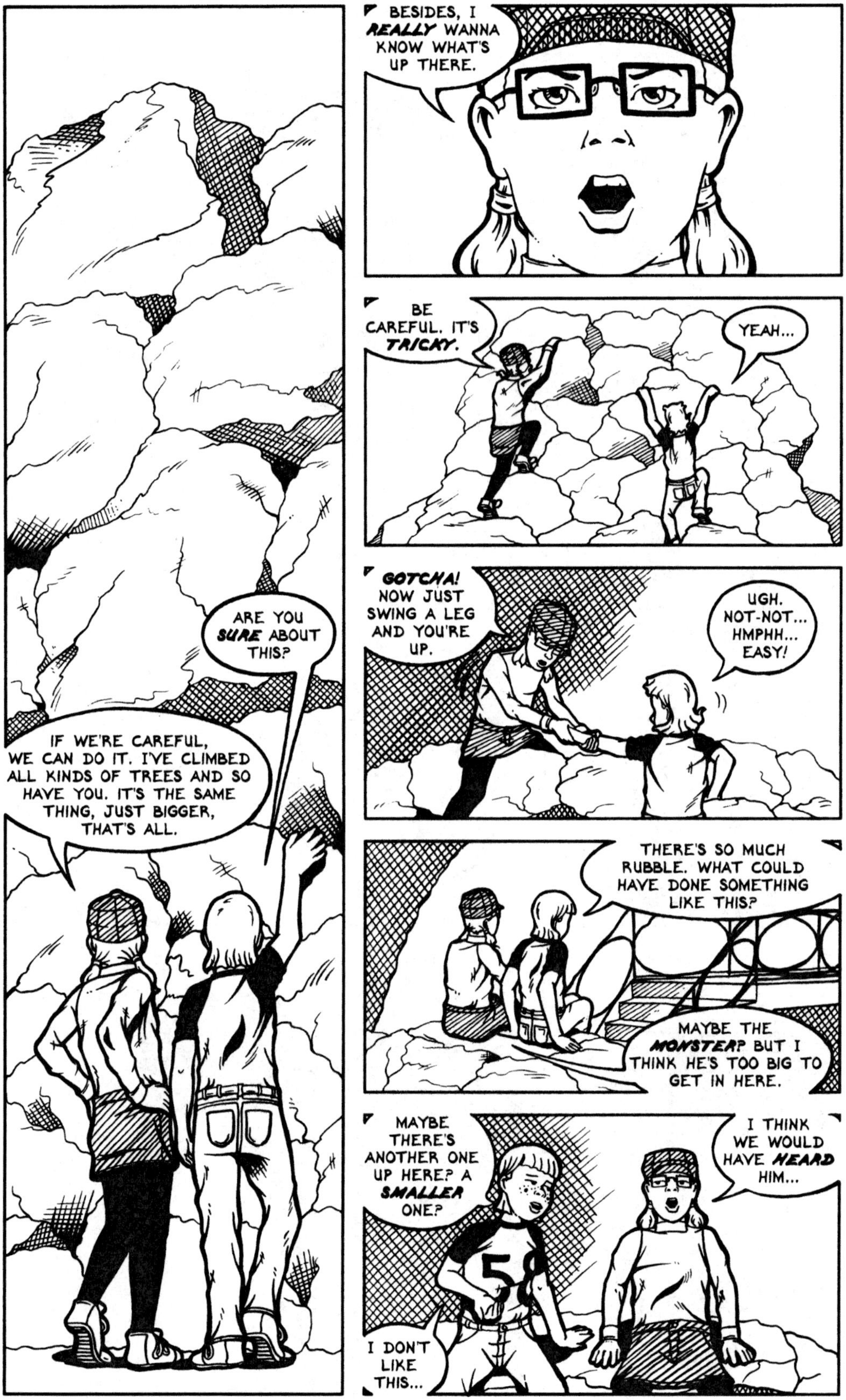
ARE YOU SURE ABOUT THIS?
IF WE'RE CAREFUL, WE CAN DO IT. I'VE CLIMBED ALL KINDS OF TREES AND SO HAVE YOU. IT'S THE SAME THING, JUST BIGGER, THAT'S ALL.
BESIDES, I REALLY WANNA KNOW WHAT'S UP THERE.
BE CAREFUL. IT'S TRICKY.
YEAH...
GOTCHA! NOW JUST SWING A LEG AND YOU'RE UP.
UGH. NOT-NOT... HMPHH... EASY!
THERE'S SO MUCH RUBBLE. WHAT COULD HAVE DONE SOMETHING LIKE THIS?
MAYBE THE MONSTER? BUT I THINK HE'S TOO BIG TO GET IN HERE.
MAYBE THERE'S ANOTHER ONE UP HERE? A SMALLER ONE?
I THINK WE WOULD HAVE HEARD HIM...
I DON'T LIKE THIS...

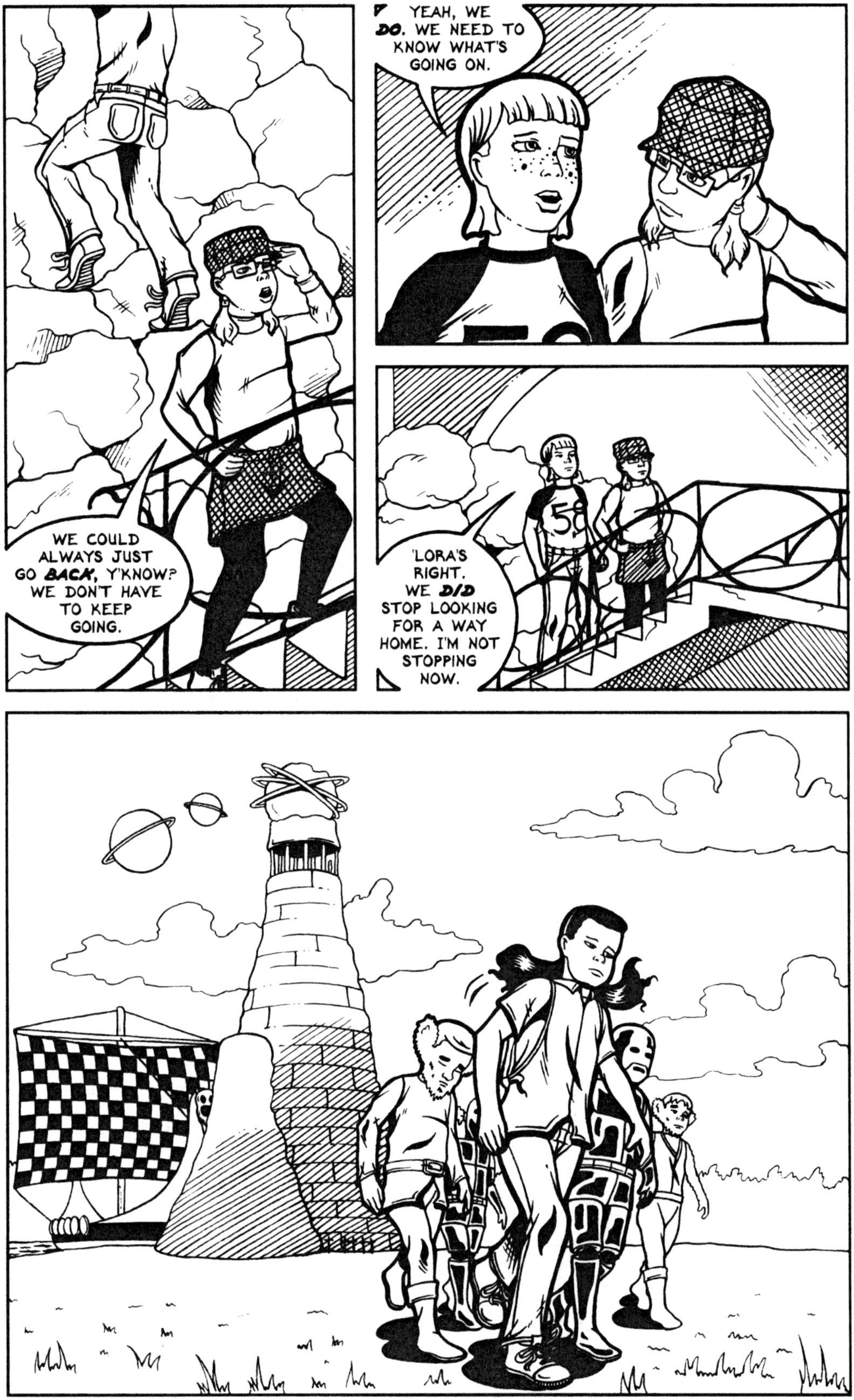
WE COULD ALWAYS JUST GO BACK, Y'KNOW? WE DON'T HAVE TO KEEP GOING.
YEAH, WE DO. WE NEED TO KNOW WHAT'S GOING ON.
'LORA'S RIGHT. WE DID STOP LOOKING FOR A WAY HOME. I'M NOT STOPPING NOW.

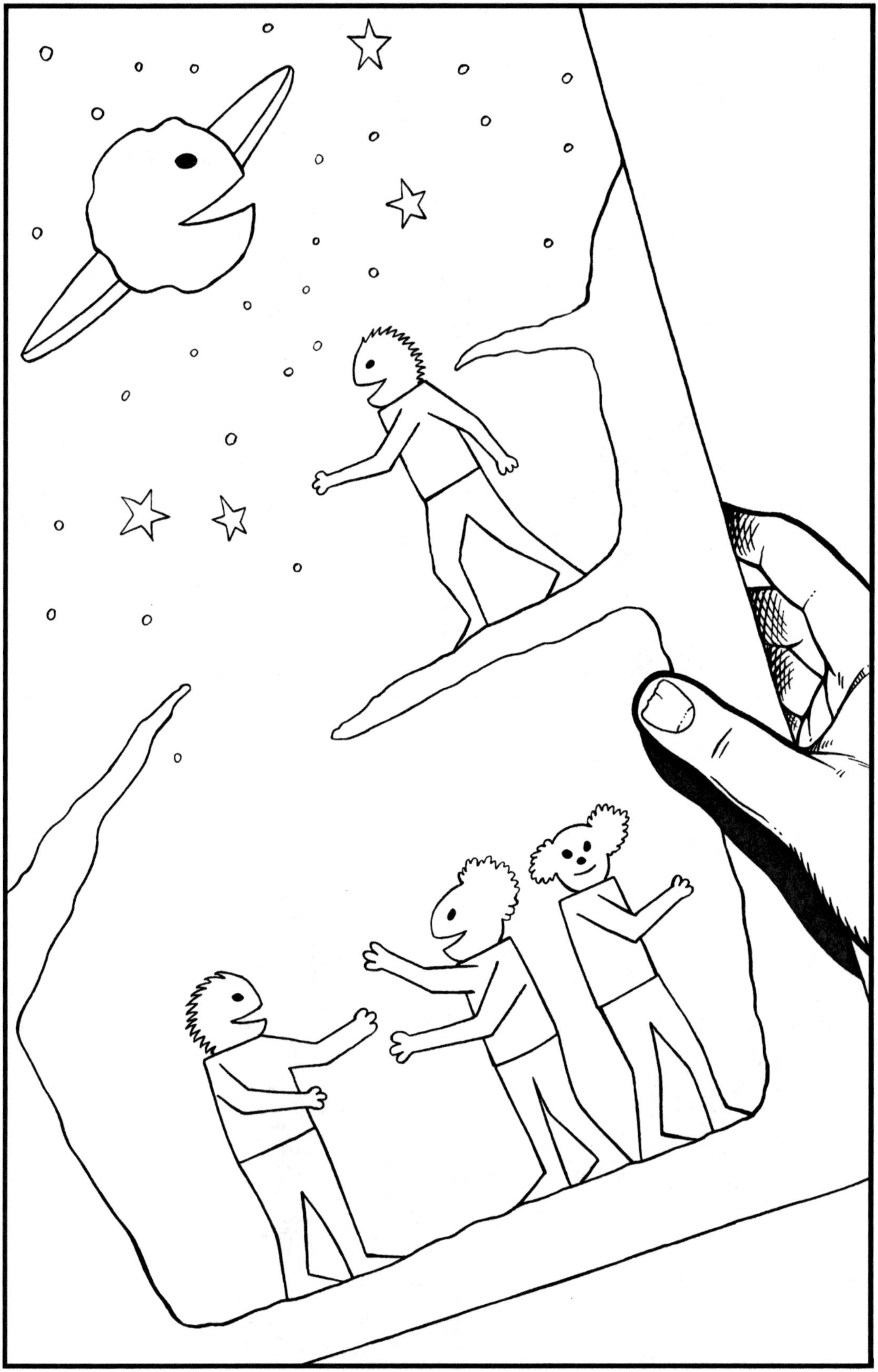

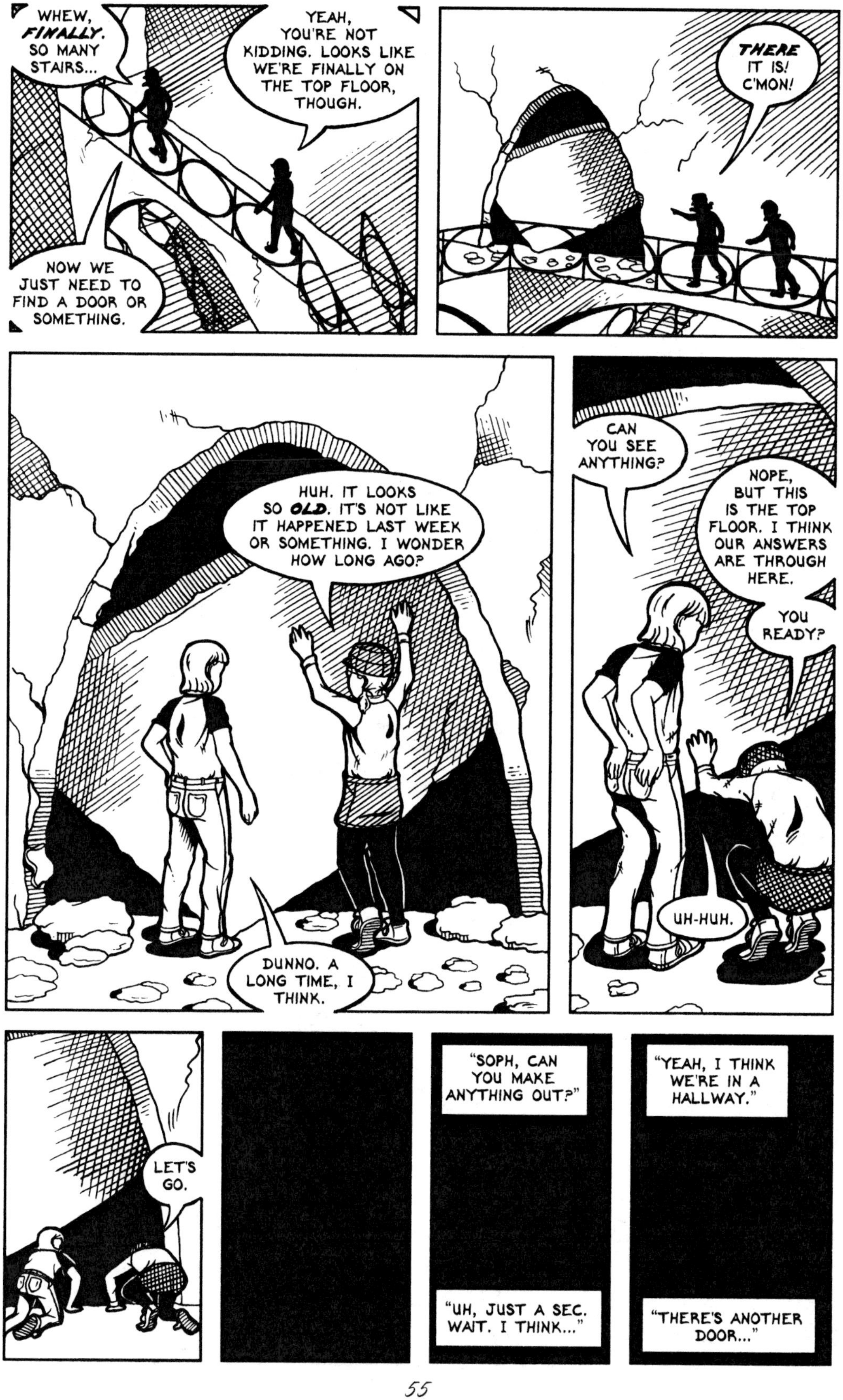
WHEW, **FINALLY**. SO MANY STAIRS...
YEAH, YOU'RE NOT KIDDING. LOOKS LIKE WE'RE FINALLY ON THE TOP FLOOR, THOUGH.
NOW WE JUST NEED TO FIND A DOOR OR SOMETHING.
THERE IT IS! C'MON!
HUH. IT LOOKS SO **OLD**. IT'S NOT LIKE IT HAPPENED LAST WEEK OR SOMETHING. I WONDER HOW LONG AGO?
DUNNO. A LONG TIME, I THINK.
CAN YOU SEE ANYTHING?
NOPE, BUT THIS IS THE TOP FLOOR. I THINK OUR ANSWERS ARE THROUGH HERE.
YOU READY?
UH-HUH.
LET'S GO.
"SOPH, CAN YOU MAKE ANYTHING OUT?"
"UH, JUST A SEC. WAIT. I THINK..."
"YEAH, I THINK WE'RE IN A HALLWAY."
"THERE'S ANOTHER DOOR..."

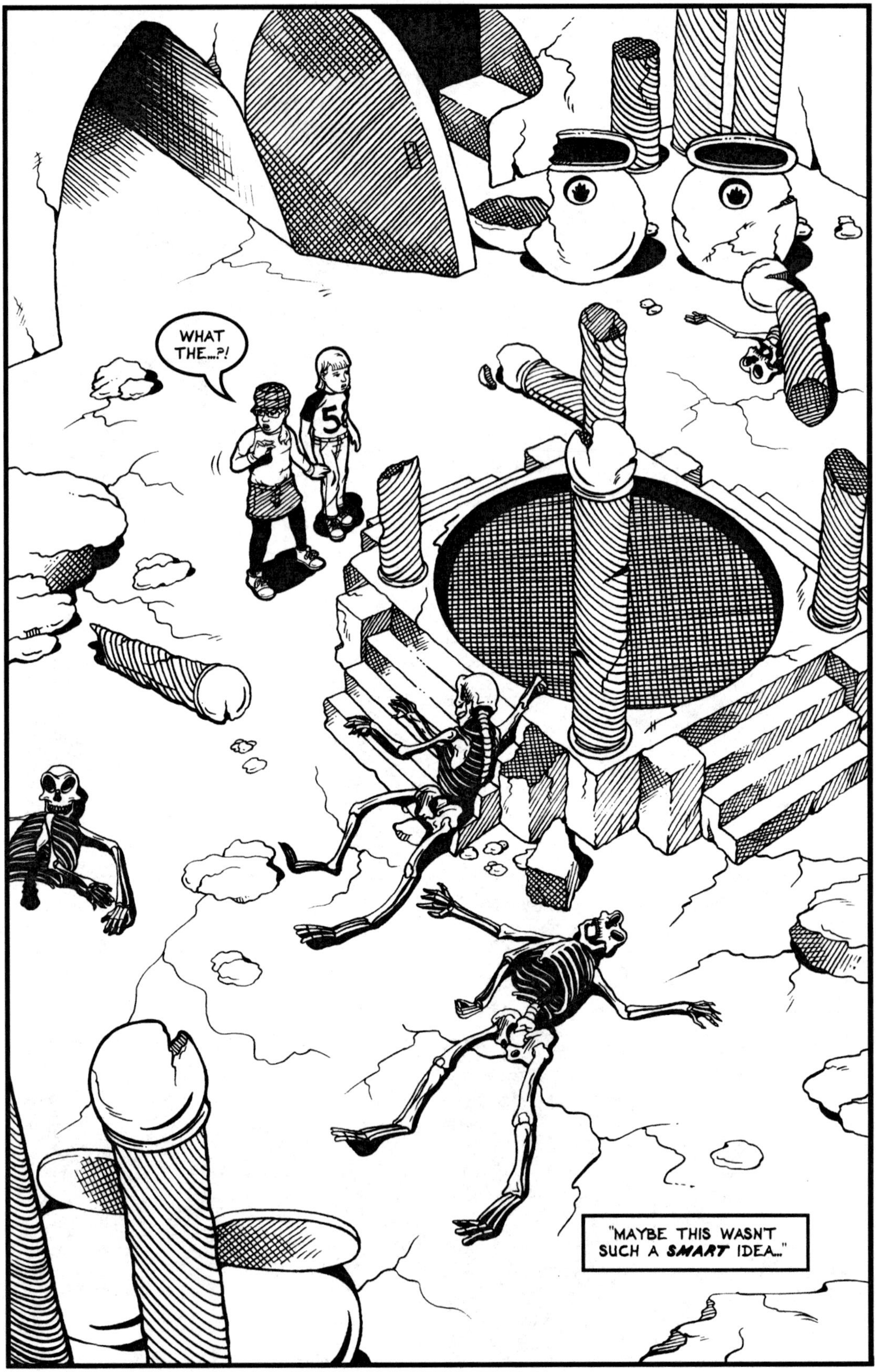
WHAT THE...?!
"MAYBE THIS WASN'T SUCH A SMART IDEA..."

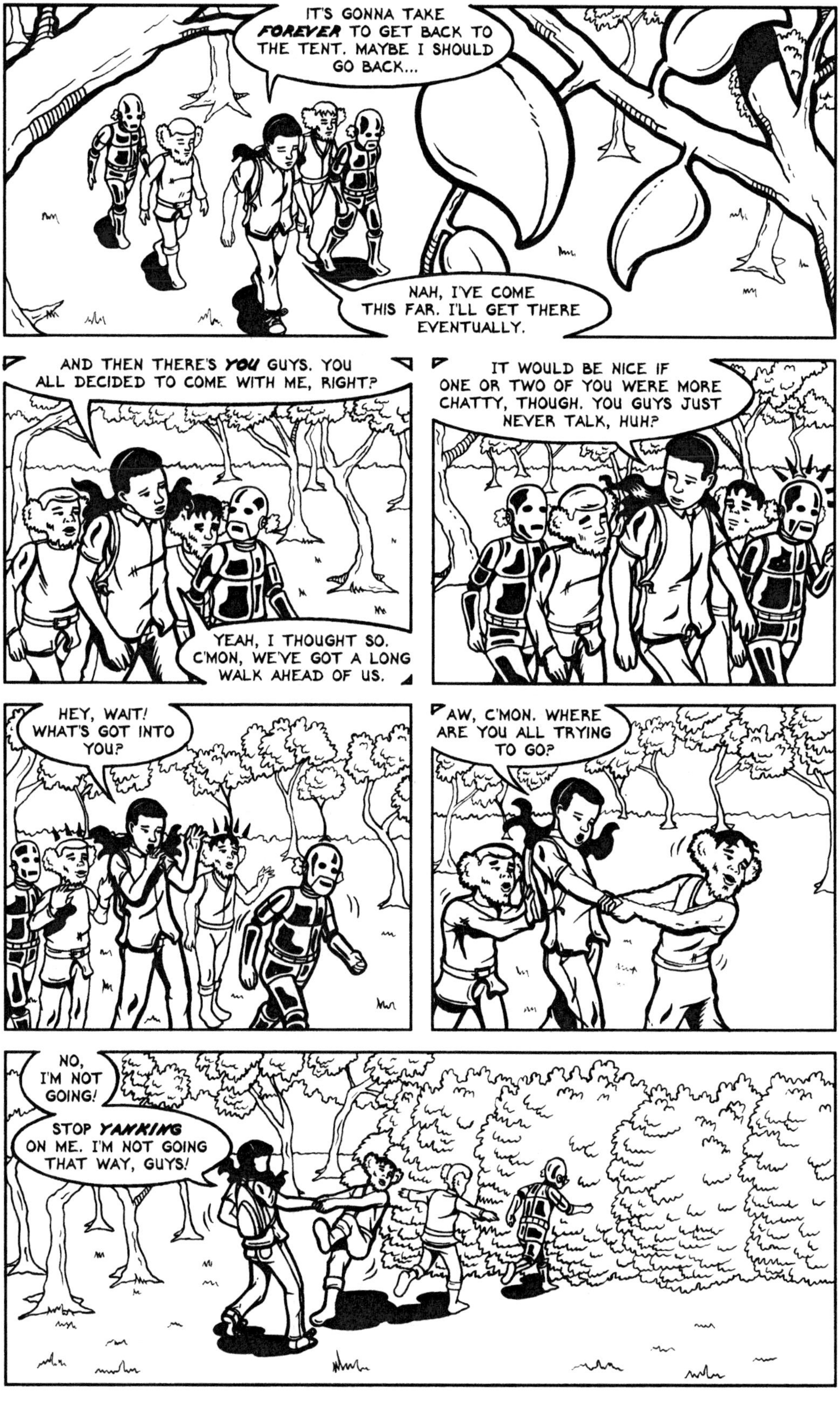
IT'S GONNA TAKE *FOREVER* TO GET BACK TO THE TENT. MAYBE I SHOULD GO BACK...
NAH, I'VE COME THIS FAR. I'LL GET THERE EVENTUALLY.
AND THEN THERE'S *YOU* GUYS. YOU ALL DECIDED TO COME WITH ME, RIGHT?
YEAH, I THOUGHT SO. C'MON, WE'VE GOT A LONG WALK AHEAD OF US.
IT WOULD BE NICE IF ONE OR TWO OF YOU WERE MORE CHATTY, THOUGH. YOU GUYS JUST NEVER TALK, HUH?
HEY, WAIT! WHAT'S GOT INTO YOU?
AW, C'MON. WHERE ARE YOU ALL TRYING TO GO?
NO, I'M NOT GOING!
STOP *YANKING* ON ME. I'M NOT GOING THAT WAY, GUYS!

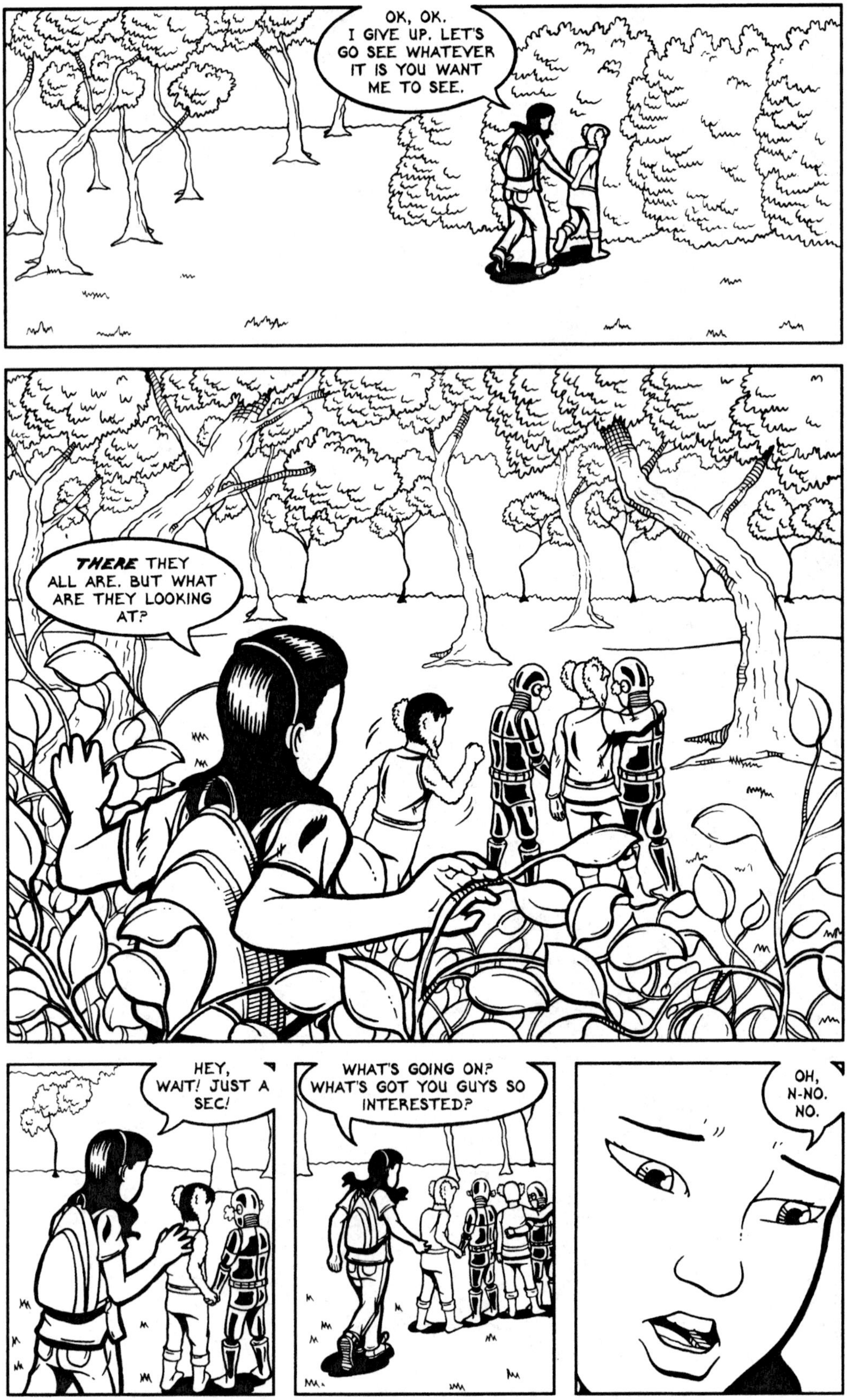
OK, OK. I GIVE UP. LET'S GO SEE WHATEVER IT IS YOU WANT ME TO SEE.
THERE THEY ALL ARE. BUT WHAT ARE THEY LOOKING AT?
HEY, WAIT! JUST A SEC!
WHAT'S GOING ON? WHAT'S GOT YOU GUYS SO INTERESTED?
OH, N-NO. NO.

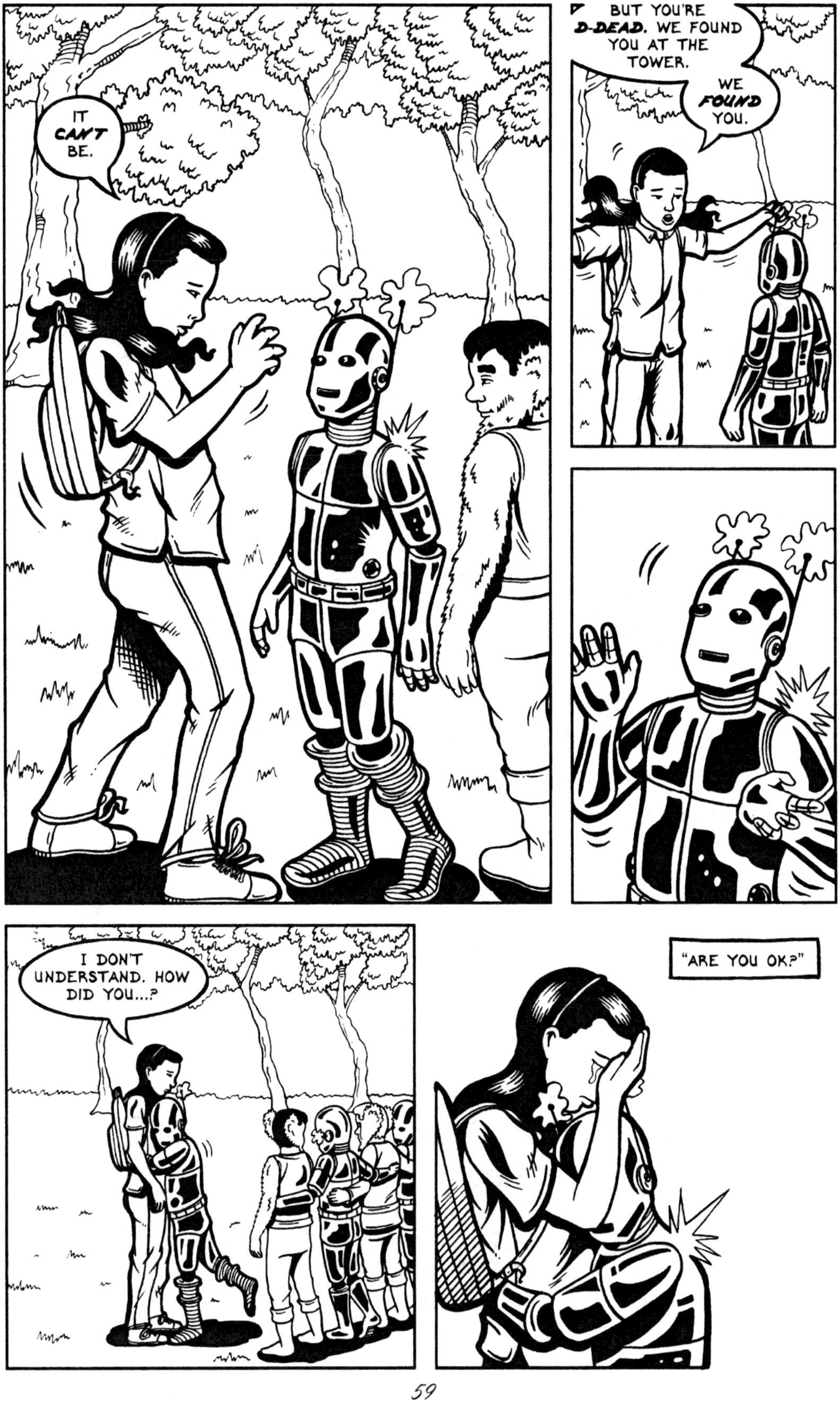
IT CAN'T BE.
BUT YOU'RE D-DEAD. WE FOUND YOU AT THE TOWER.
WE FOUND YOU.
I DON'T UNDERSTAND. HOW DID YOU...?
"ARE YOU OK?"

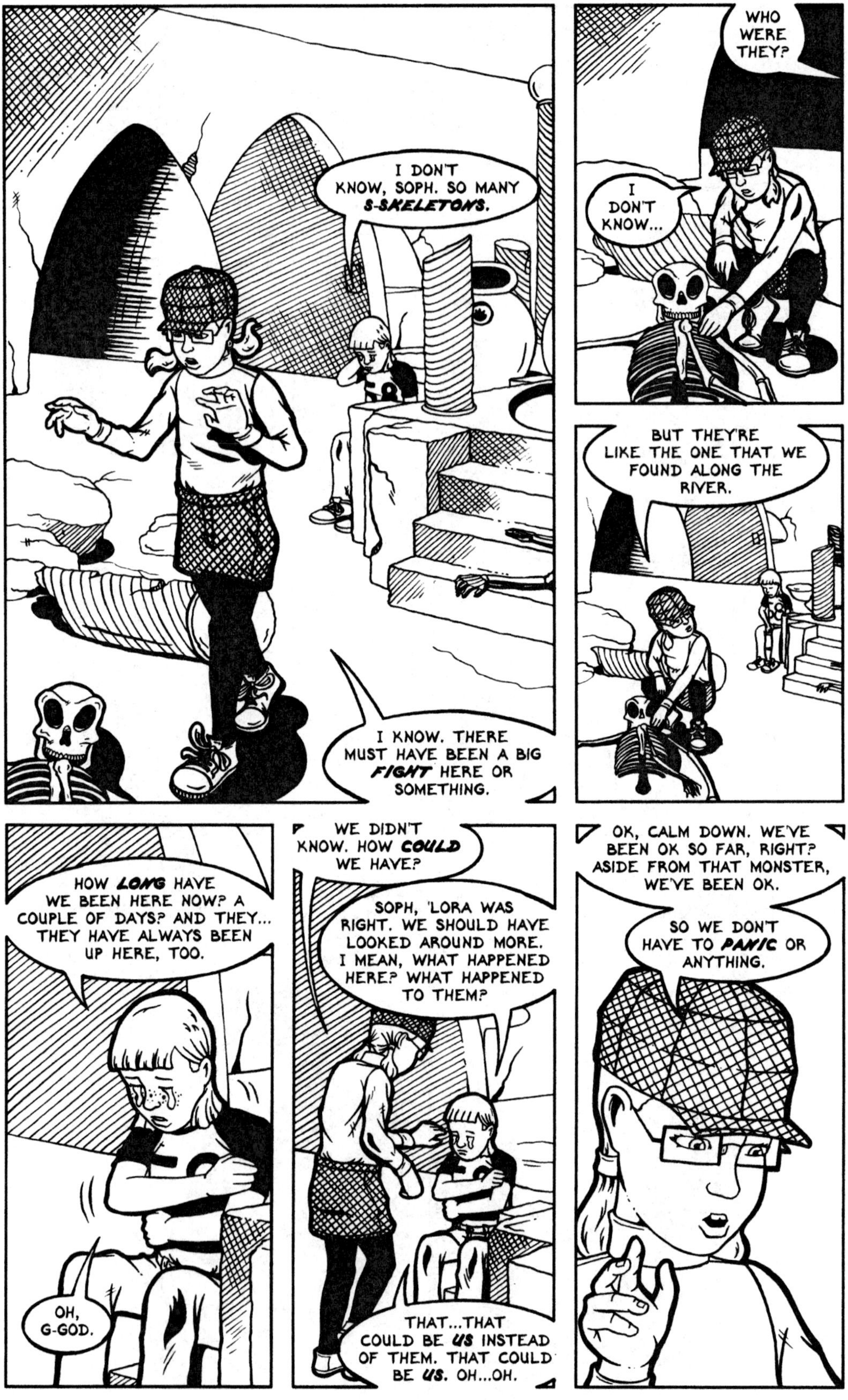
I DON'T KNOW, SOPH. SO MANY S-SKELETONS.
I KNOW. THERE MUST HAVE BEEN A BIG FIGHT HERE OR SOMETHING.
WHO WERE THEY?
I DON'T KNOW...
BUT THEY'RE LIKE THE ONE THAT WE FOUND ALONG THE RIVER.
HOW LONG HAVE WE BEEN HERE NOW? A COUPLE OF DAYS? AND THEY... THEY HAVE ALWAYS BEEN UP HERE, TOO.
OH, G-GOD.
WE DIDN'T KNOW. HOW COULD WE HAVE?
SOPH, 'LORA WAS RIGHT. WE SHOULD HAVE LOOKED AROUND MORE. I MEAN, WHAT HAPPENED HERE? WHAT HAPPENED TO THEM?
THAT...THAT COULD BE US INSTEAD OF THEM. THAT COULD BE US. OH...OH.
OK, CALM DOWN. WE'VE BEEN OK SO FAR, RIGHT? ASIDE FROM THAT MONSTER, WE'VE BEEN OK.
SO WE DON'T HAVE TO PANIC OR ANYTHING.

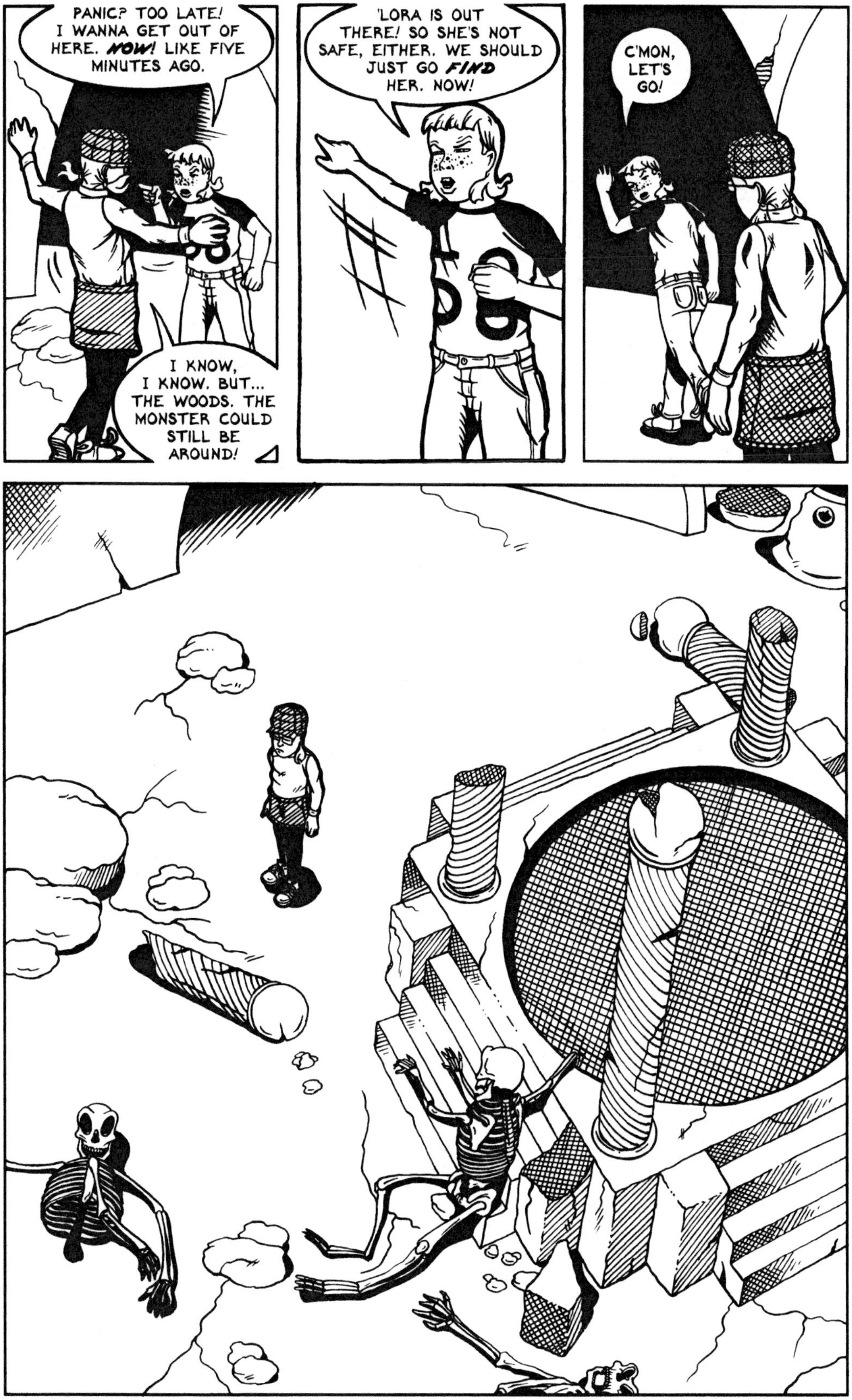
PANIC? TOO LATE! I WANNA GET OUT OF HERE. NOW! LIKE FIVE MINUTES AGO.
I KNOW, I KNOW. BUT... THE WOODS. THE MONSTER COULD STILL BE AROUND!
'LORA IS OUT THERE! SO SHE'S NOT SAFE, EITHER. WE SHOULD JUST GO FIND HER. NOW!
C'MON, LET'S GO!

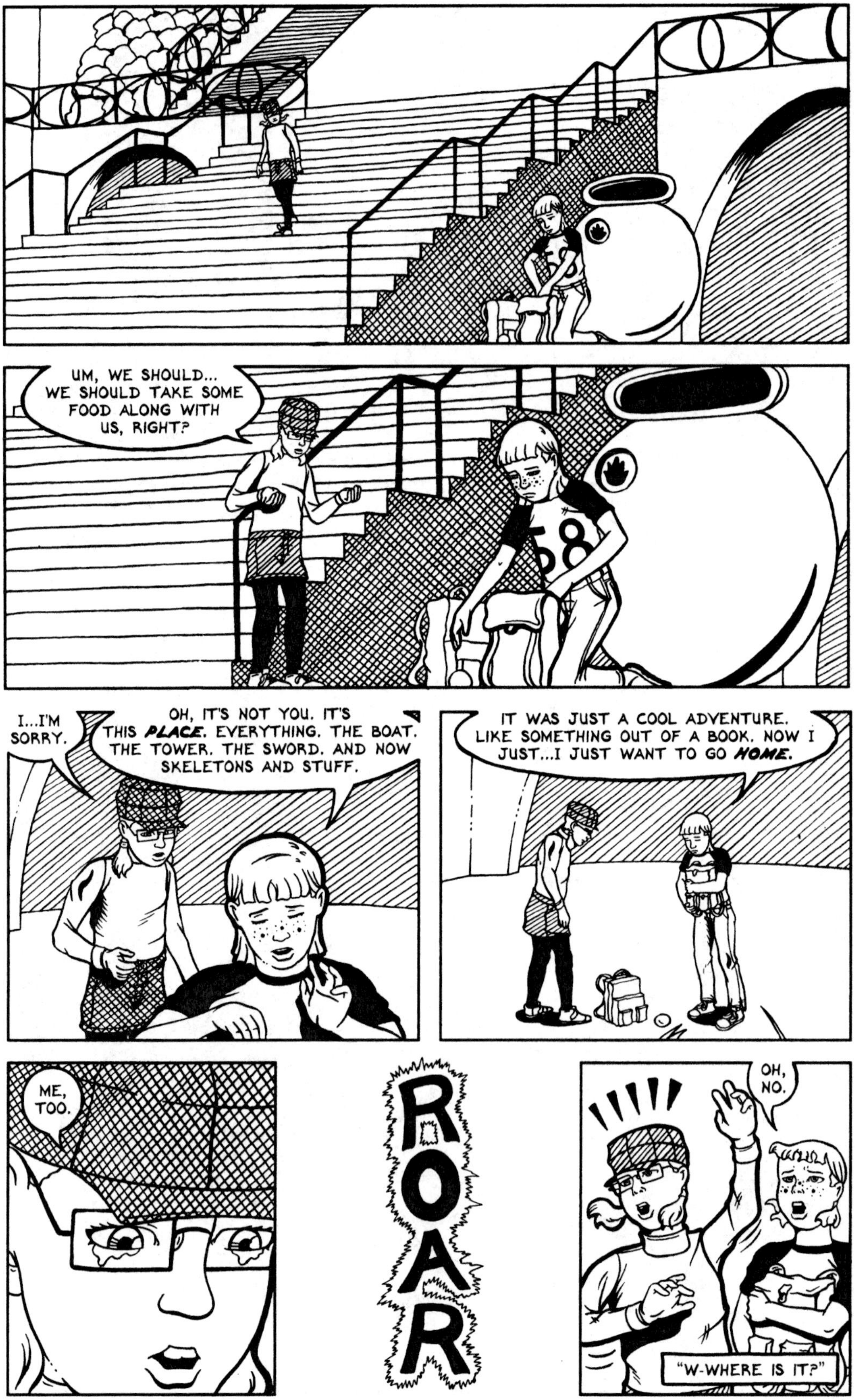
UM, WE SHOULD... WE SHOULD TAKE SOME FOOD ALONG WITH US, RIGHT?
I...I'M SORRY.
OH, IT'S NOT YOU. IT'S THIS *PLACE*. EVERYTHING. THE BOAT. THE TOWER. THE SWORD. AND NOW SKELETONS AND STUFF.
IT WAS JUST A COOL ADVENTURE. LIKE SOMETHING OUT OF A BOOK. NOW I JUST...I JUST WANT TO GO *HOME*.
ME, TOO.
ROAR
OH, NO.
"W-WHERE IS IT?"

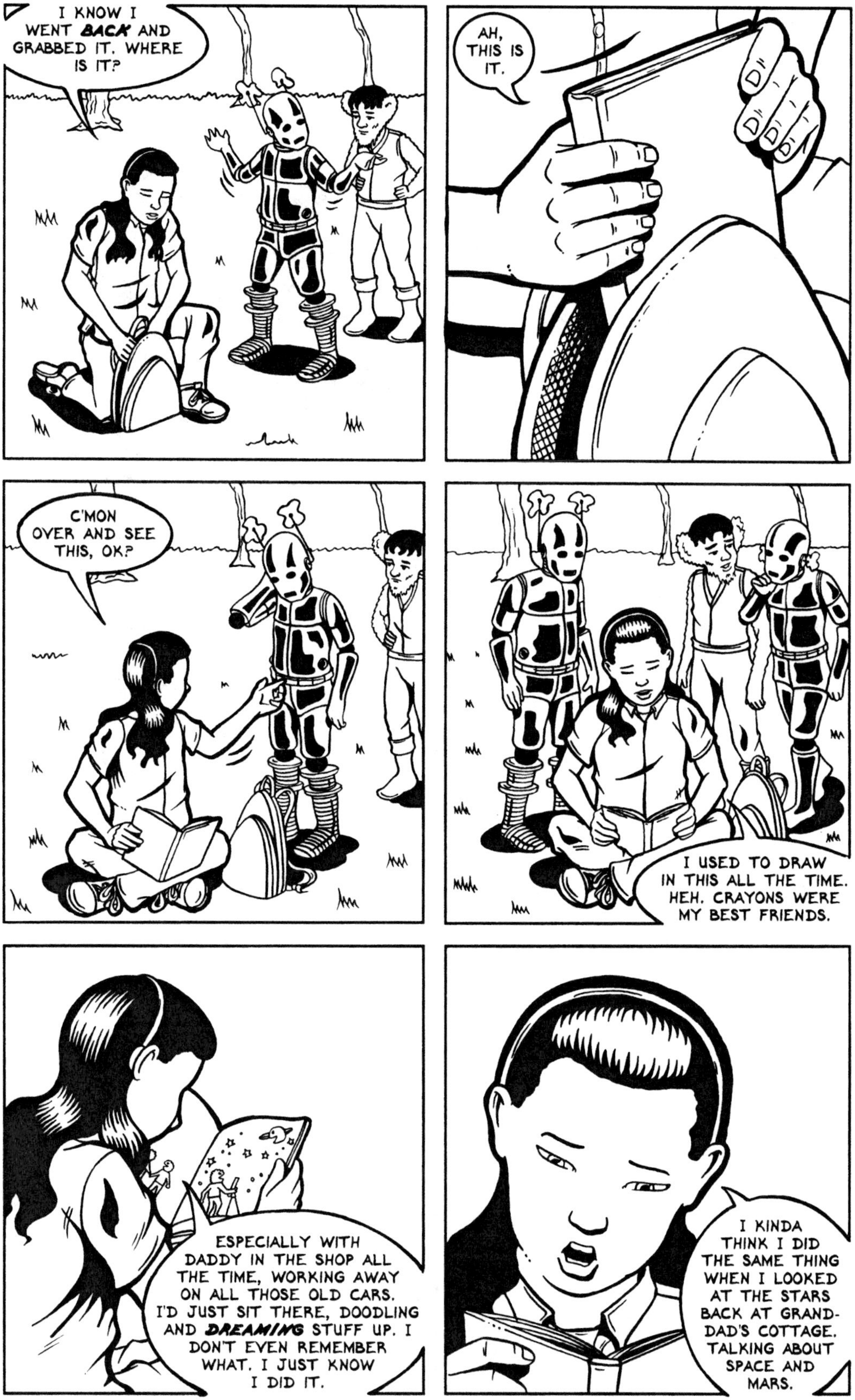
I KNOW I WENT BACK AND GRABBED IT. WHERE IS IT?
AH, THIS IS IT.
C'MON OVER AND SEE THIS, OK?
I USED TO DRAW IN THIS ALL THE TIME. HEH. CRAYONS WERE MY BEST FRIENDS.
ESPECIALLY WITH DADDY IN THE SHOP ALL THE TIME, WORKING AWAY ON ALL THOSE OLD CARS. I'D JUST SIT THERE, DOODLING AND DREAMING STUFF UP. I DON'T EVEN REMEMBER WHAT. I JUST KNOW I DID IT.
I KINDA THINK I DID THE SAME THING WHEN I LOOKED AT THE STARS BACK AT GRAND-DAD'S COTTAGE. TALKING ABOUT SPACE AND MARS.

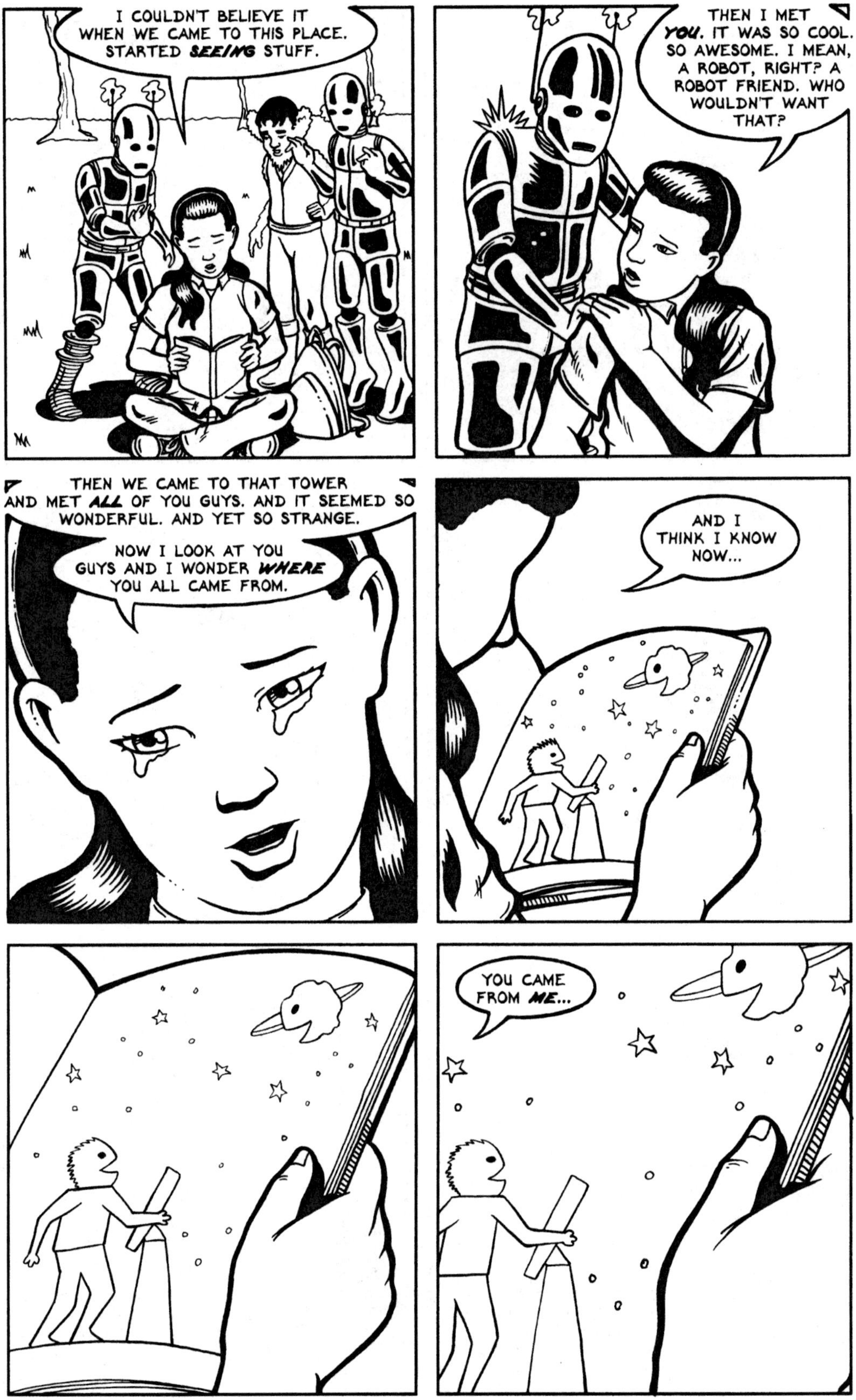
I COULDN'T BELIEVE IT WHEN WE CAME TO THIS PLACE. STARTED SEEING STUFF.
THEN I MET YOU. IT WAS SO COOL. SO AWESOME. I MEAN, A ROBOT, RIGHT? A ROBOT FRIEND. WHO WOULDN'T WANT THAT?
THEN WE CAME TO THAT TOWER AND MET ALL OF YOU GUYS. AND IT SEEMED SO WONDERFUL. AND YET SO STRANGE.
NOW I LOOK AT YOU GUYS AND I WONDER WHERE YOU ALL CAME FROM.
AND I THINK I KNOW NOW...
YOU CAME FROM ME...

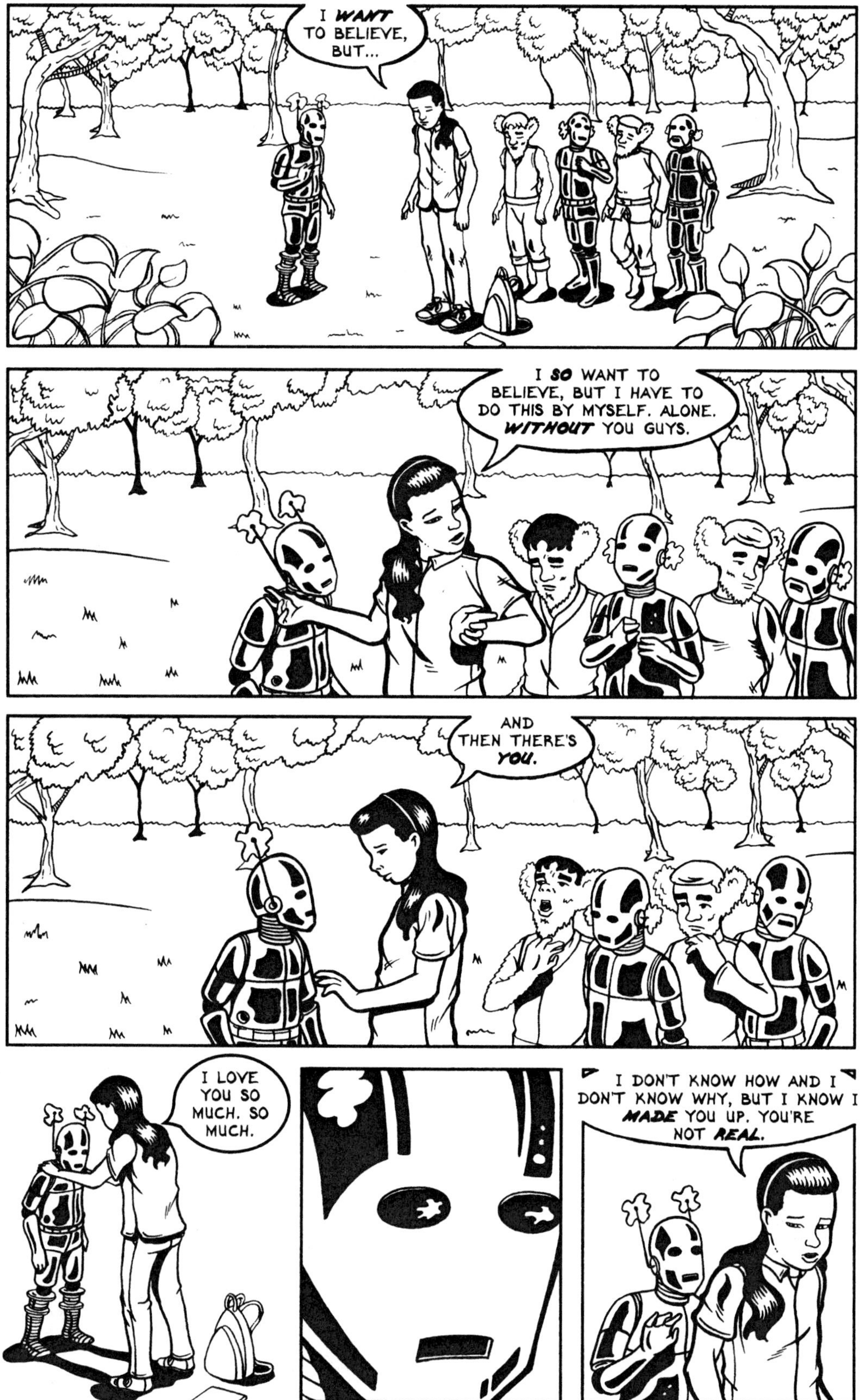
I WANT TO BELIEVE, BUT...
I SO WANT TO BELIEVE, BUT I HAVE TO DO THIS BY MYSELF. ALONE. WITHOUT YOU GUYS.
AND THEN THERE'S YOU.
I LOVE YOU SO MUCH. SO MUCH.
I DON'T KNOW HOW AND I DON'T KNOW WHY, BUT I KNOW I MADE YOU UP. YOU'RE NOT REAL.

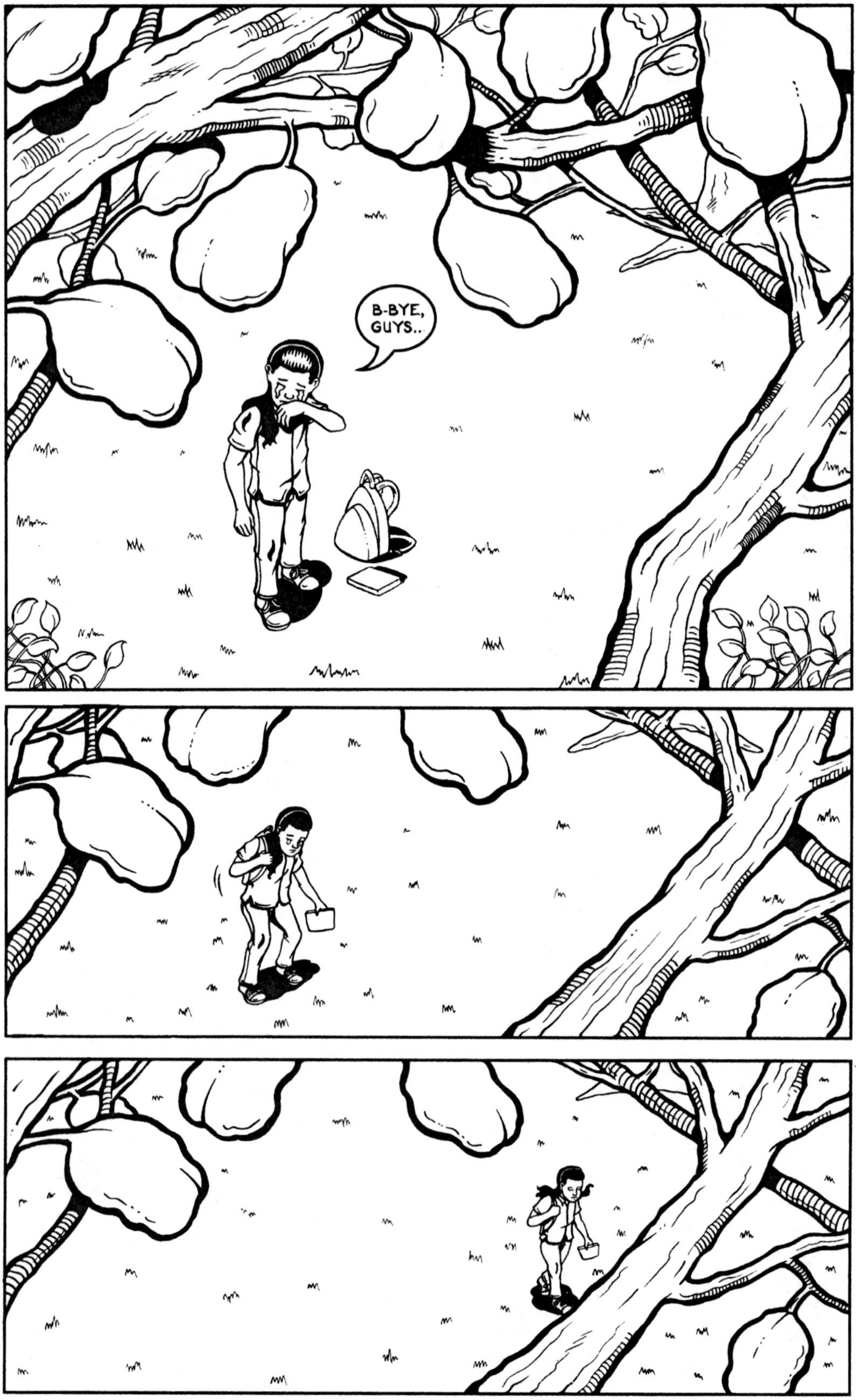
B-BYE, GUYS..

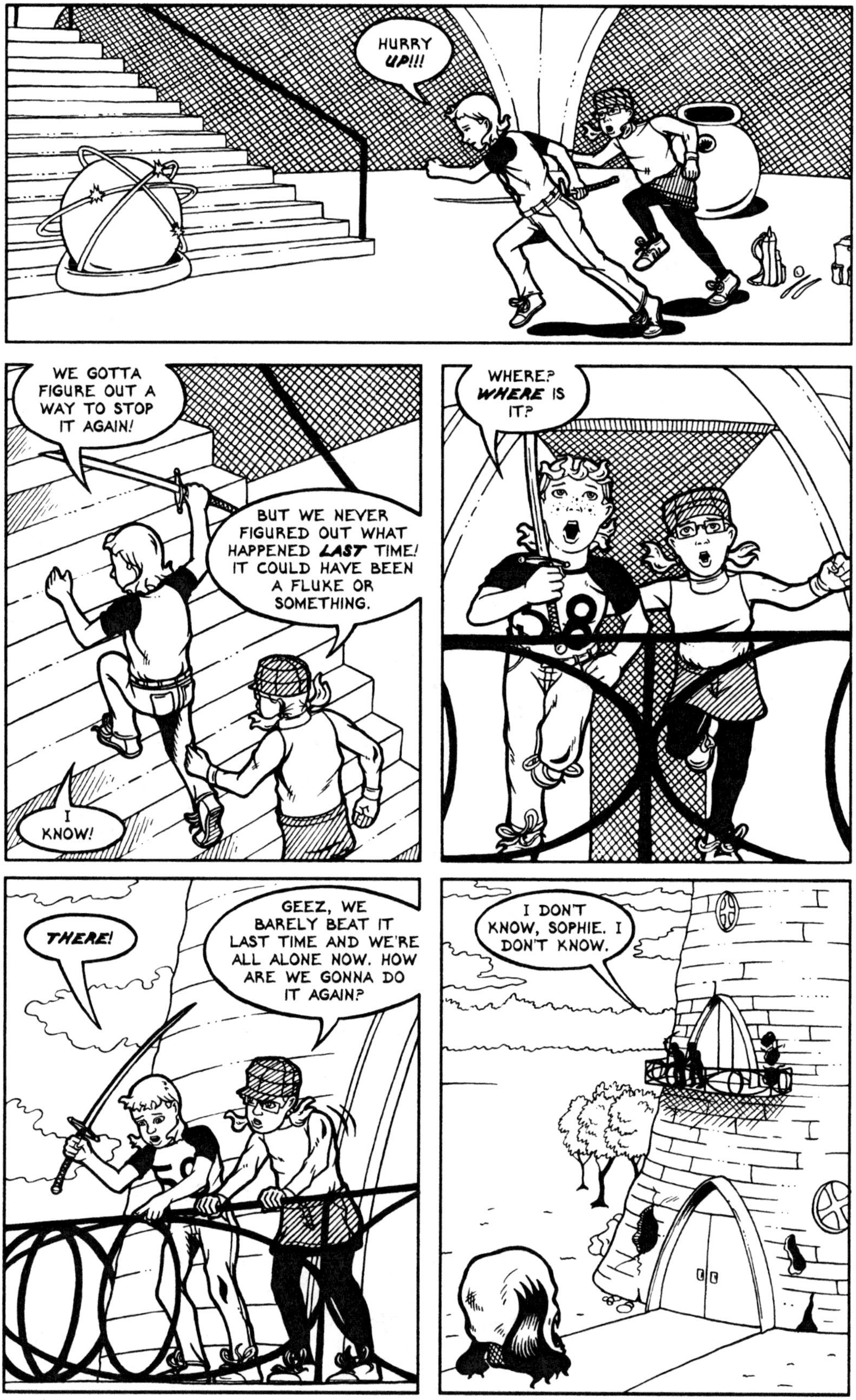
HURRY UP!!!
WE GOTTA FIGURE OUT A WAY TO STOP IT AGAIN!
BUT WE NEVER FIGURED OUT WHAT HAPPENED LAST TIME! IT COULD HAVE BEEN A FLUKE OR SOMETHING.
I KNOW!
WHERE? WHERE IS IT?
THERE!
GEEZ, WE BARELY BEAT IT LAST TIME AND WE'RE ALL ALONE NOW. HOW ARE WE GONNA DO IT AGAIN?
I DON'T KNOW, SOPHIE. I DON'T KNOW.

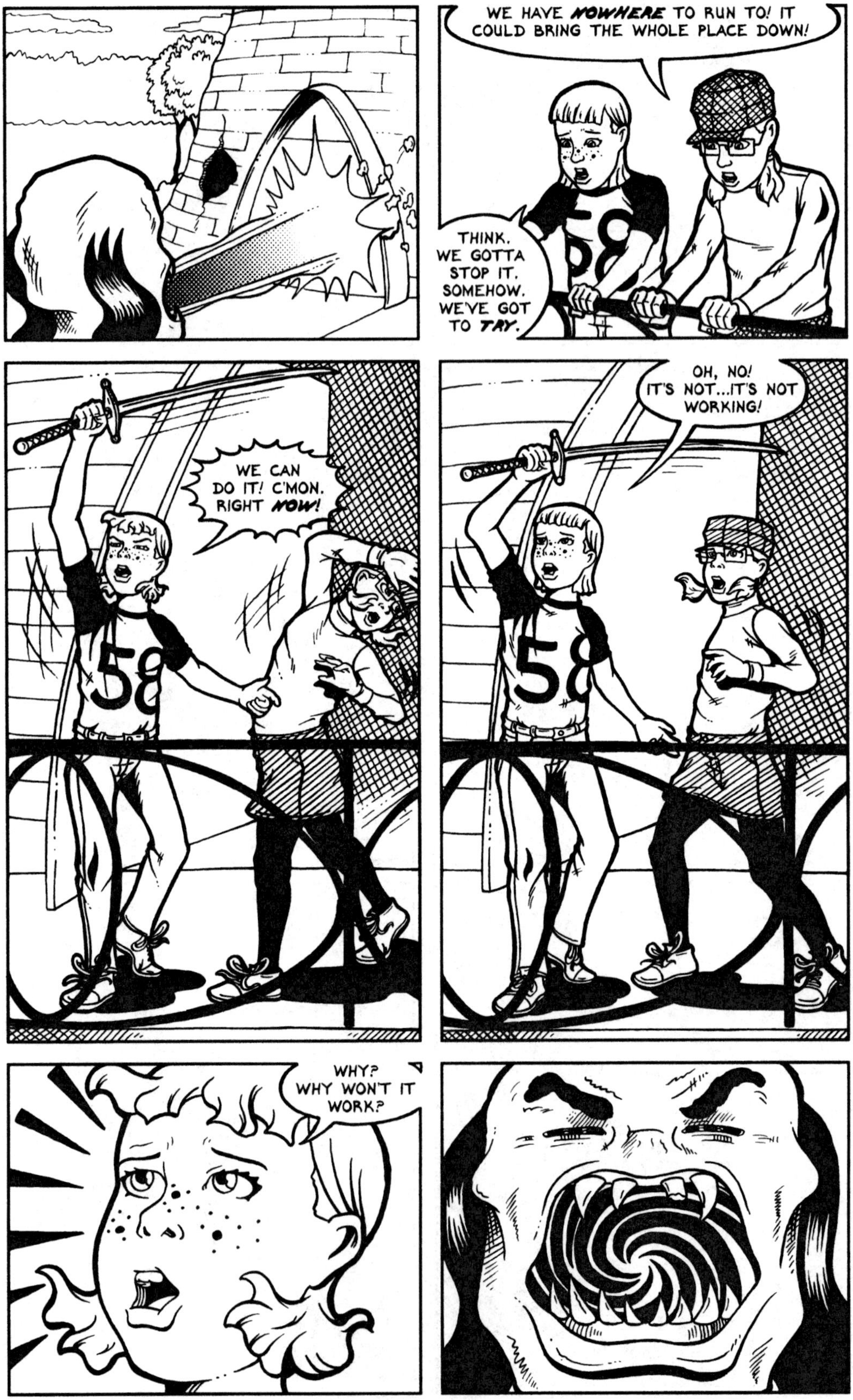
WE HAVE NOWHERE TO RUN TO! IT COULD BRING THE WHOLE PLACE DOWN!
THINK. WE GOTTA STOP IT. SOMEHOW. WE'VE GOT TO TRY.
WE CAN DO IT! C'MON. RIGHT NOW!
OH, NO! IT'S NOT...IT'S NOT WORKING!
WHY? WHY WON'T IT WORK?

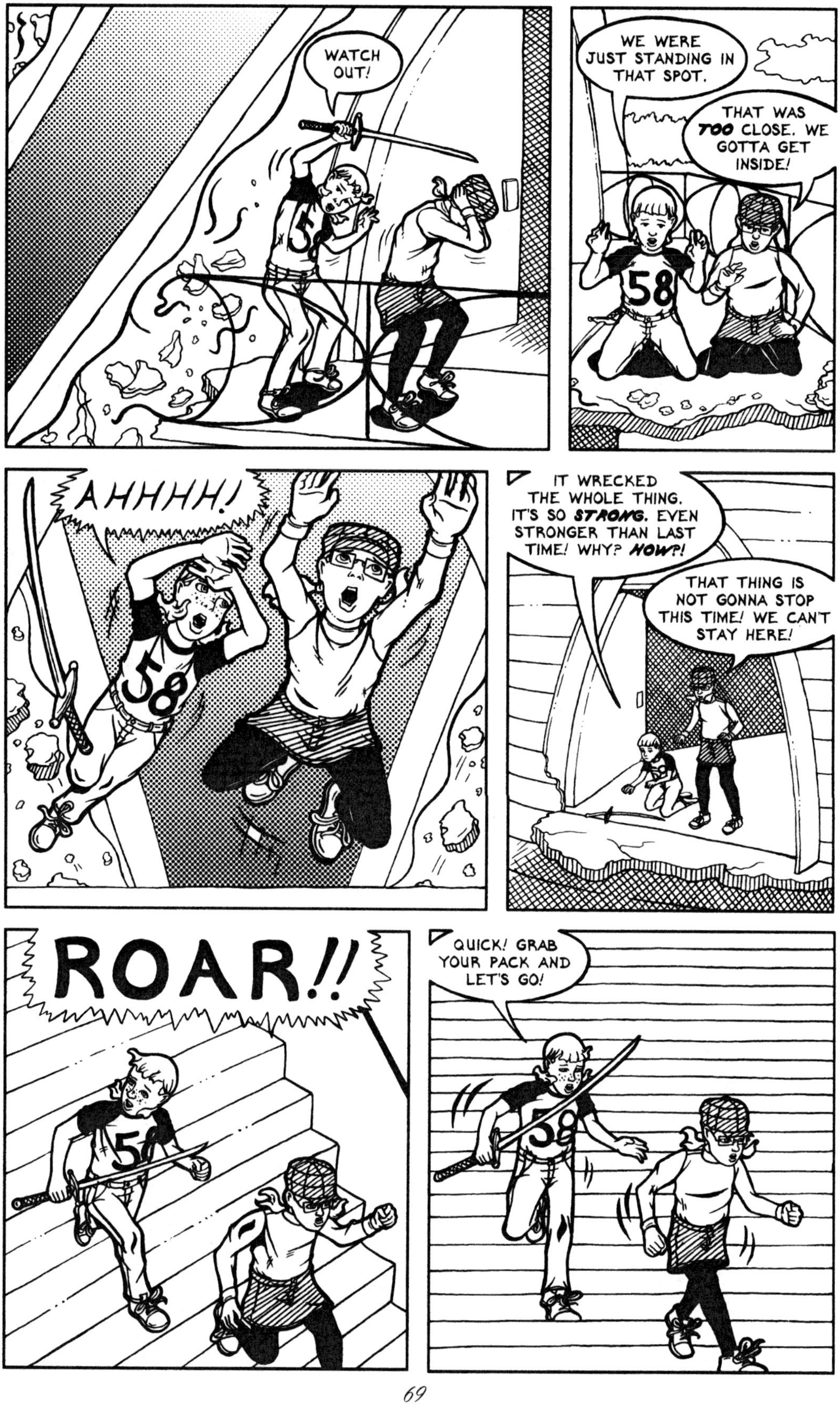
WATCH OUT!
WE WERE JUST STANDING IN THAT SPOT.
THAT WAS TOO CLOSE. WE GOTTA GET INSIDE!
AHHHH!
IT WRECKED THE WHOLE THING. IT'S SO STRONG. EVEN STRONGER THAN LAST TIME! WHY? NOW?!
THAT THING IS NOT GONNA STOP THIS TIME! WE CAN'T STAY HERE!
ROAR!!
QUICK! GRAB YOUR PACK AND LET'S GO!

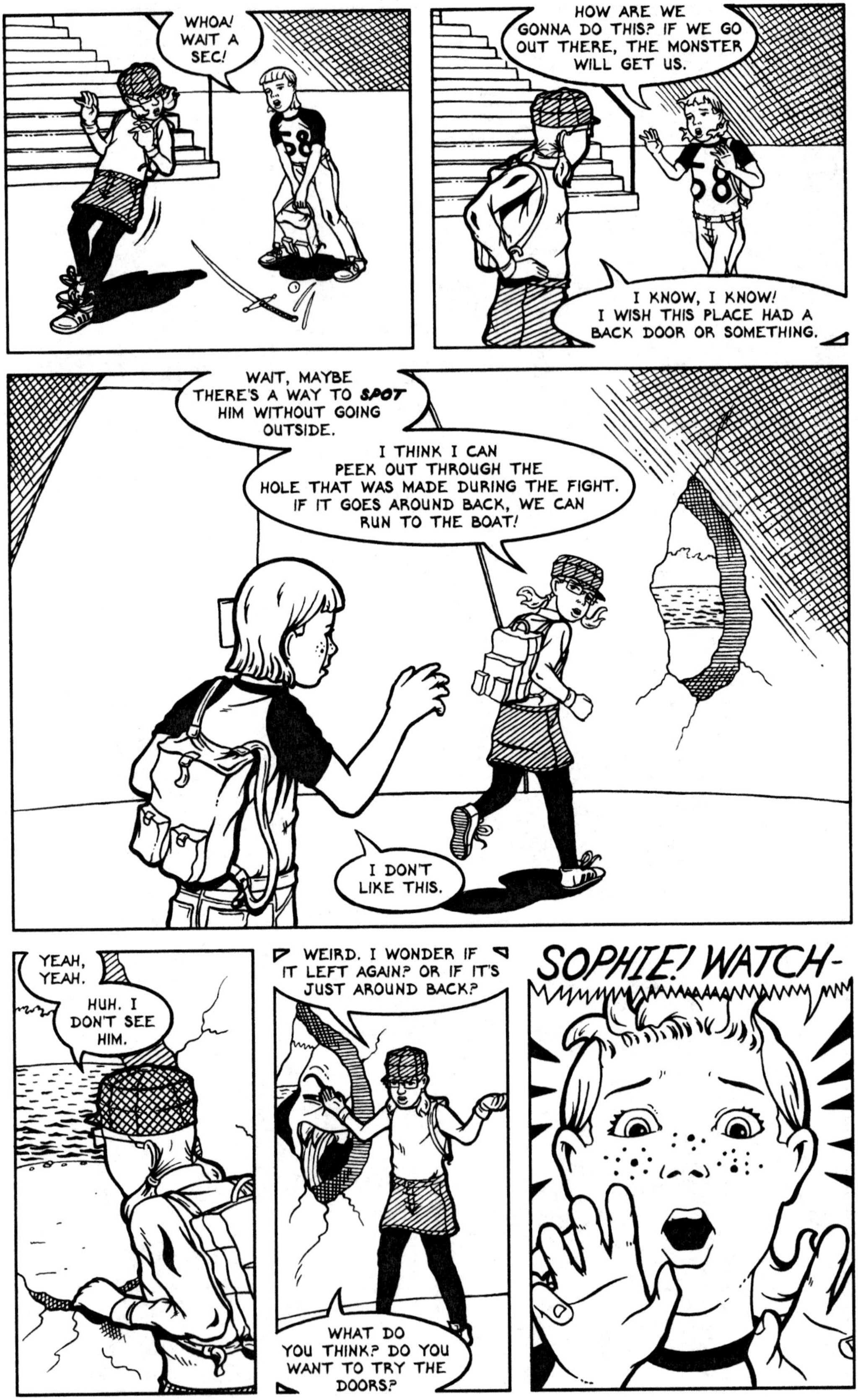
WHOA! WAIT A SEC!
HOW ARE WE GONNA DO THIS? IF WE GO OUT THERE, THE MONSTER WILL GET US.
I KNOW, I KNOW! I WISH THIS PLACE HAD A BACK DOOR OR SOMETHING.
WAIT, MAYBE THERE'S A WAY TO SPOT HIM WITHOUT GOING OUTSIDE.
I THINK I CAN PEEK OUT THROUGH THE HOLE THAT WAS MADE DURING THE FIGHT. IF IT GOES AROUND BACK, WE CAN RUN TO THE BOAT!
I DON'T LIKE THIS.
YEAH, YEAH.
HUH. I DON'T SEE HIM.
WEIRD. I WONDER IF IT LEFT AGAIN? OR IF IT'S JUST AROUND BACK?
WHAT DO YOU THINK? DO YOU WANT TO TRY THE DOORS?
SOPHIE! WATCH-

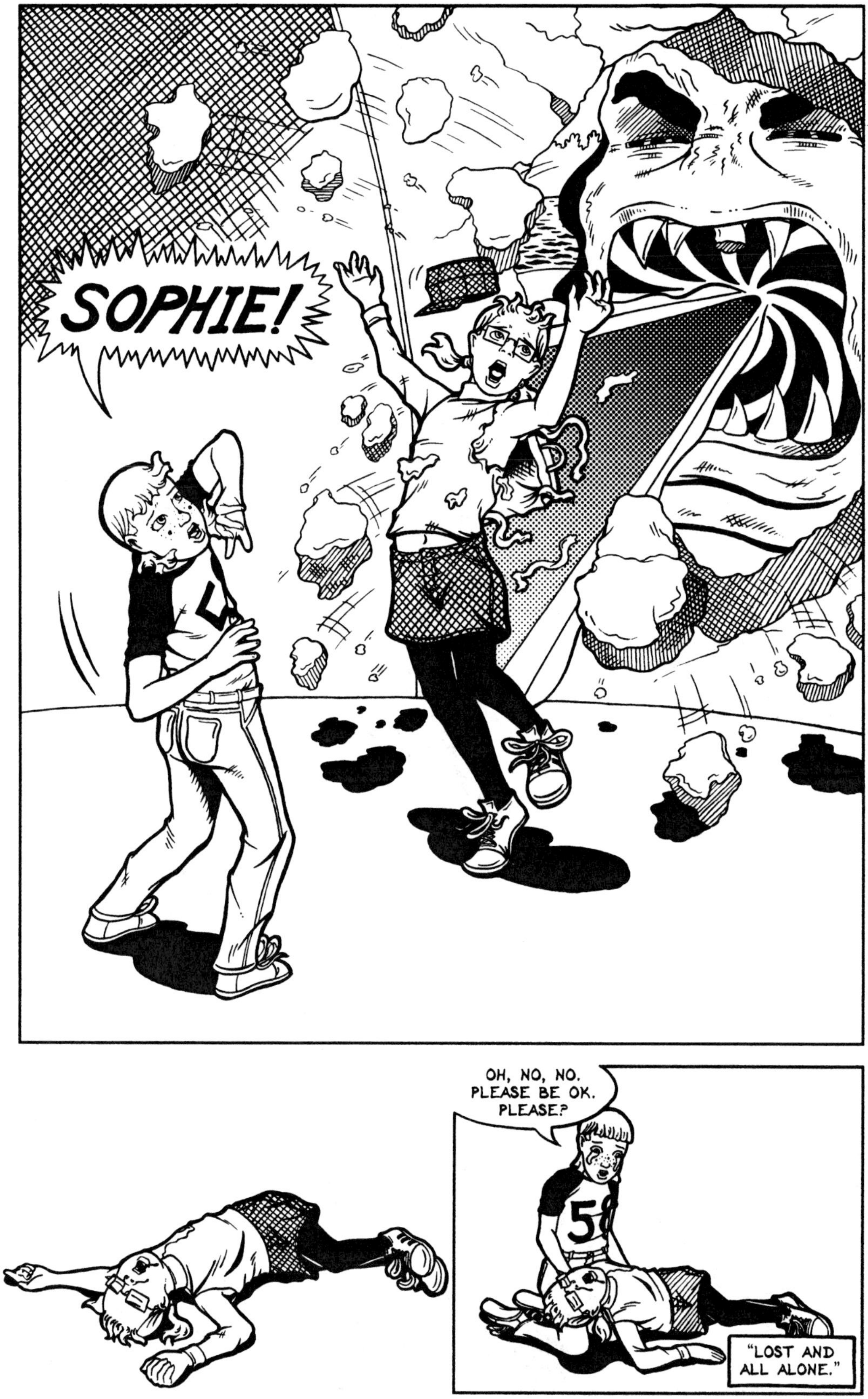
SOPHIE!
OH, NO, NO. PLEASE BE OK. PLEASE?
"LOST AND ALL ALONE."

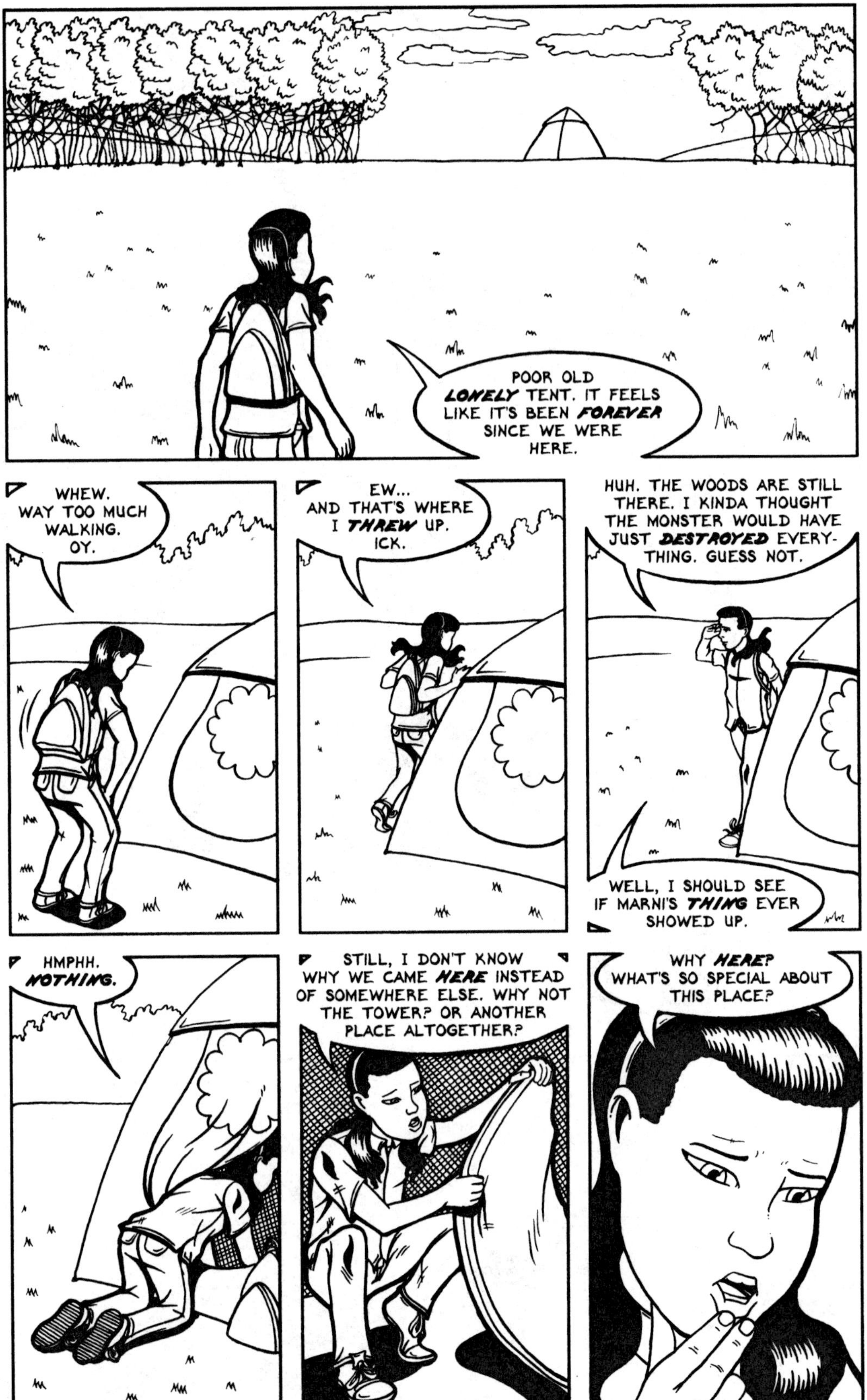
POOR OLD LONELY TENT. IT FEELS LIKE IT'S BEEN FOREVER SINCE WE WERE HERE.
WHEW. WAY TOO MUCH WALKING. OY.
EW... AND THAT'S WHERE I THREW UP. ICK.
HUH. THE WOODS ARE STILL THERE. I KINDA THOUGHT THE MONSTER WOULD HAVE JUST DESTROYED EVERY-THING. GUESS NOT.
WELL, I SHOULD SEE IF MARNI'S THING EVER SHOWED UP.
HMPHH. NOTHING.
STILL, I DON'T KNOW WHY WE CAME HERE INSTEAD OF SOMEWHERE ELSE. WHY NOT THE TOWER? OR ANOTHER PLACE ALTOGETHER?
WHY HERE? WHAT'S SO SPECIAL ABOUT THIS PLACE?

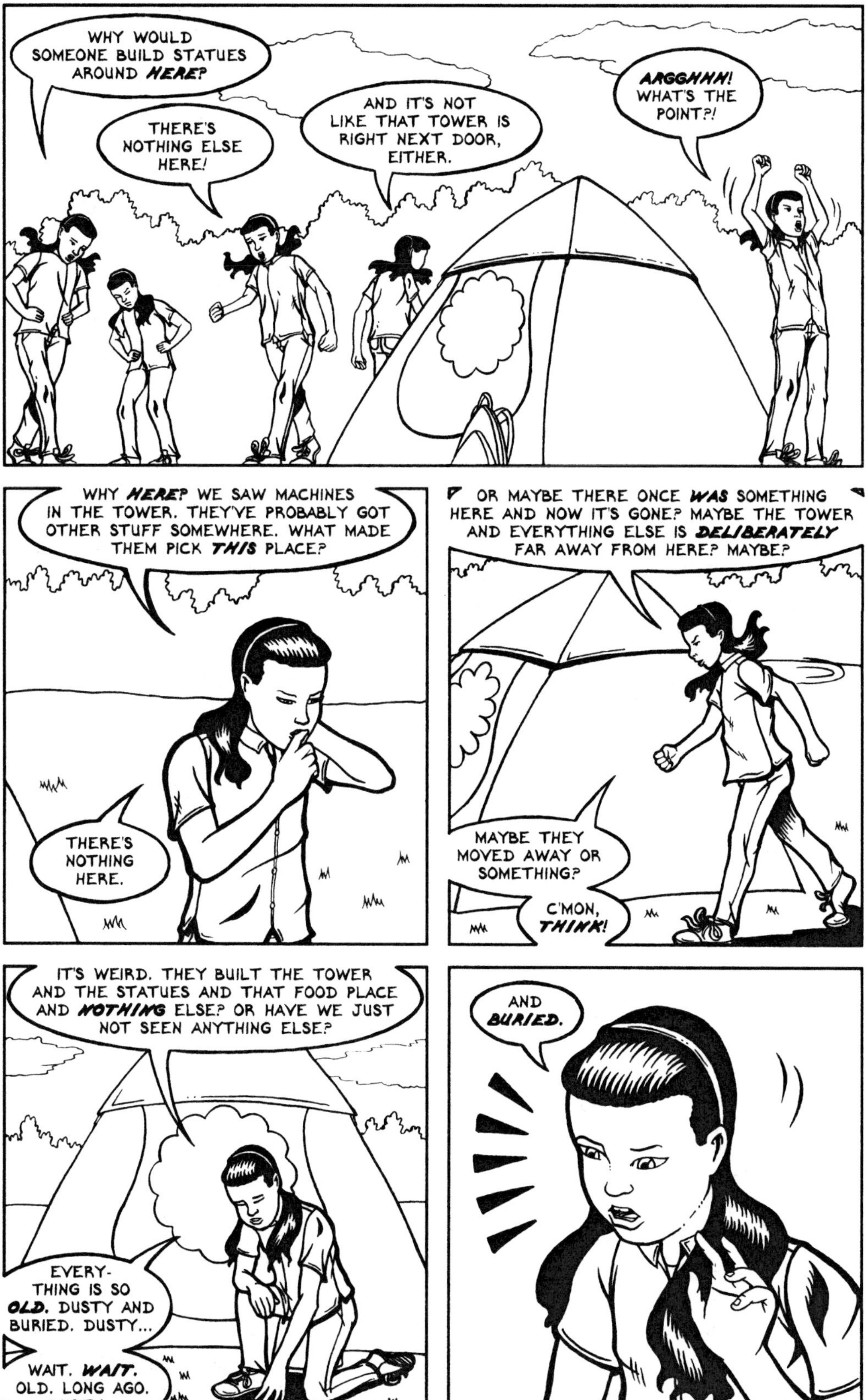
WHY WOULD SOMEONE BUILD STATUES AROUND HERE?
THERE'S NOTHING ELSE HERE!
AND IT'S NOT LIKE THAT TOWER IS RIGHT NEXT DOOR, EITHER.
ARGGHHH! WHAT'S THE POINT?!
WHY HERE? WE SAW MACHINES IN THE TOWER. THEY'VE PROBABLY GOT OTHER STUFF SOMEWHERE. WHAT MADE THEM PICK THIS PLACE?
THERE'S NOTHING HERE.
OR MAYBE THERE ONCE WAS SOMETHING HERE AND NOW IT'S GONE? MAYBE THE TOWER AND EVERYTHING ELSE IS DELIBERATELY FAR AWAY FROM HERE? MAYBE?
MAYBE THEY MOVED AWAY OR SOMETHING?
C'MON, THINK!
IT'S WEIRD. THEY BUILT THE TOWER AND THE STATUES AND THAT FOOD PLACE AND NOTHING ELSE? OR HAVE WE JUST NOT SEEN ANYTHING ELSE?
EVERYTHING IS SO OLD. DUSTY AND BURIED. DUSTY...
WAIT. WAIT. OLD. LONG AGO. DUSTY...
AND BURIED.

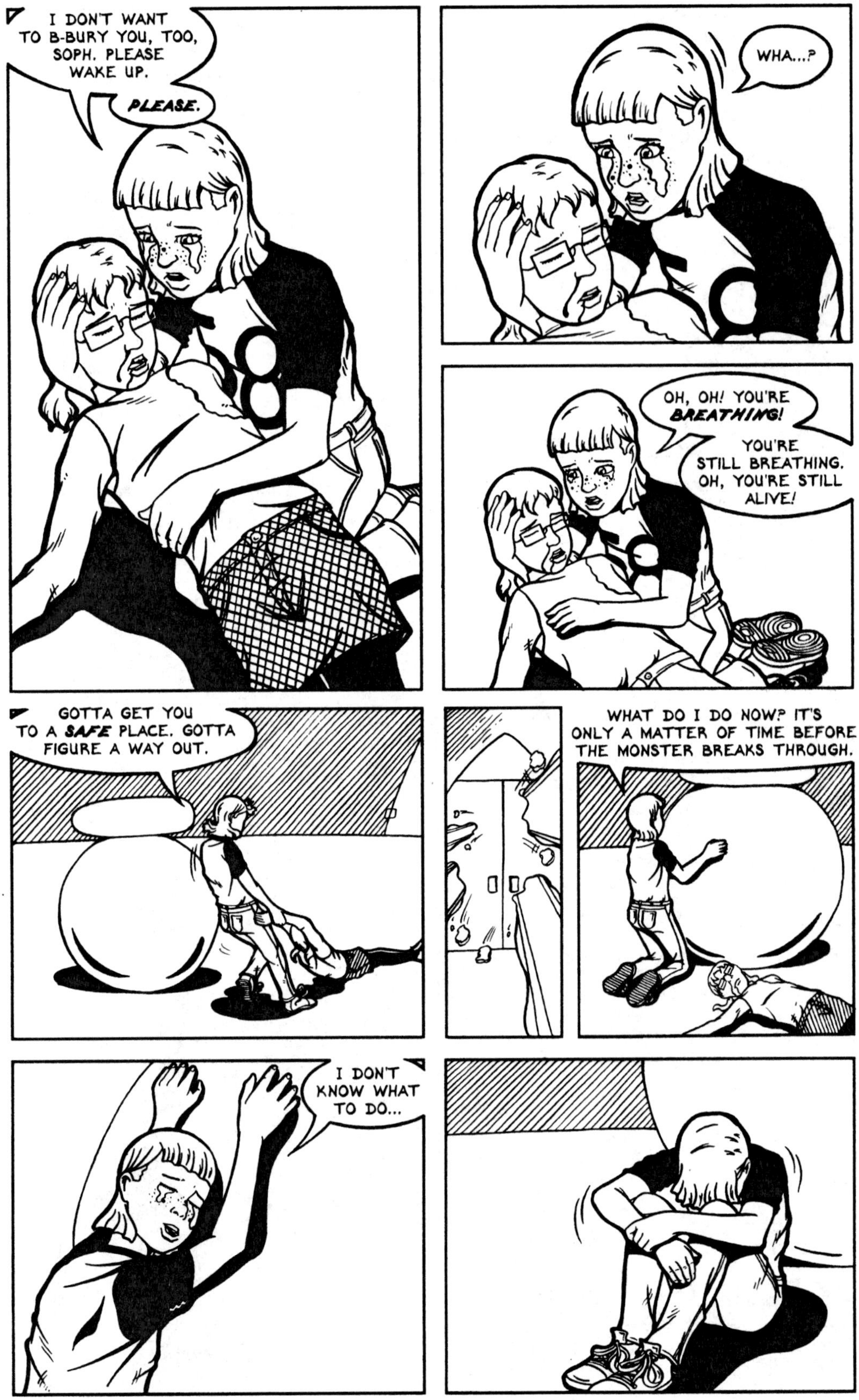
I DON'T WANT TO B-BURY YOU, TOO, SOPH. PLEASE WAKE UP.
PLEASE.
WHA...?
OH, OH! YOU'RE BREATHING!
YOU'RE STILL BREATHING. OH, YOU'RE STILL ALIVE!
GOTTA GET YOU TO A SAFE PLACE. GOTTA FIGURE A WAY OUT.
WHAT DO I DO NOW? IT'S ONLY A MATTER OF TIME BEFORE THE MONSTER BREAKS THROUGH.
I DON'T KNOW WHAT TO DO...

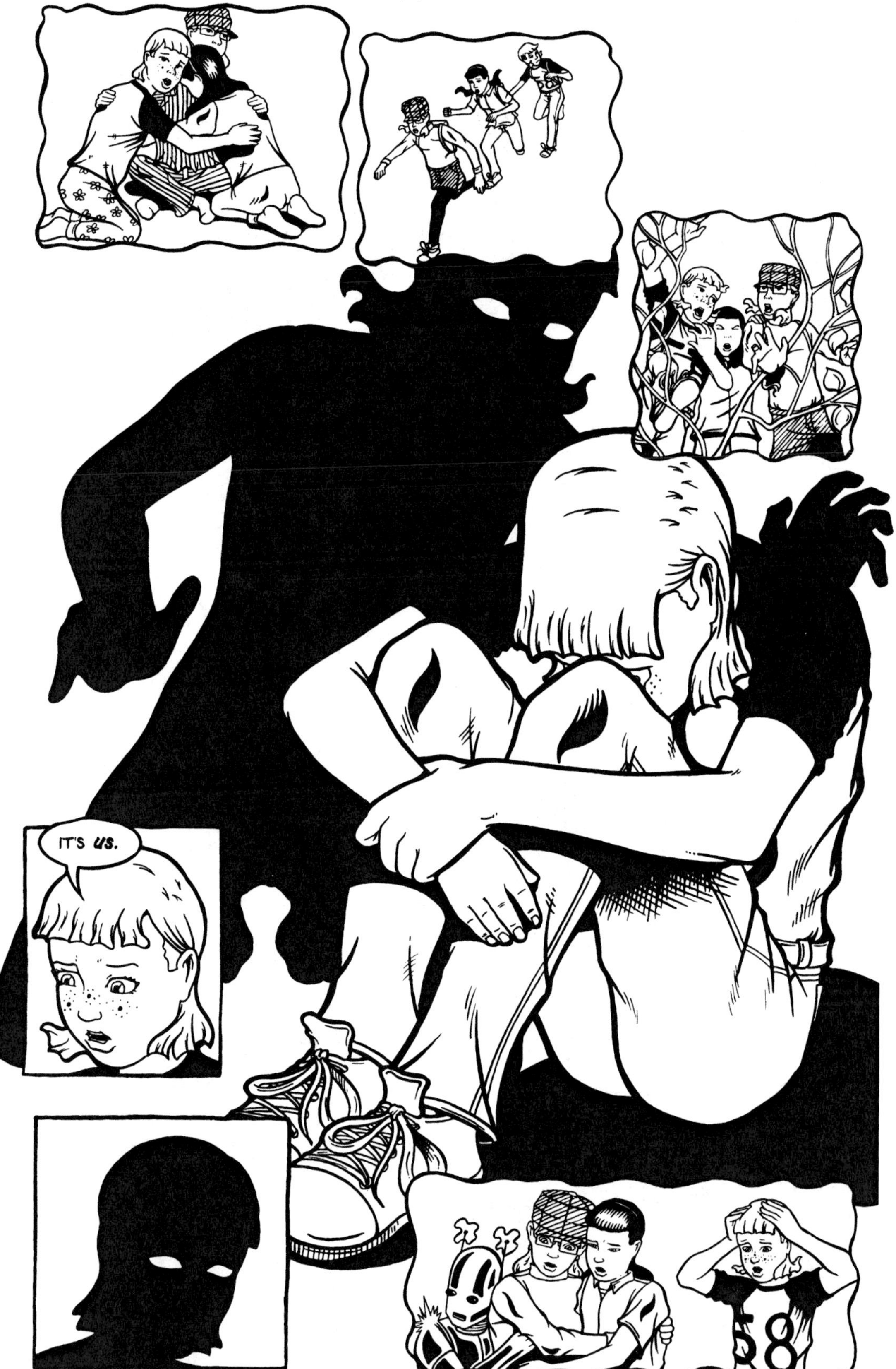
IT'S US.

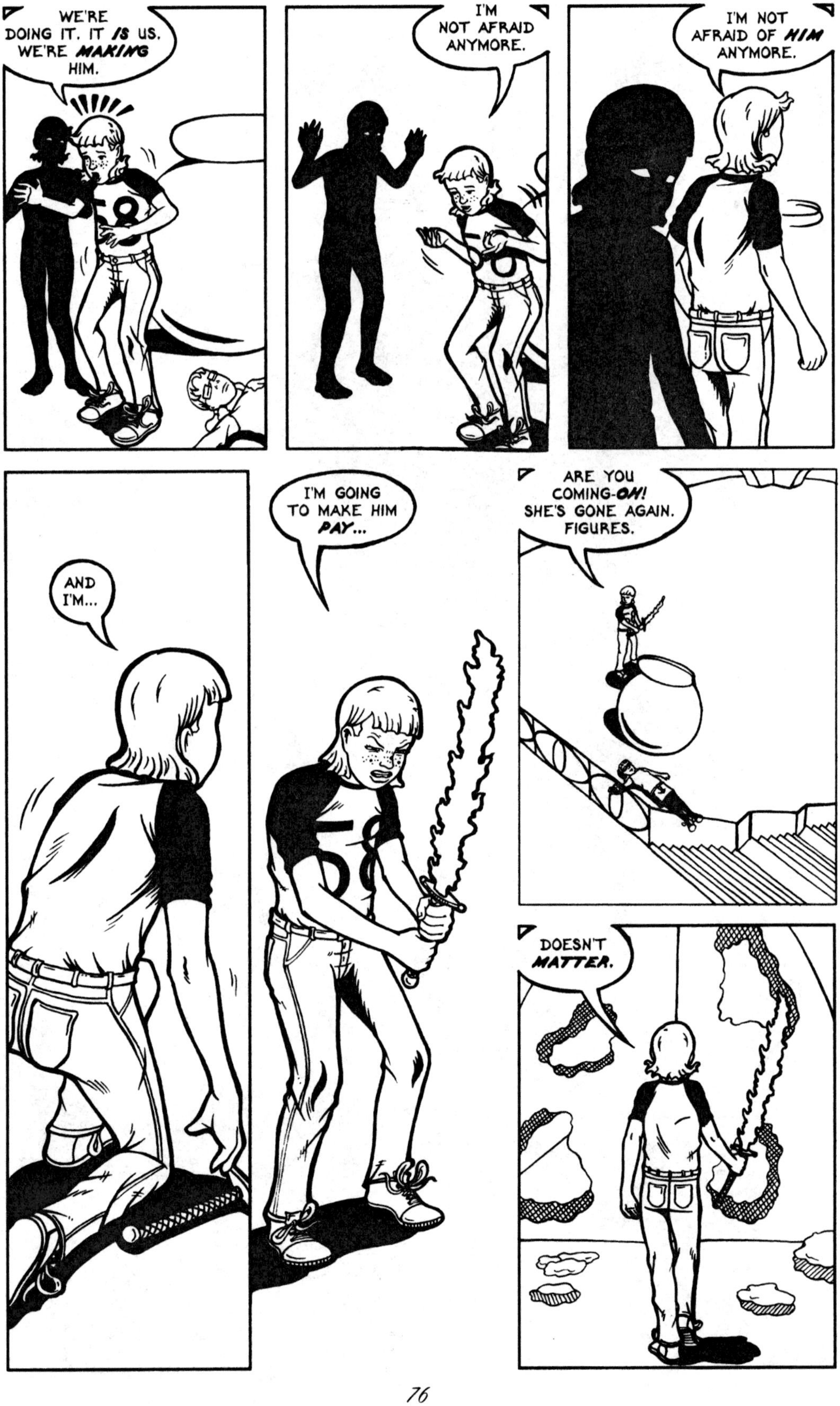
WE'RE DOING IT. IT *IS* US. WE'RE *MAKING* HIM.
I'M NOT AFRAID ANYMORE.
I'M NOT AFRAID OF *HIM* ANYMORE.
AND I'M...
I'M GOING TO MAKE HIM *PAY*...
ARE YOU COMING-*OH!* SHE'S GONE AGAIN. FIGURES.
DOESN'T *MATTER*.

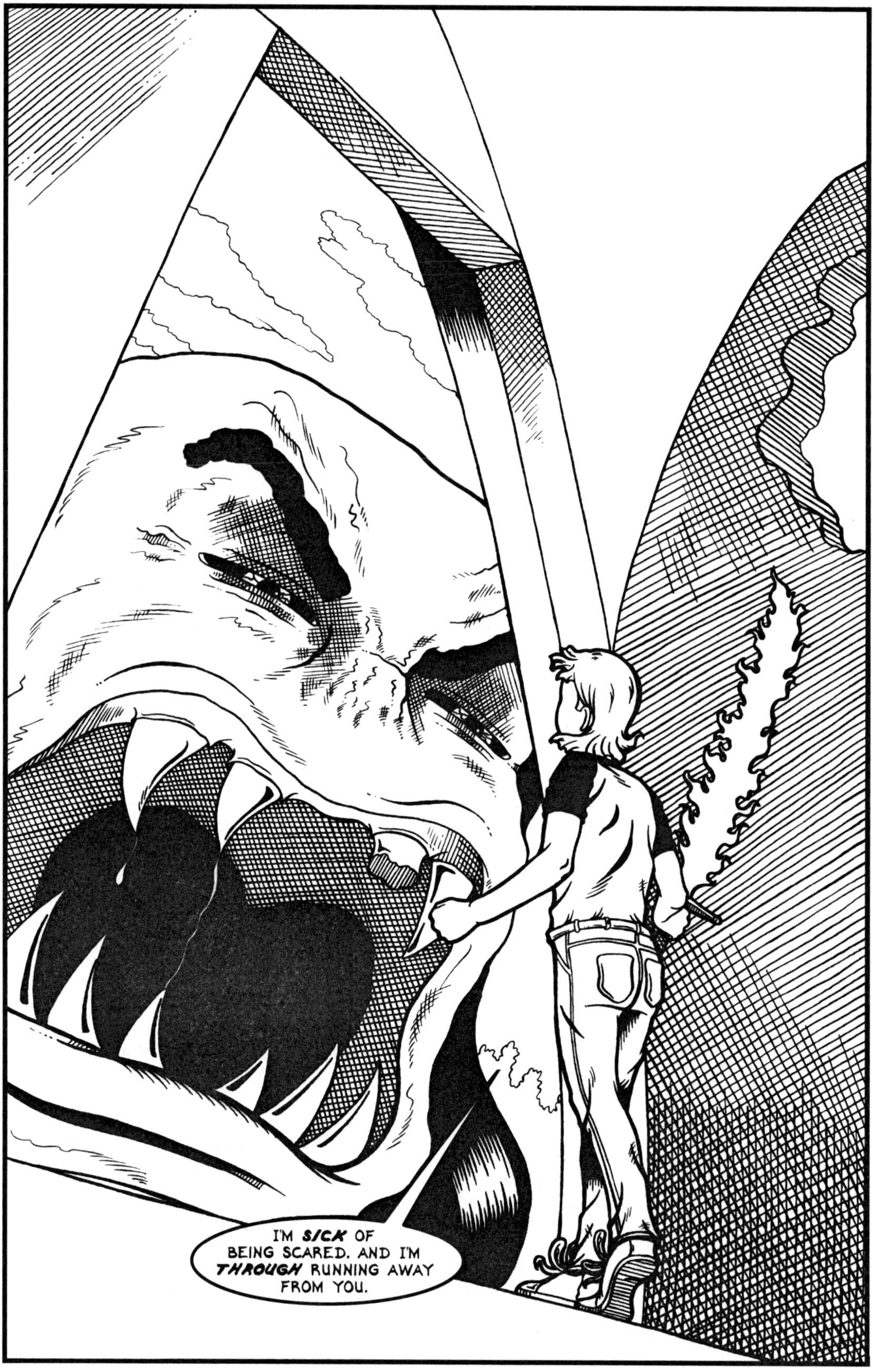
I'M SICK OF BEING SCARED. AND I'M THROUGH RUNNING AWAY FROM YOU.

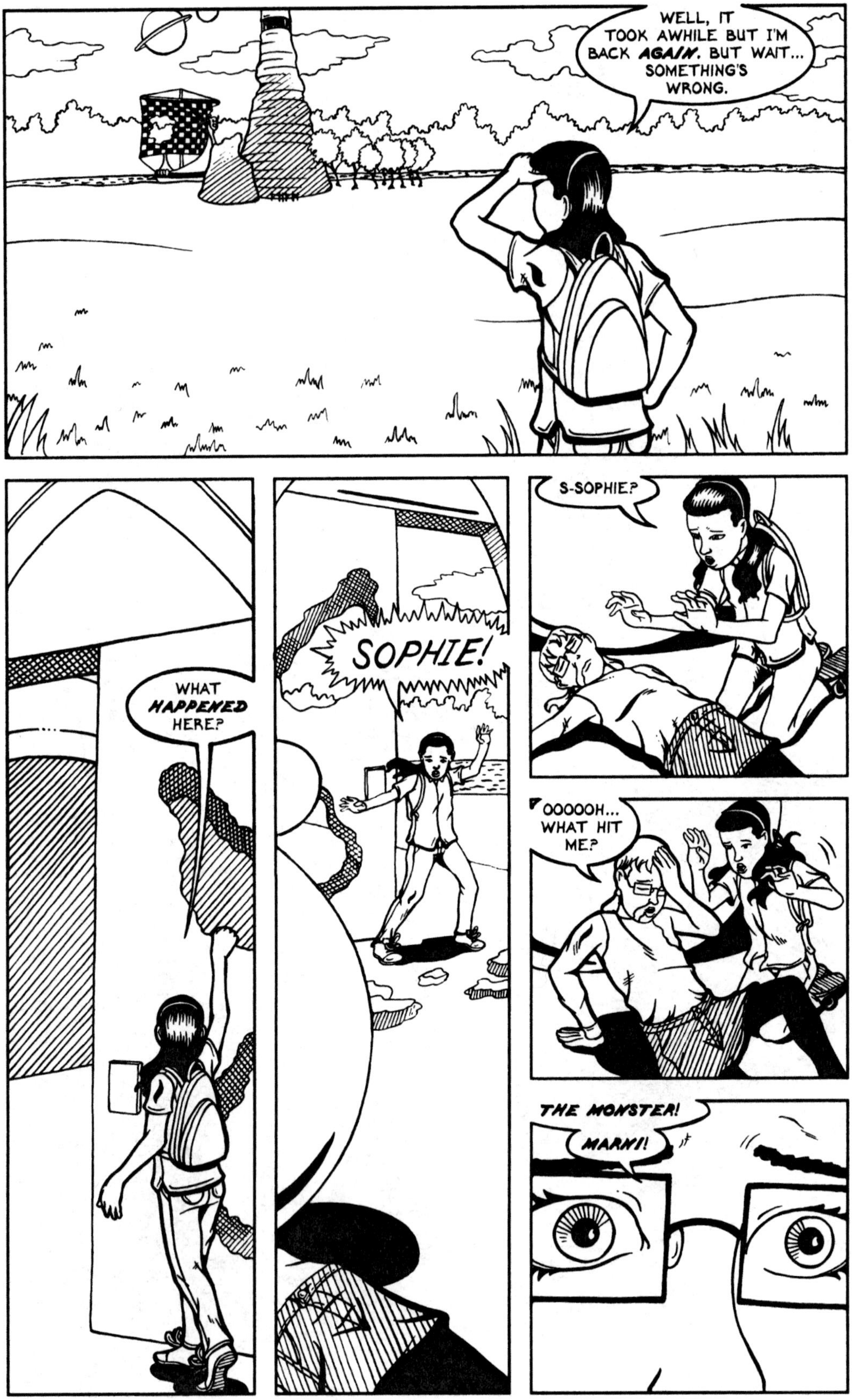
WELL, IT TOOK AWHILE BUT I'M BACK AGAIN. BUT WAIT... SOMETHING'S WRONG.
...
WHAT HAPPENED HERE?
SOPHIE!
S-SOPHIE?
OOOOOH... WHAT HIT ME?
THE MONSTER!
MARNI!

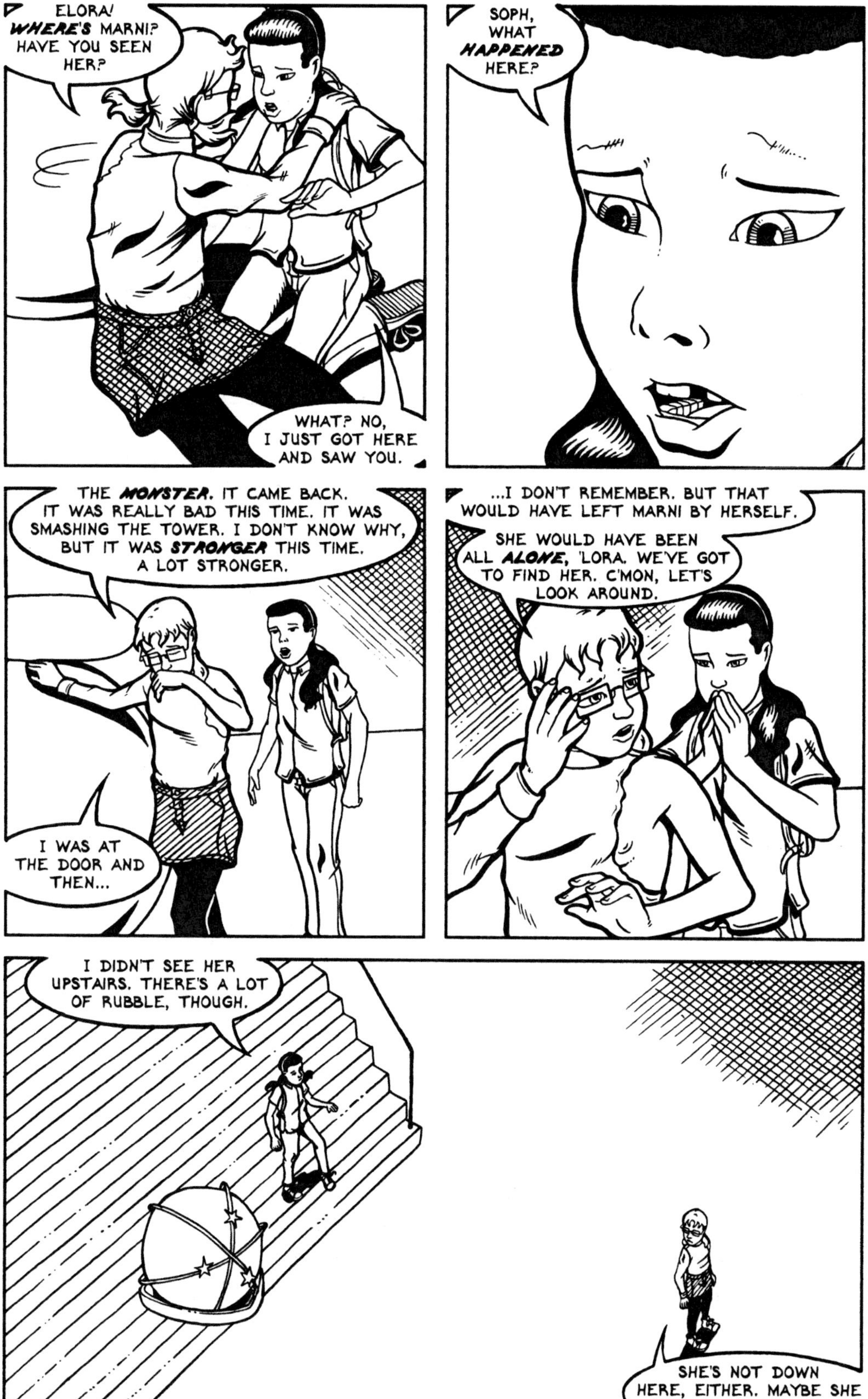
ELORA! WHERE'S MARNI? HAVE YOU SEEN HER?
WHAT? NO, I JUST GOT HERE AND SAW YOU.
SOPH, WHAT HAPPENED HERE?
THE MONSTER. IT CAME BACK. IT WAS REALLY BAD THIS TIME. IT WAS SMASHING THE TOWER. I DON'T KNOW WHY, BUT IT WAS STRONGER THIS TIME. A LOT STRONGER.
I WAS AT THE DOOR AND THEN...
...I DON'T REMEMBER. BUT THAT WOULD HAVE LEFT MARNI BY HERSELF.
SHE WOULD HAVE BEEN ALL ALONE, 'LORA. WE'VE GOT TO FIND HER. C'MON, LET'S LOOK AROUND.
I DIDN'T SEE HER UPSTAIRS. THERE'S A LOT OF RUBBLE, THOUGH.
SHE'S NOT DOWN HERE, EITHER. MAYBE SHE GOT AWAY? OUTSIDE?

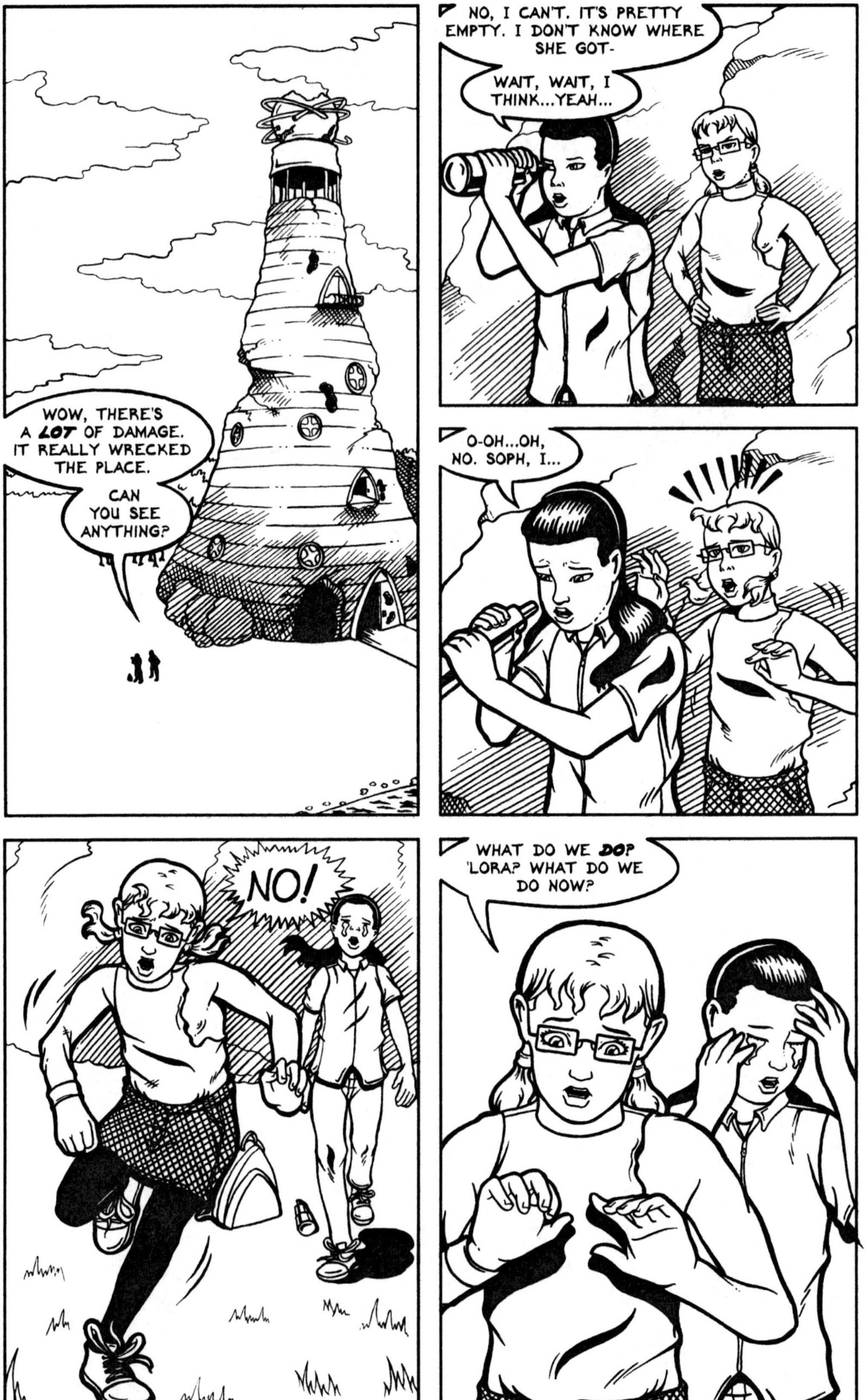
WOW, THERE'S A LOT OF DAMAGE. IT REALLY WRECKED THE PLACE.
CAN YOU SEE ANYTHING?
NO, I CAN'T. IT'S PRETTY EMPTY. I DON'T KNOW WHERE SHE GOT-
WAIT, WAIT, I THINK...YEAH...
O-OH...OH, NO. SOPH, I...
NO!
WHAT DO WE DO? 'LORA? WHAT DO WE DO NOW?

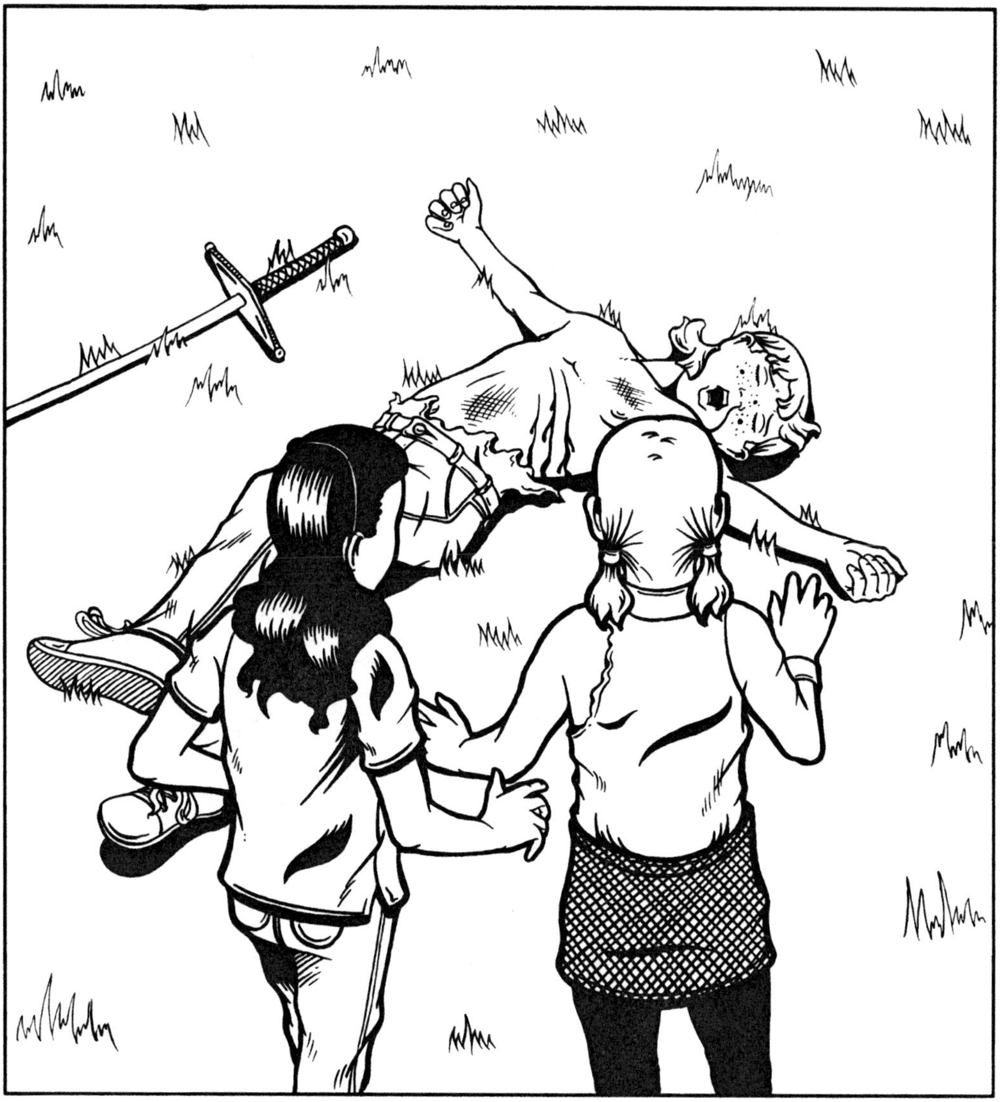

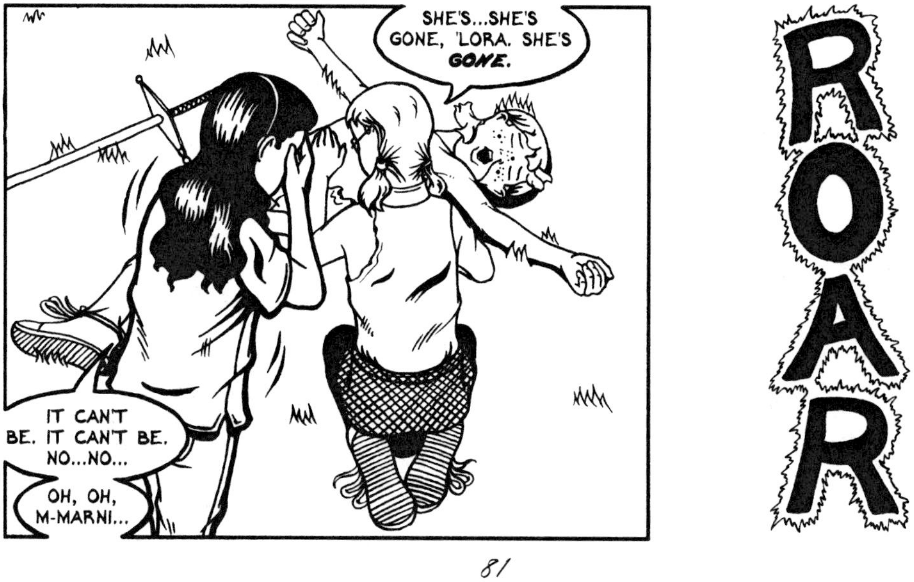
SHE'S...SHE'S GONE, 'LORA. SHE'S GONE.
IT CAN'T BE. IT CAN'T BE. NO...NO...
OH, OH, M-MARNI...
ROAR

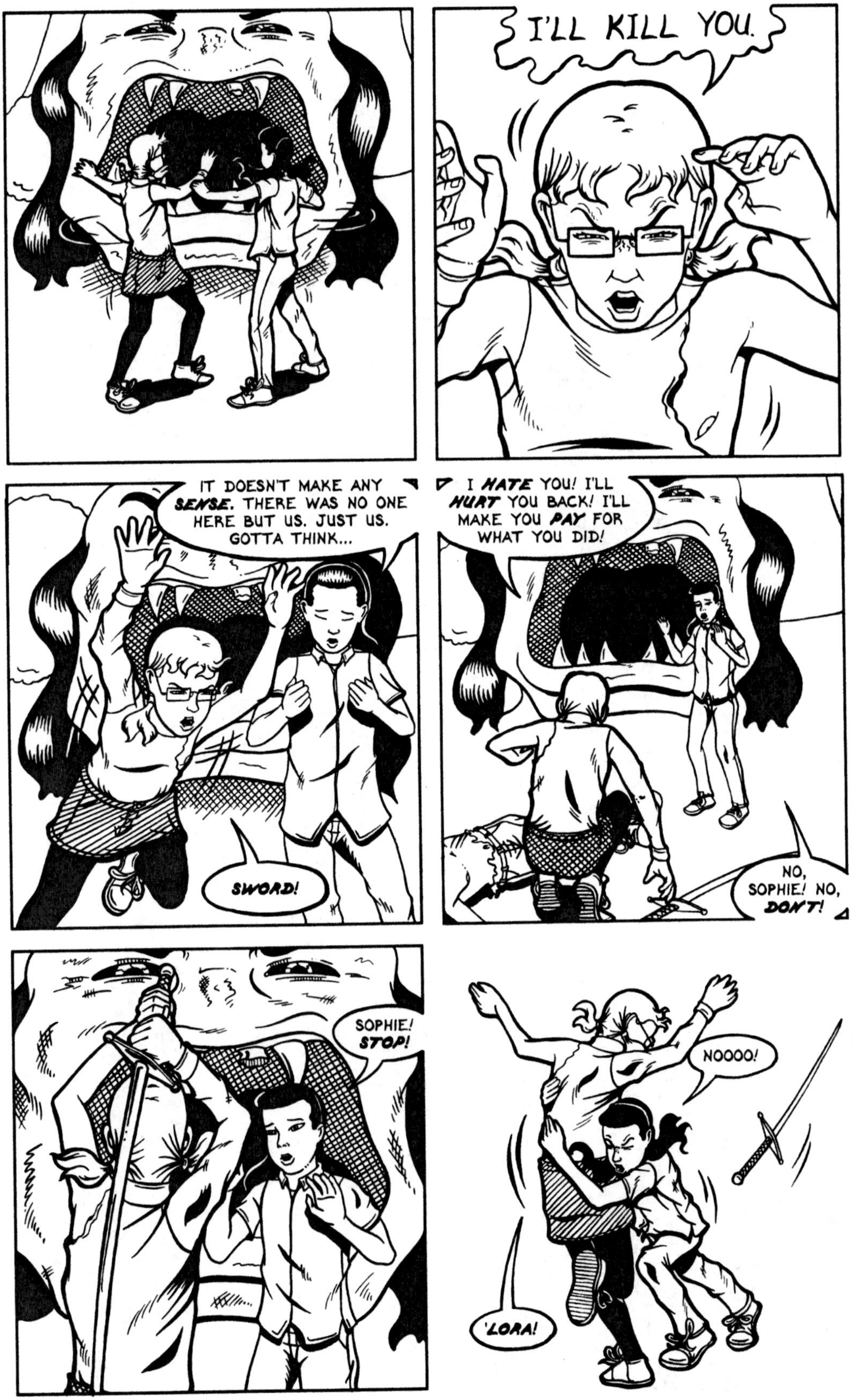
I'LL KILL YOU.
IT DOESN'T MAKE ANY SENSE. THERE WAS NO ONE HERE BUT US. JUST US. GOTTA THINK...
SWORD!
I HATE YOU! I'LL HURT YOU BACK! I'LL MAKE YOU PAY FOR WHAT YOU DID!
NO, SOPHIE! NO, DON'T!
SOPHIE! STOP!
NOOOO!
'LORA!

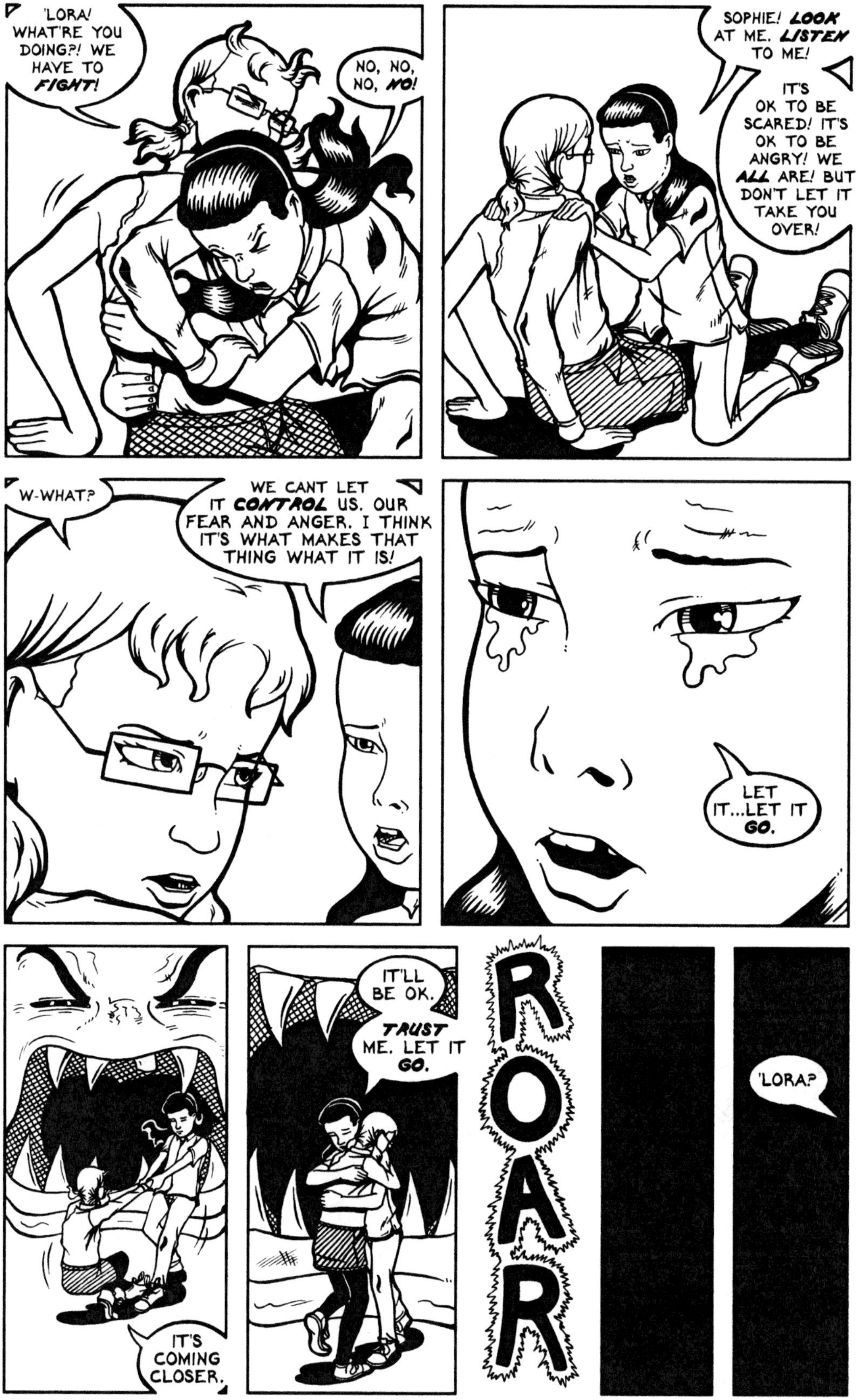
'LORA! WHAT'RE YOU DOING?! WE HAVE TO FIGHT!
NO, NO, NO, NO!
SOPHIE! LOOK AT ME. LISTEN TO ME!
IT'S OK TO BE SCARED! IT'S OK TO BE ANGRY! WE ALL ARE! BUT DON'T LET IT TAKE YOU OVER!
W-WHAT?
WE CANT LET IT CONTROL US. OUR FEAR AND ANGER. I THINK IT'S WHAT MAKES THAT THING WHAT IT IS!
LET IT...LET IT GO.
IT'S COMING CLOSER.
IT'LL BE OK. TRUST ME. LET IT GO.
ROAR
'LORA?

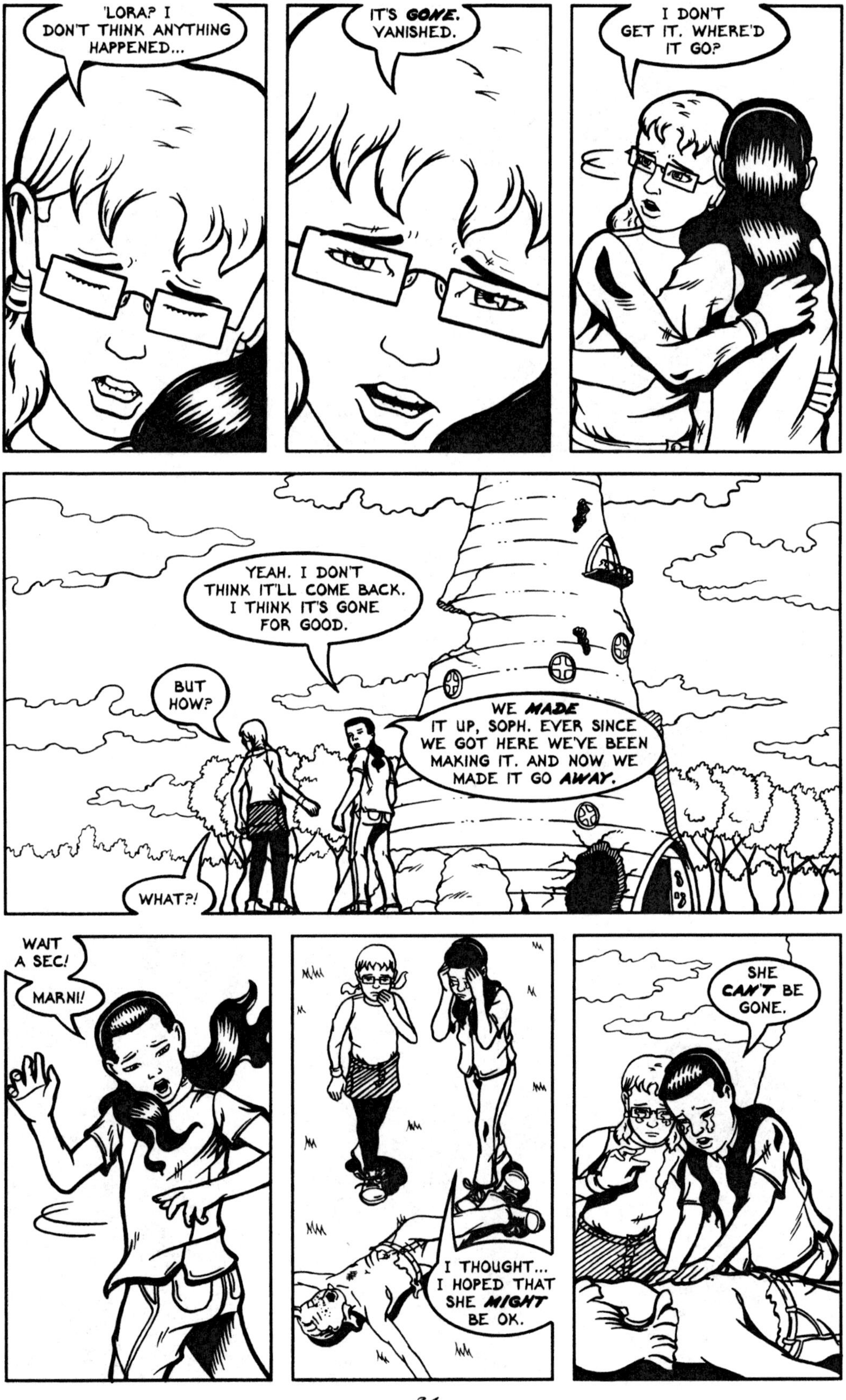
'LORA? I DON'T THINK ANYTHING HAPPENED...
IT'S GONE. VANISHED.
I DON'T GET IT. WHERE'D IT GO?
YEAH. I DON'T THINK IT'LL COME BACK. I THINK IT'S GONE FOR GOOD.
BUT HOW?
WE MADE IT UP, SOPH. EVER SINCE WE GOT HERE WE'VE BEEN MAKING IT. AND NOW WE MADE IT GO AWAY.
WHAT?!
WAIT A SEC!
MARNI!
I THOUGHT... I HOPED THAT SHE MIGHT BE OK.
SHE CAN'T BE GONE.

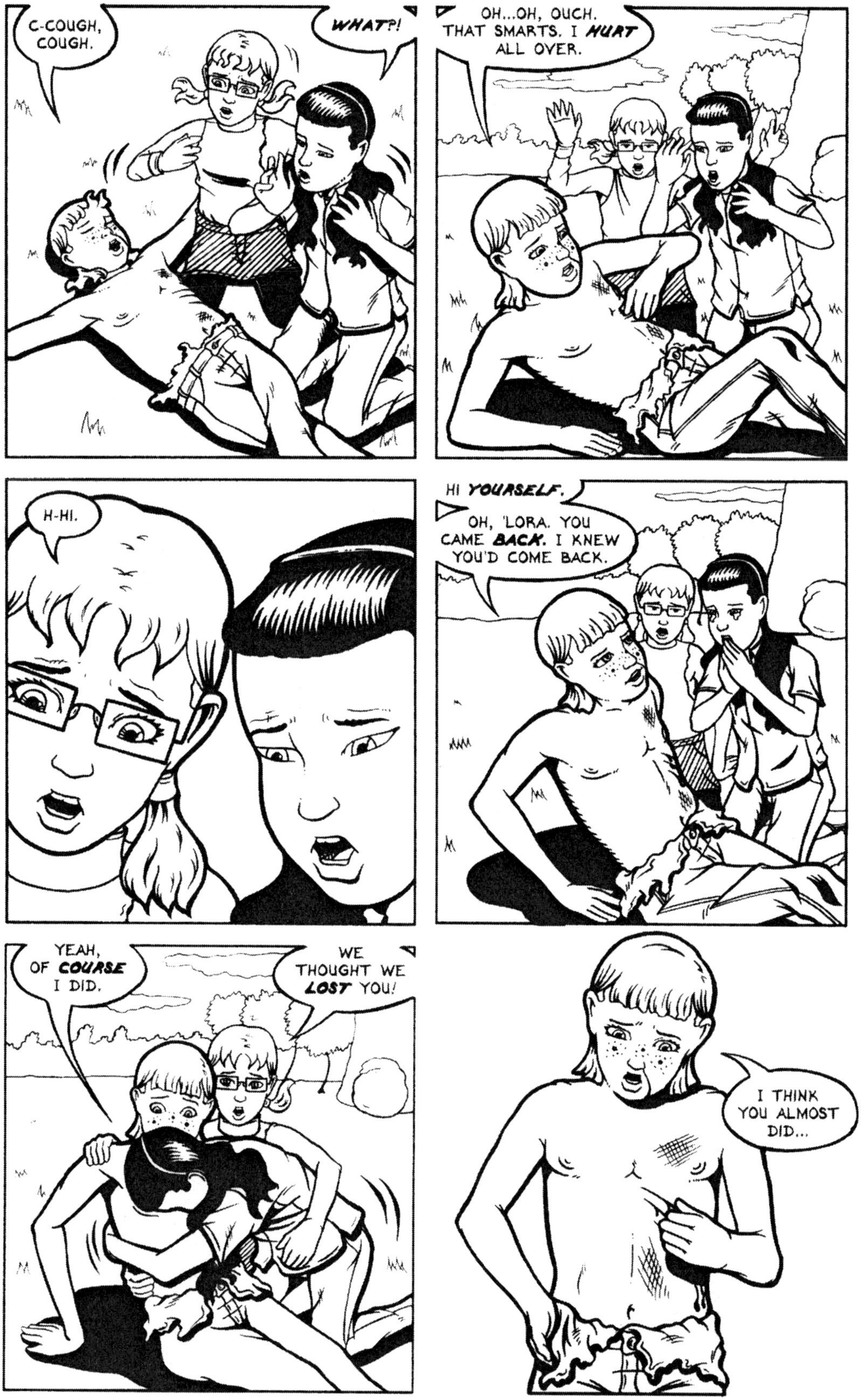
C-COUGH, COUGH.
WHAT?!
OH...OH, OUCH. THAT SMARTS. I HURT ALL OVER.
H-HI.
HI YOURSELF.
OH, 'LORA. YOU CAME BACK. I KNEW YOU'D COME BACK.
YEAH, OF COURSE I DID.
WE THOUGHT WE LOST YOU!
I THINK YOU ALMOST DID...

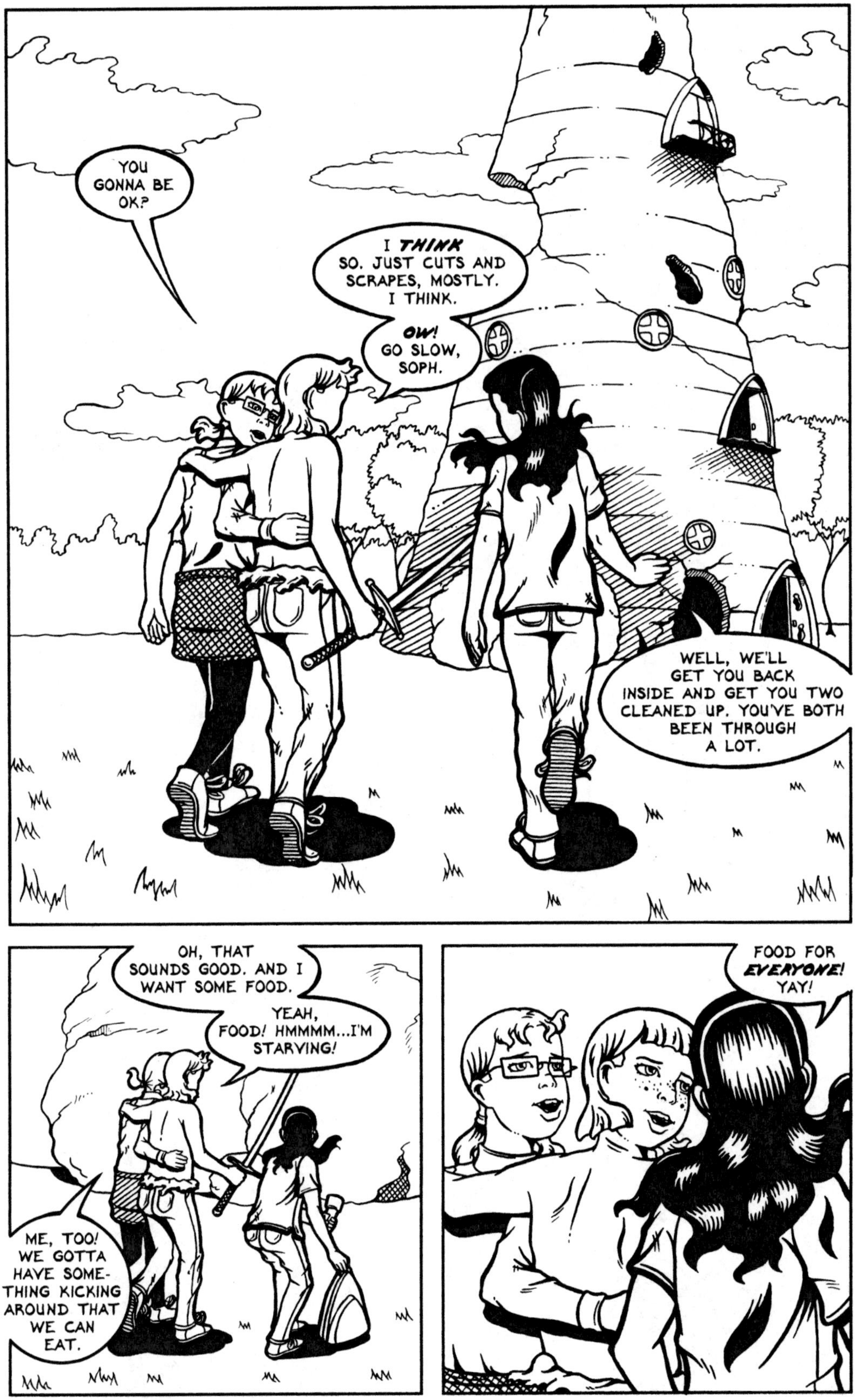
YOU GONNA BE OK?
I *THINK* SO. JUST CUTS AND SCRAPES, MOSTLY. I THINK.
OW! GO SLOW, SOPH.
WELL, WE'LL GET YOU BACK INSIDE AND GET YOU TWO CLEANED UP. YOU'VE BOTH BEEN THROUGH A LOT.
OH, THAT SOUNDS GOOD. AND I WANT SOME FOOD.
YEAH, FOOD! HMMMM...I'M STARVING!
ME, TOO! WE GOTTA HAVE SOME-THING KICKING AROUND THAT WE CAN EAT.
FOOD FOR *EVERYONE!* YAY!

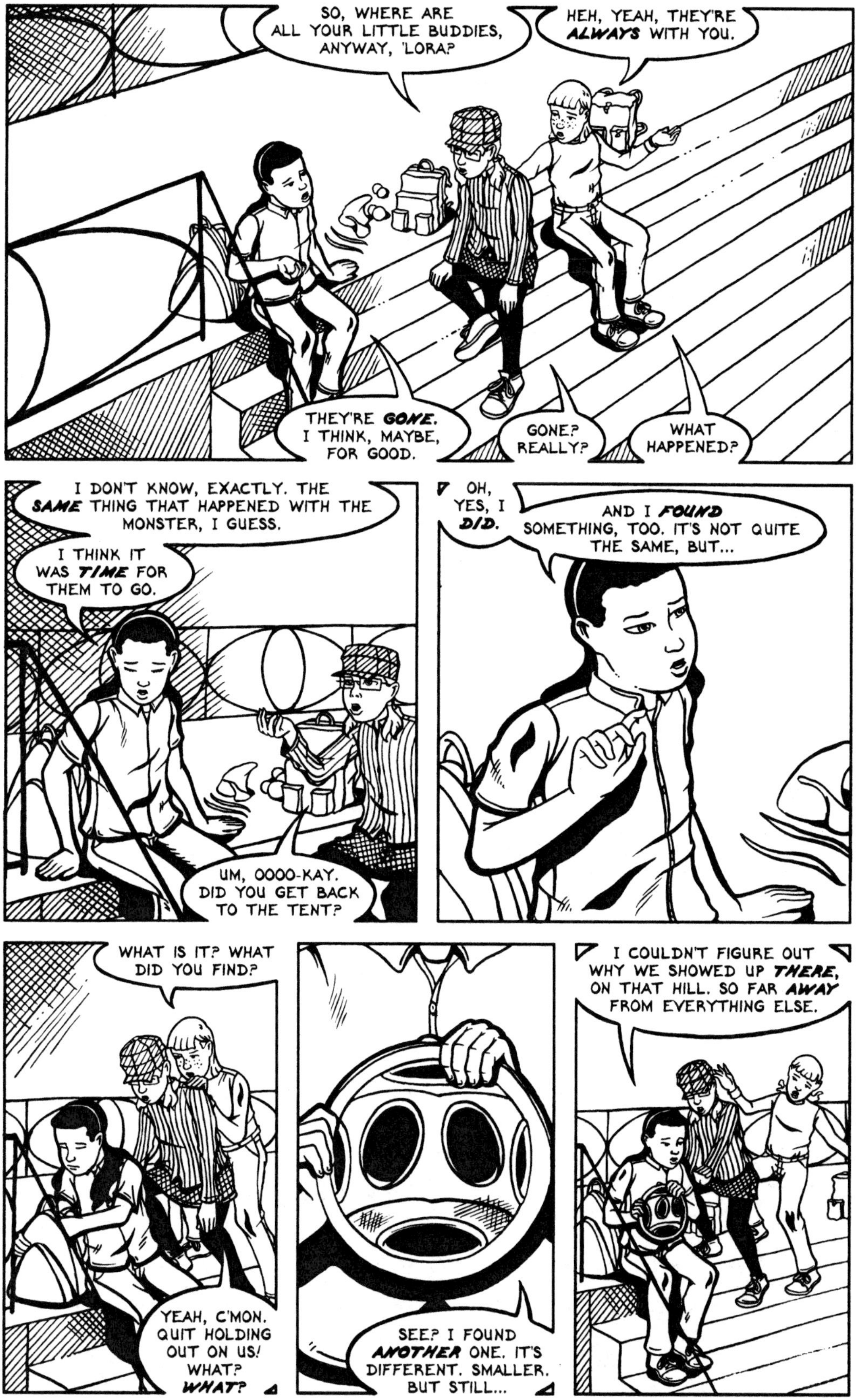
SO, WHERE ARE ALL YOUR LITTLE BUDDIES, ANYWAY, 'LORA?
HEH, YEAH, THEY'RE ALWAYS WITH YOU.
THEY'RE GONE. I THINK, MAYBE, FOR GOOD.
GONE? REALLY?
WHAT HAPPENED?
I DON'T KNOW, EXACTLY. THE SAME THING THAT HAPPENED WITH THE MONSTER, I GUESS.
I THINK IT WAS TIME FOR THEM TO GO.
UM, OOOO-KAY. DID YOU GET BACK TO THE TENT?
OH, YES, I DID.
AND I FOUND SOMETHING, TOO. IT'S NOT QUITE THE SAME, BUT...
WHAT IS IT? WHAT DID YOU FIND?
YEAH, C'MON. QUIT HOLDING OUT ON US! WHAT? WHAT?
SEE? I FOUND ANOTHER ONE. IT'S DIFFERENT. SMALLER. BUT STILL...
I COULDN'T FIGURE OUT WHY WE SHOWED UP THERE, ON THAT HILL. SO FAR AWAY FROM EVERYTHING ELSE.

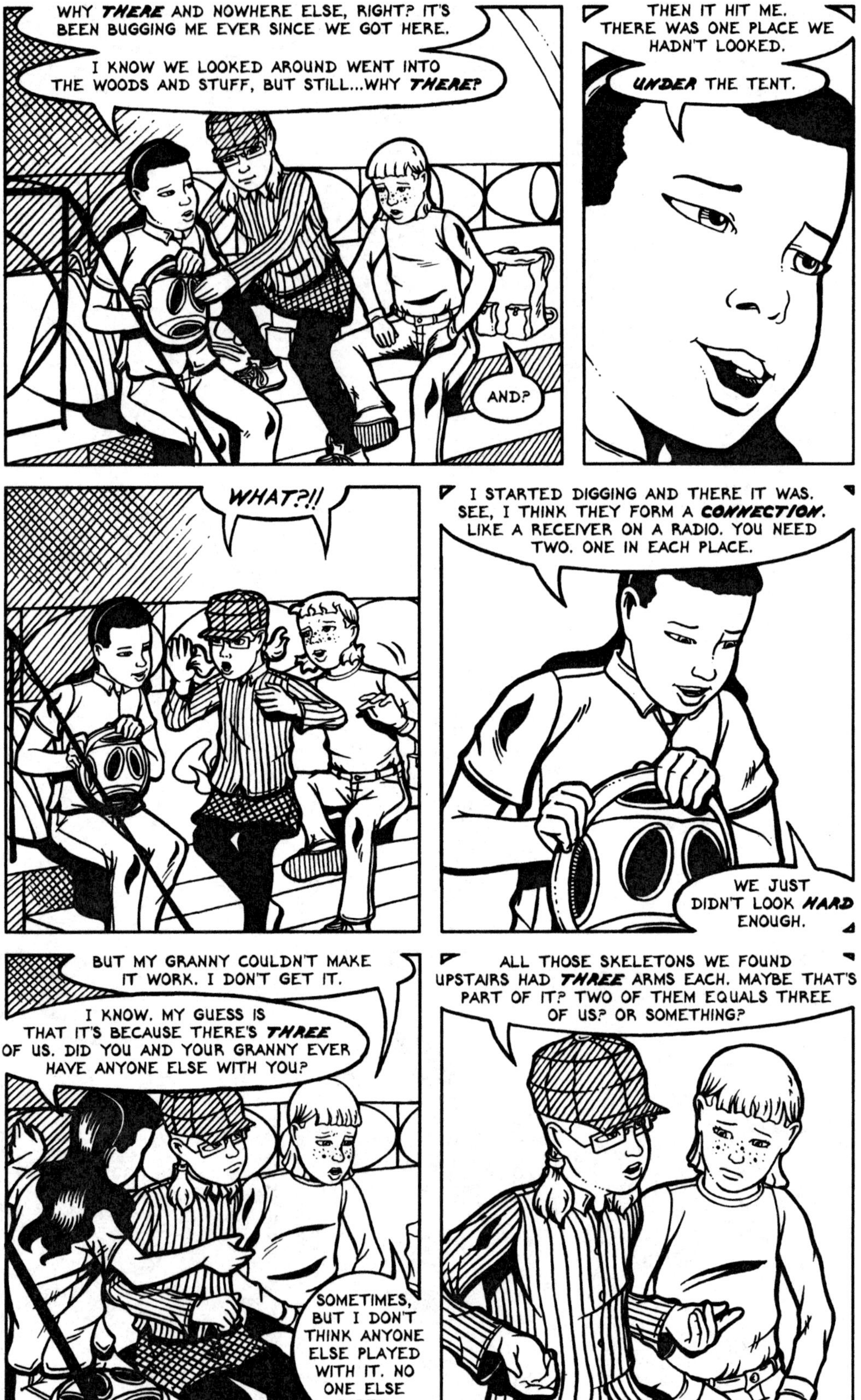
WHY *THERE* AND NOWHERE ELSE, RIGHT? IT'S BEEN BUGGING ME EVER SINCE WE GOT HERE.
I KNOW WE LOOKED AROUND WENT INTO THE WOODS AND STUFF, BUT STILL...WHY *THERE*?
AND?
THEN IT HIT ME. THERE WAS ONE PLACE WE HADN'T LOOKED.
UNDER THE TENT.
WHAT?!!
I STARTED DIGGING AND THERE IT WAS. SEE, I THINK THEY FORM A *CONNECTION*. LIKE A RECEIVER ON A RADIO. YOU NEED TWO. ONE IN EACH PLACE.
WE JUST DIDN'T LOOK *HARD* ENOUGH.
BUT MY GRANNY COULDN'T MAKE IT WORK. I DON'T GET IT.
I KNOW. MY GUESS IS THAT IT'S BECAUSE THERE'S *THREE* OF US. DID YOU AND YOUR GRANNY EVER HAVE ANYONE ELSE WITH YOU?
SOMETIMES, BUT I DON'T THINK ANYONE ELSE PLAYED WITH IT. NO ONE ELSE CARED.
ALL THOSE SKELETONS WE FOUND UPSTAIRS HAD *THREE* ARMS EACH. MAYBE THAT'S PART OF IT? TWO OF THEM EQUALS THREE OF US? OR SOMETHING?

YOU FOUND **SKELETONS** UPSTAIRS? EW...

ANYWAY, I'M WILLING TO TRY THIS THING OUT. YOU GUYS **UP** FOR IT? IF IT WORKS, WE COULD BE **HOME** IN JUST A FEW MINUTES.

WELL, IT DOESN'T LOOK BIG ENOUGH TO GET ALL OUR HANDS IN, BUT YEAH, LET'S DO IT.

I THINK...I THINK IT'S TIME TO SAY **GOODBYE.**

DO YOU GUYS REMEMBER WHAT WE DID?

DIDN'T WE JUST PUT OUR HANDS **INSIDE** IT? THAT'S ALL I REMEMBER. OUR HANDS WERE IN IT, THERE WAS A **FLASH**, AND THEN THE LIGHTS WENT OUT.

OK, THEN. HERE GOES NOTHING.

ACK, IT'S KINDA AWKWARD!

WHOA!

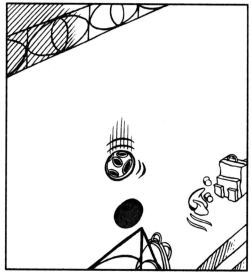

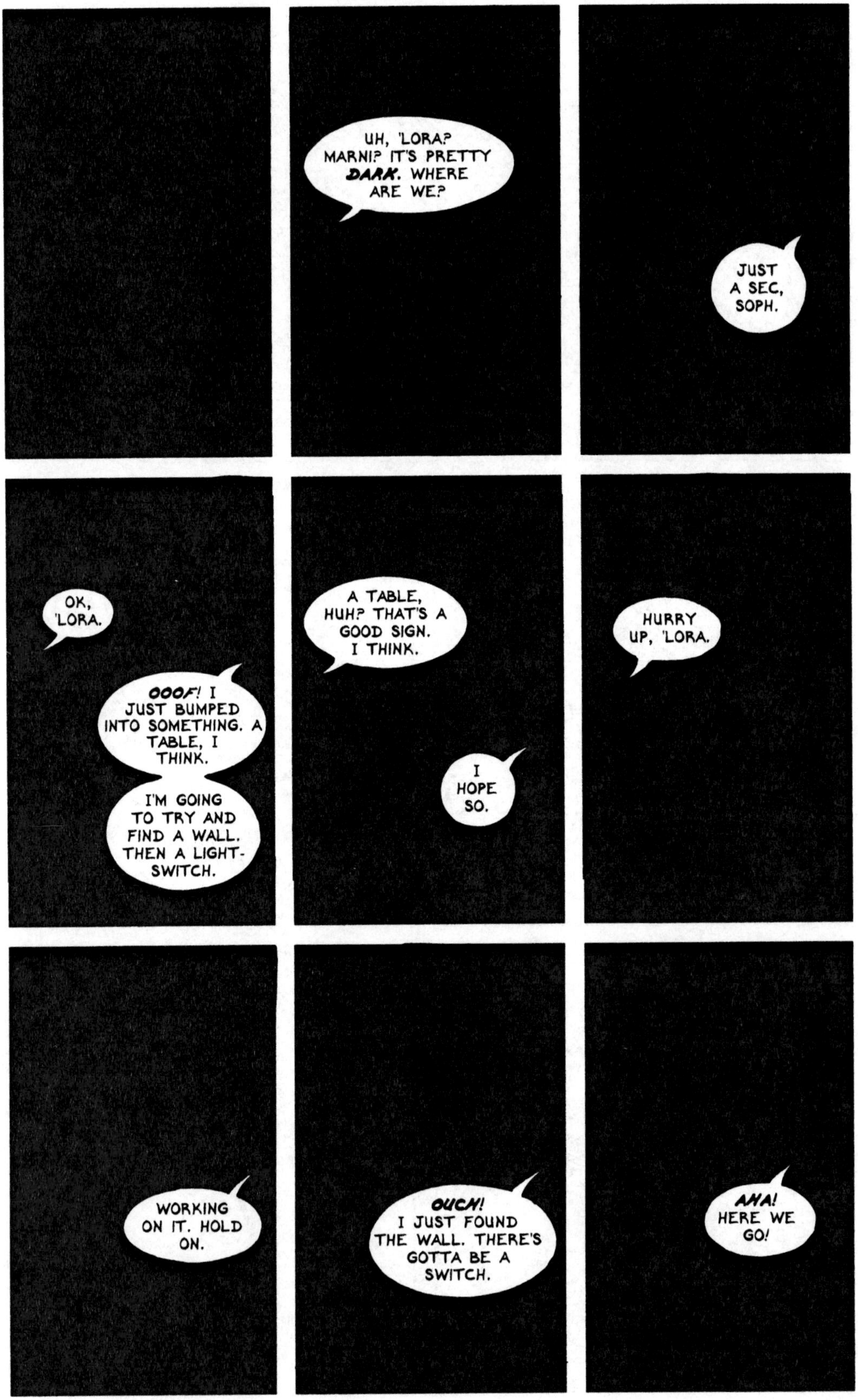
UH, 'LORA? MARNI? IT'S PRETTY DARK. WHERE ARE WE?
JUST A SEC, SOPH.
OK, 'LORA.
OOOF! I JUST BUMPED INTO SOMETHING. A TABLE, I THINK.
I'M GOING TO TRY AND FIND A WALL. THEN A LIGHT-SWITCH.
A TABLE, HUH? THAT'S A GOOD SIGN. I THINK.
I HOPE SO.
HURRY UP, 'LORA.
WORKING ON IT. HOLD ON.
OUCH! I JUST FOUND THE WALL. THERE'S GOTTA BE A SWITCH.
AHA! HERE WE GO!

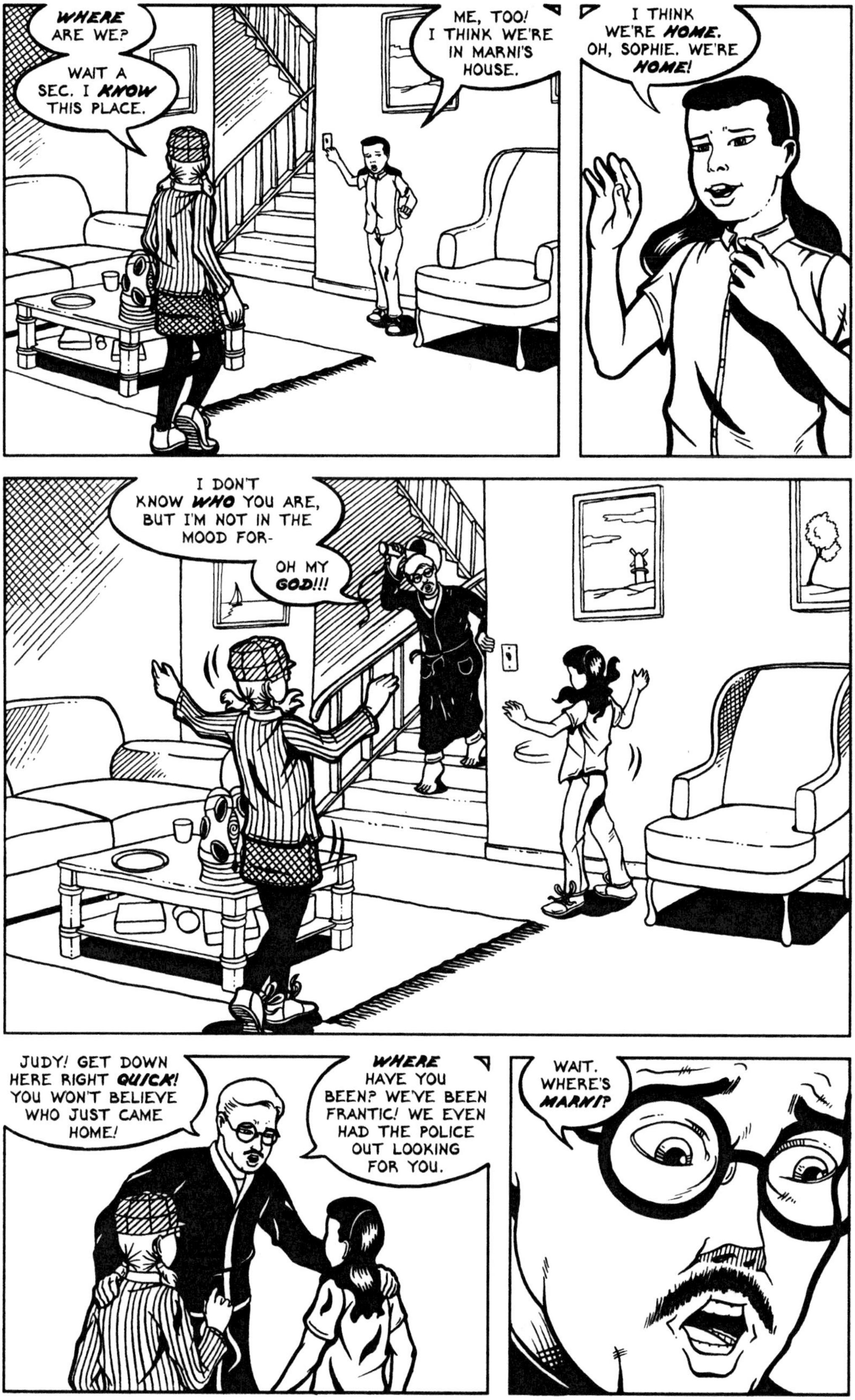
WHERE ARE WE?
WAIT A SEC. I KNOW THIS PLACE.
ME, TOO! I THINK WE'RE IN MARNI'S HOUSE.
I THINK WE'RE HOME. OH, SOPHIE. WE'RE HOME!
I DON'T KNOW WHO YOU ARE, BUT I'M NOT IN THE MOOD FOR-
OH MY GOD!!!
JUDY! GET DOWN HERE RIGHT QUICK! YOU WON'T BELIEVE WHO JUST CAME HOME!
WHERE HAVE YOU BEEN? WE'VE BEEN FRANTIC! WE EVEN HAD THE POLICE OUT LOOKING FOR YOU.
WAIT. WHERE'S MARNI?

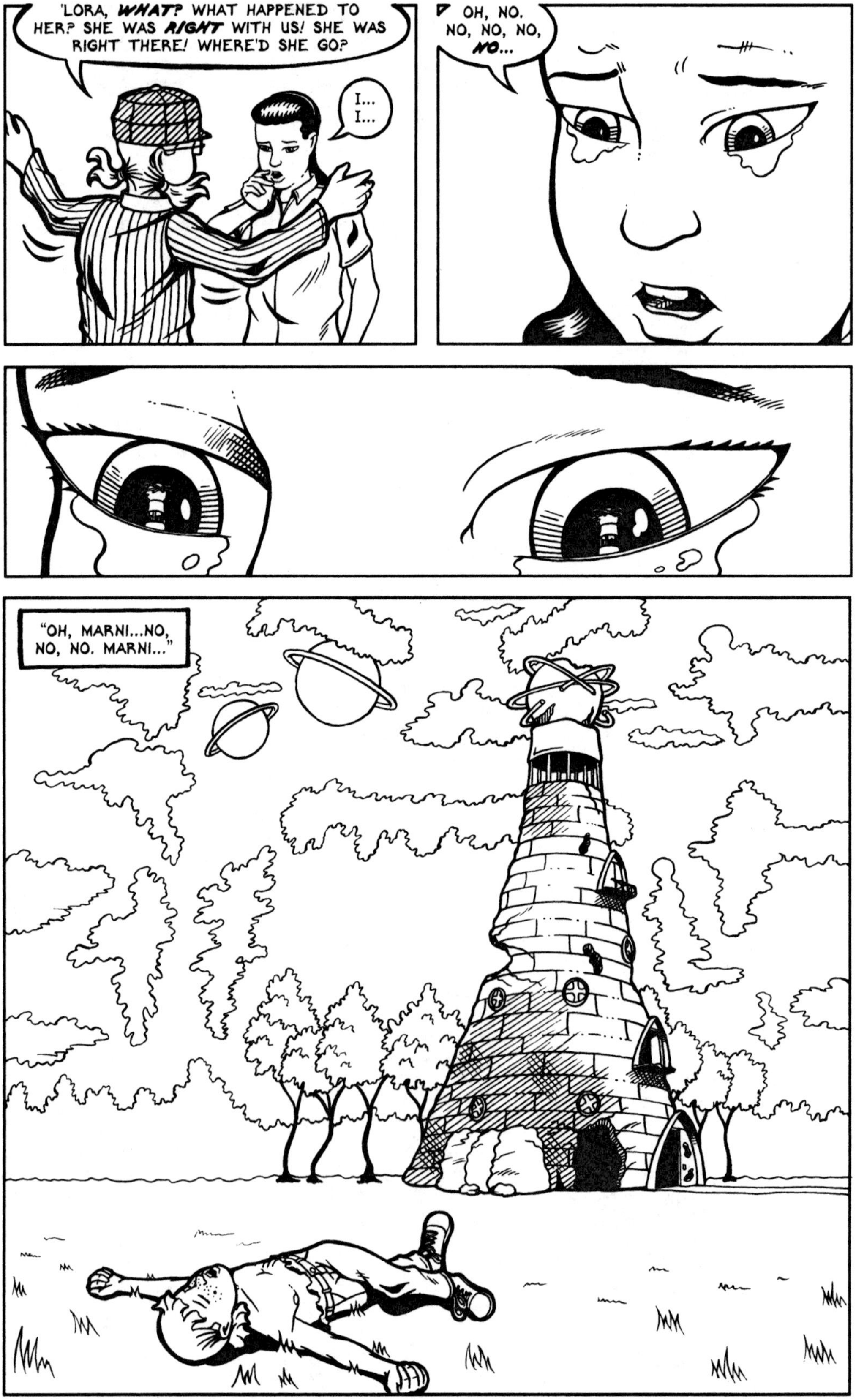
'LORA, WHAT? WHAT HAPPENED TO HER? SHE WAS RIGHT WITH US! SHE WAS RIGHT THERE! WHERE'D SHE GO?
I... I...
OH, NO. NO, NO, NO, NO...
"OH, MARNI...NO, NO, NO. MARNI..."

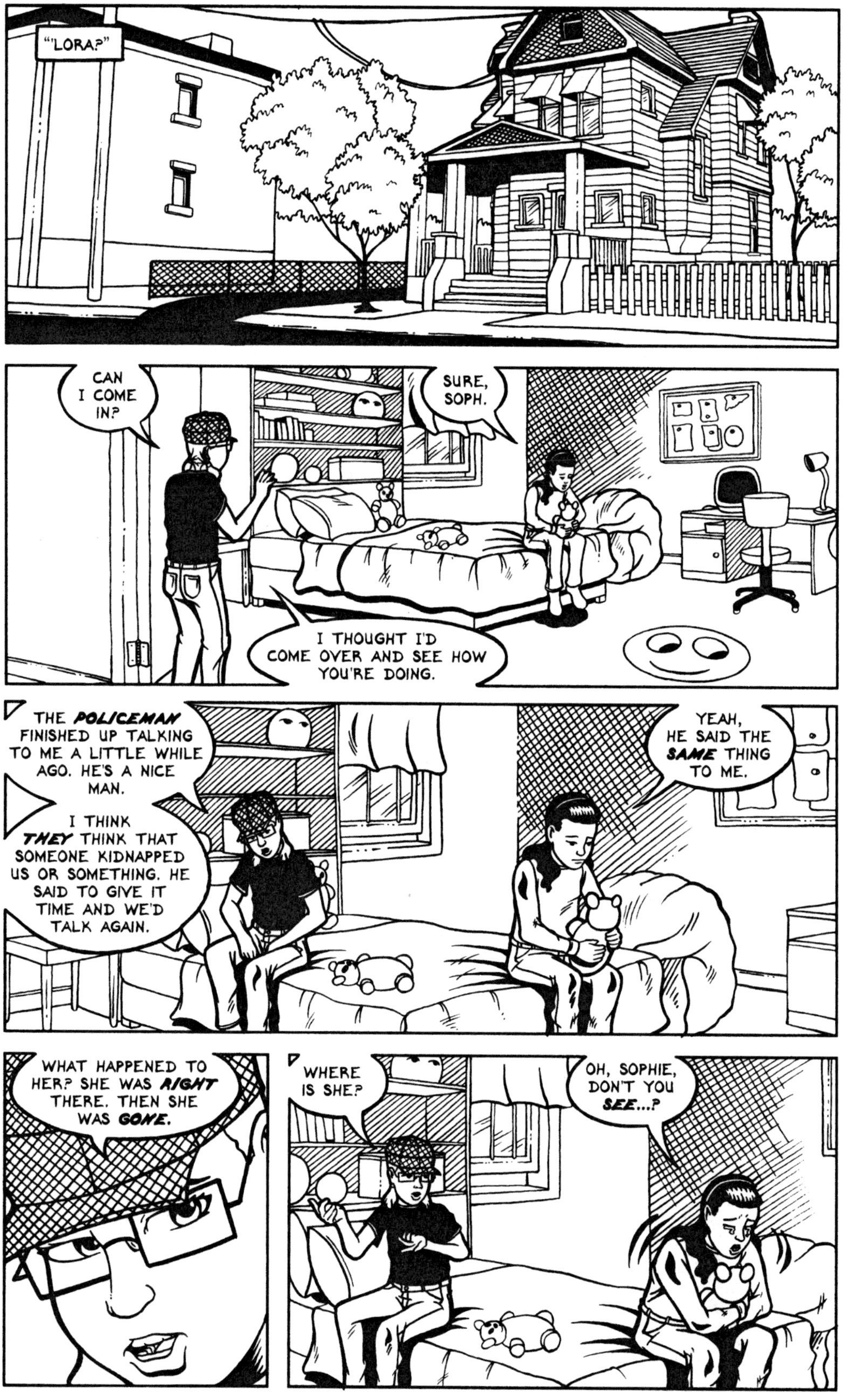
"LORA?"
CAN I COME IN?
SURE, SOPH.
I THOUGHT I'D COME OVER AND SEE HOW YOU'RE DOING.
THE POLICEMAN FINISHED UP TALKING TO ME A LITTLE WHILE AGO. HE'S A NICE MAN.
I THINK THEY THINK THAT SOMEONE KIDNAPPED US OR SOMETHING. HE SAID TO GIVE IT TIME AND WE'D TALK AGAIN.
YEAH, HE SAID THE SAME THING TO ME.
WHAT HAPPENED TO HER? SHE WAS RIGHT THERE. THEN SHE WAS GONE.
WHERE IS SHE?
OH, SOPHIE, DON'T YOU SEE...?

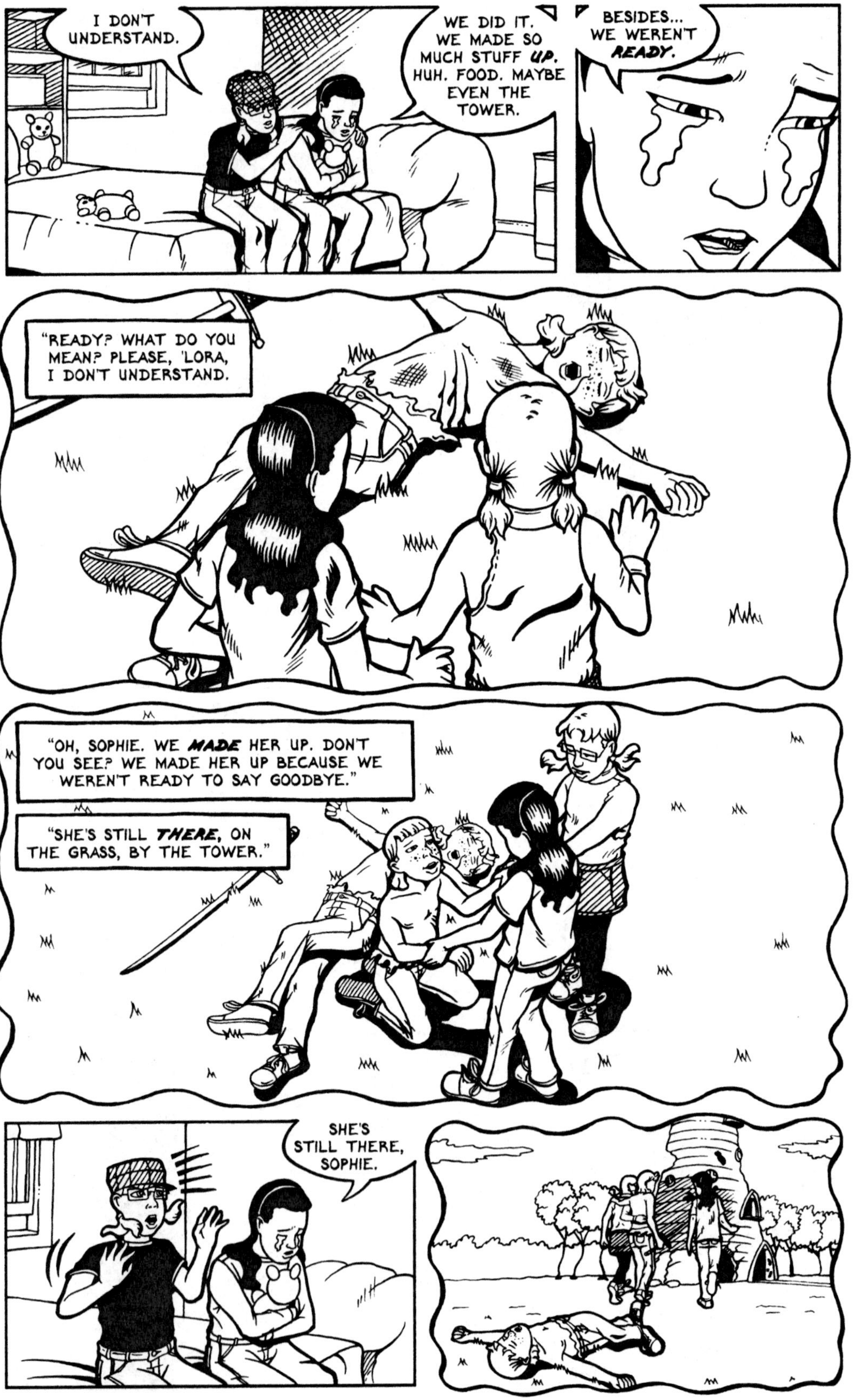
I DON'T UNDERSTAND.
WE DID IT. WE MADE SO MUCH STUFF UP. HUH. FOOD. MAYBE EVEN THE TOWER.
BESIDES... WE WERENT READY.
"READY? WHAT DO YOU MEAN? PLEASE, 'LORA, I DON'T UNDERSTAND.
"OH, SOPHIE. WE MADE HER UP. DON'T YOU SEE? WE MADE HER UP BECAUSE WE WEREN'T READY TO SAY GOODBYE."
"SHE'S STILL THERE, ON THE GRASS, BY THE TOWER."
SHE'S STILL THERE, SOPHIE.

Extras

Thumbnailing

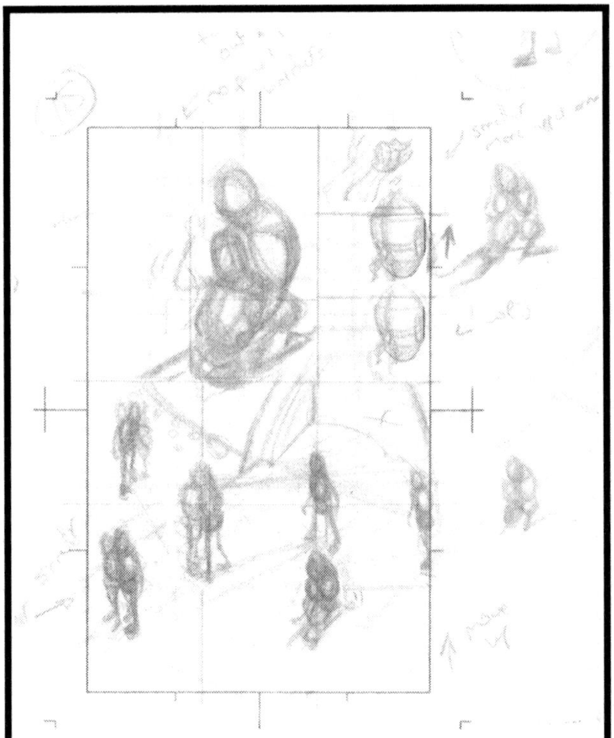

Drawing 1: Stage One Thumbnail of Page 36

In *Stargazer Volume One* I discussed how I approached writing the story and I presented some concept art and pinups. This time I wanted to show you how I approach drawing a page. I want to clarify one thing right off the bat, though: I don't believe there are any hard and fast rules when it comes to creating comics; there are multiple approaches and no single way is correct. I think the best advice is to learn everything you can and then figure out, through trial and error, which approach works best for you. In other words, much of learning to draw involves learning to use *tools* rather than learning hard and fast *rules*.

Most artists I know of (and this applies to many kinds of visual art and not just comics) try to thumbnail a page first. All this means is doing a small drawing (often many small drawings) in an attempt to work out what will be on the final page before completing a final drawing. Thumbnails should be very loose and typically very small. The script describes what's happening on the page and then the artist needs to visualize it and put it down on paper. What you don't want to do is start drawing the final page without figuring things out first. Why? Well, if you run into a problem with the page, you may have to discard it and start all over again, which is a lot of time wasted. With thumbnails, if you make a mistake or if you simply change your mind, you can start over again without too much trouble.

There are many approaches to thumbnailing but it generally involves sketching out little stick figures with loose perspective to try and get a feel for the final page. Always keep the script in mind but try to get things down on the page quickly, simply, and clearly. A good example of this is the above thumbnail from page 36. This is small (approximately 1.75" by 2.75") and very loose, but there's lots of information in it. I really try to focus on composition and narrative at this stage. Making sure that things are "explained" visually is very important to me and, despite the simplicity of the drawing, in many ways I find that thumbnailing is where I do the hardest work; the most thinking, figuring, and problem solving. As you can see in the example, I also often make a few notes on my thumbnails. Once I'm happy with a thumbnail, I scan it into my computer and blow it up to a larger size. The notes I make allow me to make some changes digitally rather than erasing something or simply starting over with a new drawing.

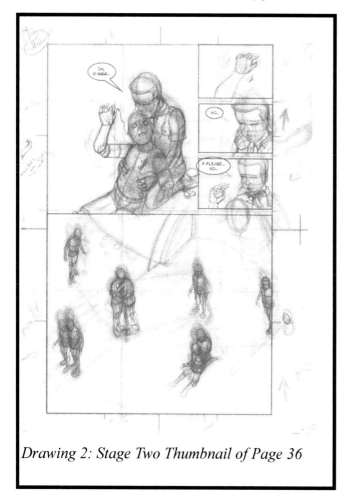

Drawing 2: Stage Two Thumbnail of Page 36

Stage Two Thumbnails

Once I've scanned in the little thumbnail and blown it up so that it will fit on a standard piece of paper (i.e.: 8.5" by 11"), I start to figure out a number of things, including the panel borders and the dialogue and speech balloons. For simplicity's sake, I prefer doing it at this stage rather than on the final page. By doing it this way I can figure out if a particular panel has too many words or if the art is too big (or small) in relation to both the dialogue and the panel. And so on. I also apply the little notes I made in the first thumbnail. Basically, I move elements around, resize figures and objects, and "muck around" until I'm happy with it.

Once I'm happy with all of that, I print the revised thumbnail out and start drawing right on top of the printout. That's what you can see in the example on this page. It's still loose and simple, but it's tighter and more complete than what was in the earlier thumbnail. Once I'm happy with it, I scan it *back* into my computer and blow it up once again. This time I make it large enough to fit on the final page, a sheet of Bristol board, which is where I do my pencilling and inking.

Recall that I mentioned "tools and not rules." Doing two stages of thumbnails, working digitally to move things around, even scanning, it all took me awhile to figure out. When I did my first graphic novel *the road to god knows...* I didn't know any of this and I worked very differently. I would typically do only one thumbnail and I did it on tracing paper. It was about the size of the stage two thumbnail above, but I didn't scan it in. Instead, I would just put it beside my drawing board and try to copy it onto Bristol board. It didn't work very well. I was still struggling with drawing and this approach made things far more complex. It was also time consuming since I'd have to re-draw so much. My approach on *Stargazer* works much better for me. Live and learn.

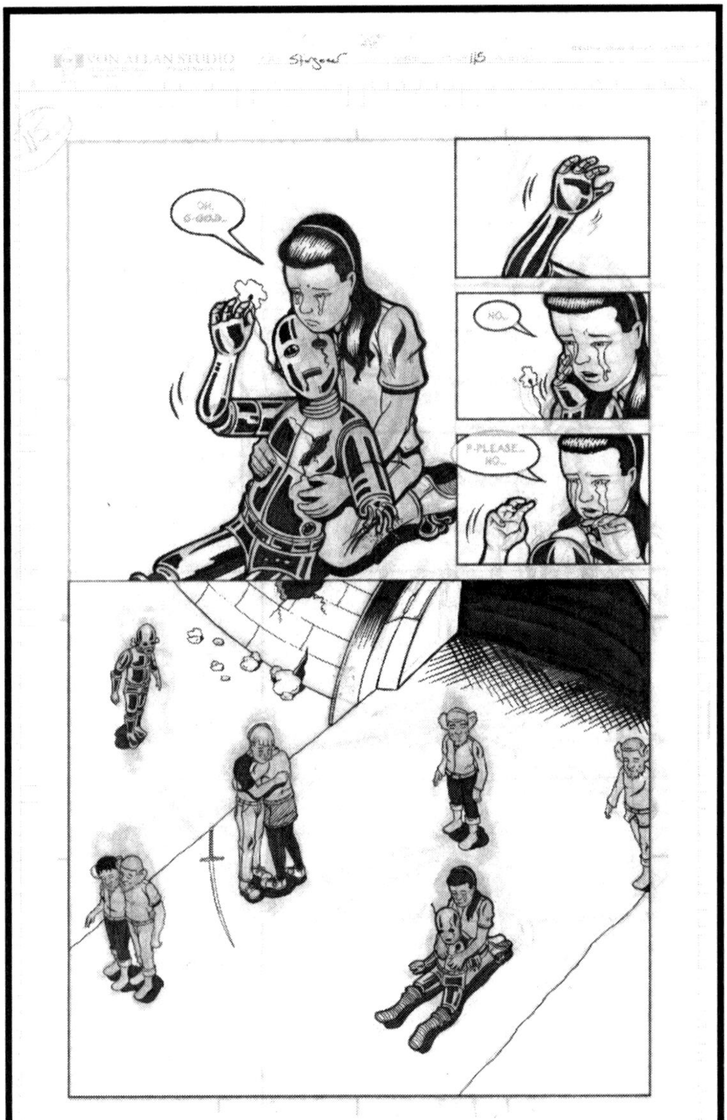
OH.
G-GOD..
NO..
P-PLEASE..
NO..

Drawing 3: Stage Three Final Page 36 Pencils and Inks

Stage Three Pencils and Inks

This is the final art board now pencilled and inked. This is done on a sheet of Bristol board that measures approximately 13" by 19." That's a little bigger than the typical 11" by 17" but I wanted to work a bit bigger on *Stargazer.* That decision was also based on my experiences with *the road to god knows...* I felt hampered by working smaller and the larger size gave me more room to work. Everything is printed in blue but, since this graphic novel is printed in black and white, the blue lines show up as grey. You'll have to use your imagination to see the blue! Once I've finished the tight blue pencilling, I then ink the page using my trusty brush and black ink. Sometimes people ink with pens (either nib pens or technical pens) and sometimes people ink digitally. Occasionally people even draw digitally and avoid using pencils and paper altogether; there is no right way, just the right way for *you.* Again, it takes a lot of trial and error to figure out the best approach for you; keep an open mind and don't be afraid to go back and try things you've previously abandoned. Sometimes something you hate at one point becomes something you love a few years later. Learning through experimenting, playing, and thinking is an excellent approach; it worked for me and could do the same for you!

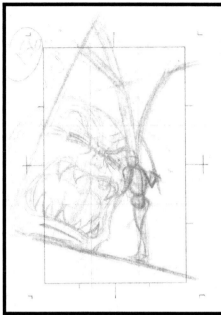

The same methodology applies to splash pages as well as pages with a large number of panels. For instance, Page 77 detailed the final confrontation between Marni and the Monster. The first stage thumbnail is where I spent a lot of time figuring things out; I wanted the page to be dynamic and with good composition, but the emotion had to be right. Marni's confidence mixed with the fear that the Monster hopefully invokes. It's tough to know how well I accomplished the latter (that depends on you), but I think the page is dynamic. There are really no absolutes in art. So much of it, at least in my own case, is based on gut feelings about what I'm working on and the emotions I'm trying to evoke.

I'M SICK OF BEING SCARED, AND I'M THROUGH RUNNING AWAY FROM YOU.

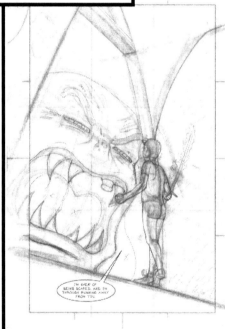

The second stage thumbnail served to tighten everything up. Of course, at this point I wasn't worried about panel borders since the page didn't call for them, so I was really only concerned with Marni's dialogue and the corresponding speech balloon.

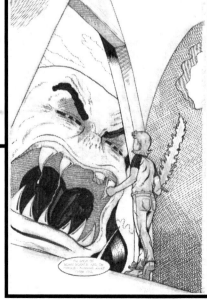

The final page has all of the actual inking and whatnot and I think it came together pretty well. While this page wasn't all that complex to draw, the emotion and narrative of the page *was*. Fundamentally it's the story that makes comics *comics*.

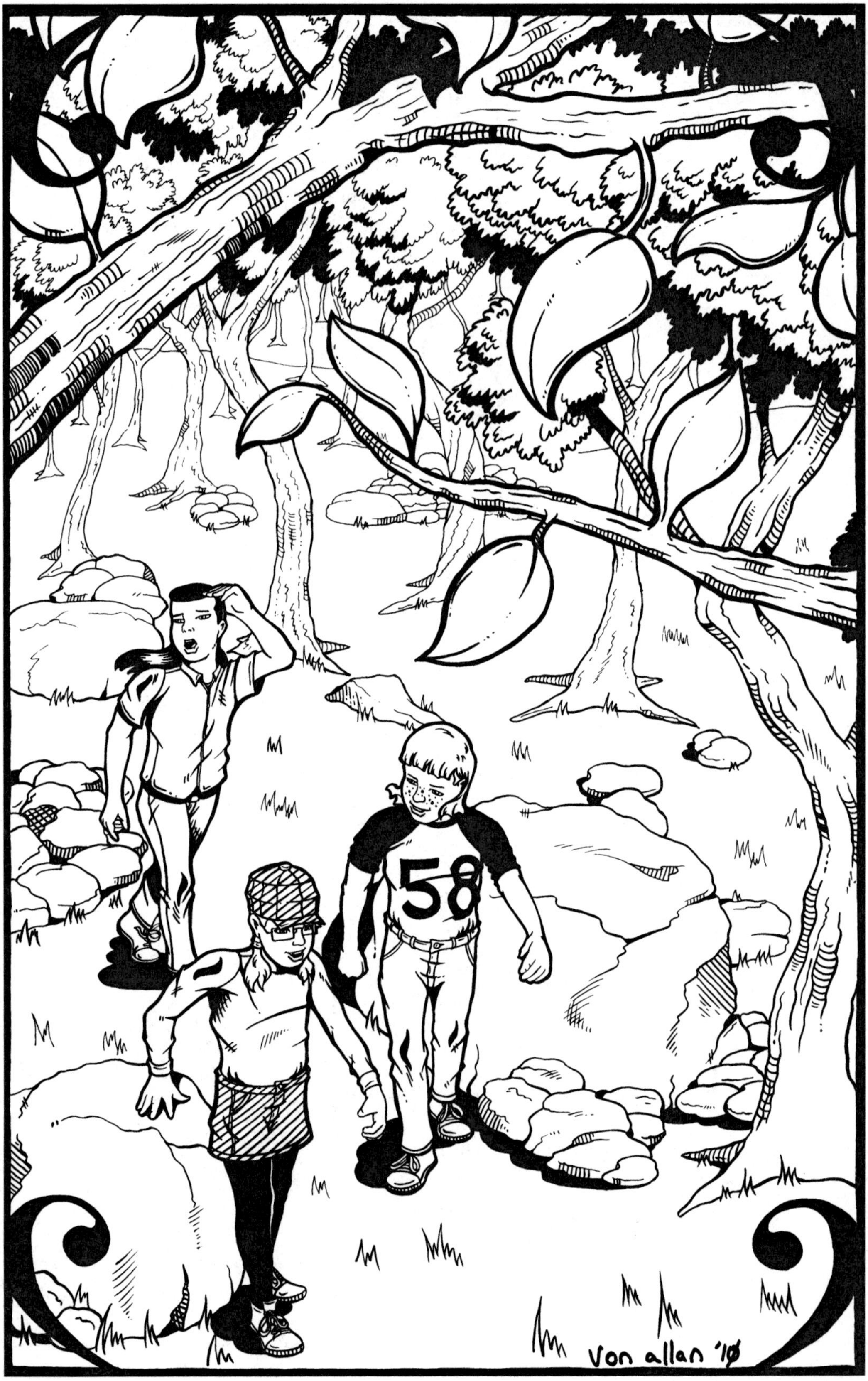
58
von allan '10

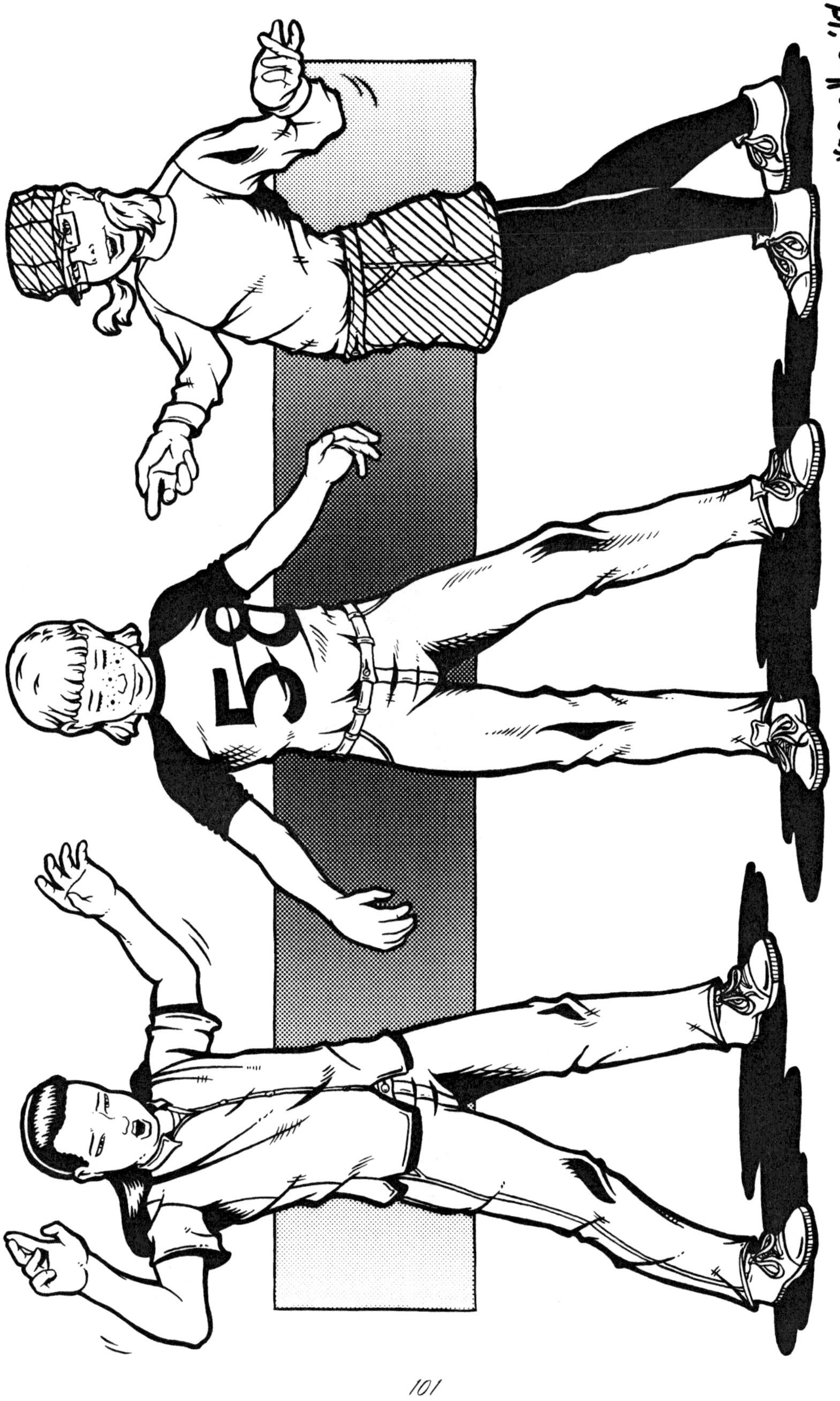
von allan '10

The first volume of the *Stargazer* saga is
available through better book stores,
comic shops, and online retailers.

Stargazer Volume One
ISBN: 978-0-9781237-2-7
Diamond Order Number: NOV101057
$14.95, 122 pages

Midwest Book Review:

"Young Marni has recently lost her grandmother,
with whom she was very close. Her grandmother
had also bequeathed a mysterious "Artifact" upon
her - and it is this object that transports Marni
and her friends, Sophie and Elora, far away from
any home they have ever known. The three girls
must pool their courage and resources to learn
more about this unreal new world...Stargazer is
a story of wonder, exploration, determination,
and inward as well as outward challenge, and is
highly recommended for readers of all ages."

And don't forget that *the road to god knows...*
is *also* available at better book stores,
comic shops, and online, too!

the road to god knows...
ISBN: 978-0-9781237-0-3
$13.99, 148 pages

Library Journal:

"Relatively few graphic novels deal with mental
illness and Allan offers an empathetic glimpse at
a realistic teen who doesn't rattle cages to seek
help even though we might wish she would.
Instead, she just keeps going and draws on the
resources she has."

Where to Buy:

Von Allan was born red-headed and freckled in Arnprior, Ontario, just in time for *Star Wars: A New Hope*. Von currently lives in Ottawa, Canada, with his writer/editor geek wife, Moggy; a husky dog, Rowen; and two feisty cats, Bonny and Reilly.

Von loves to hear from people who've read and (hopefully!) enjoyed his work. Feel free to write him at von@vonallan.com.

Von's website is at http://www.vonallan.com and is the best place to go for updates, art, essays and the like. There's a dedicated website for *Stargazer* at http://stargazer.vonallan.com. Von can also be found online in the following places:

Twitter at http://twitter.com/vonallan

Facebook at http://www.facebook.com/von.allan

CPSIA information can be obtained at www.ICGtesting.com
Printed in the USA
LVOW110331270912

300459LV00004B/6/P